Radicalism and Reverence

Radicalism and Reverence

The Political Thought of
Gerrard Winstanley

George M. Shulman

UNIVERSITY OF CALIFORNIA PRESS
Berkeley · *Los Angeles* · *London*

University of California Press
Berkeley and Los Angeles, California

University of California Press, Ltd.
London, England

© 1989 by
The Regents of the University of California

Library of Congress Cataloging-in-Publication Data

Shulman, George M.
    Radicalism and reverence: the political thought of Gerrard Winstanley/
George M. Shulman.

        p. cm.
    Began as a dissertation in political science at the University of California,
Berkeley, in 1980.
        Bibliography: p.
        Includes index.
        ISBN 0-520-06587-5 (alk. paper)
        1. Winstanley, Gerrard, b. 1609—Contributions in political
science.   2. Winstanley, Gerrard, b. 1609—Contributions in radicalism.   I. Title.
    JC153.W63S54   1989   88-7833
    320.5'312'0924—dc19   CIP

Printed in the United States of America

1   2   3   4   5   6   7   8   9

Contents

Acknowledgments

This book began in 1980 as a dissertation in political science at the University of California, Berkeley. The two years of work on it were aided considerably by my customers at a neighborhood bar in San Francisco where I worked as a bartender several nights a week. Their generous tips supported my writing, and their warm comradery, bemused encouragement, tempting distractions, and repeated questioning—"Is it done yet?"—helped my academic alter ego to thrive. The financial support of Washington University in St. Louis and the cooperation of the political science department there made it possible to begin revising the dissertation; a fellowship at the Russell Sage Institute in New York and the typing of Vivian Kaufman enabled me to create a wholly new and, I hope, better manuscript.

The dissertation was written under the direction of Hanna Pitkin and Michael Rogin. Despite their aversion to acknowledgments of their authority, they nonetheless were mentors in my intellectual development. Their great, but different, gifts as theorists, their patient reading of drafts, their illuminating criticisms, and their encouragement were also essential to this project in each of its stages. During three seemingly endless years of revising, Harvey Goldman at Columbia University provided daily, incisive, and inspiring support, both intellectual and emotional. My theoretical focus has benefited enormously from Peter Schwartz, who shared his astonishing knowledge of Puritanism and his profound theory about its meaning. Robert Merton, at the Russell Sage Foundation, read a draft of the introduction and what once was a chapter on

Hobbes with his usual meticulous and exemplary care, and Joan Tronto at Hunter College read the early chapters. Naomi Schneider, my editor at the University of California Press, provided great encouragement during the revising of the manuscript. Finally, the love and wisdom of Lynnette Taylor, my wife, helped me understand myself, and therefore Winstanley, in ways that make this book an unexpected landmark on my own road.

To such acknowledgments, of course, the usual disclaimers apply: to borrow Puritan terms, a book is a cross that is borne alone, however many have witnessed or participated in the drama. As this may seem too bleak a metaphor, I dedicate this book instead in the terms of grace and transformation:

To my parents, Grace and Martin—first birth; to Hanna and Mike—second birth.

Chronology

on the not-yet-enclosed commons land of St. George's Hill, promising to labor together to initiate a universal "community of earth and spirit." *The True Leveller's Standard* is published. September. The digger colony moves to Cobham Heath in hope of escaping physical and legal harassment.

1650   April. The digger colony is dispersed.

1652   February. *The Law of Freedom in a Platform, Or, True Magistracy Restored,* his last work, is published. (It is dedicated in the same month and year as Hobbes's *Leviathan.*)

1657   Inherits property near Cobham from his wife's father.

1665   First wife dies; marries Elizabeth Stanley, daughter of a prominent Cobham family. Establishes himself as a respectable landowner.

1659–71   Holds various county offices.

1676   Dies.

Introduction

What is past is not dead;
it is not even past.
We cut ourselves off from it;
we pretend to be strangers.
—*Christa Wolf*

The struggle against power is the struggle of memory against
forgetting.
—*Milan Kundera*

Gerrard Winstanley developed a remarkable theory of selfhood, society,
and politics in his effort to change the course of the English Revolution.
Between 1648 and 1649 he wrote an extraordinary series of pamphlets,
in which he fashioned his Puritan legacy into an explosive theoretical
synthesis of New Testament spirituality and Old Testament worldliness.
By joining a diagnosis of the Puritans' inner life to a social analysis of
their commitment to property, Winstanley tried to transform the propertied Puritan radicalism that was central to the Revolution and thereby
promote another path for England's development. Believing that his
words required the testimony of action, he also established a colony of
"diggers" or "True Levellers" in the spring of 1649. These men and
women tried to exemplify in their action an alternative to feudal social
relations, the emerging market, and Puritan radicalism.

That alternative, embodying his theories, represented a rare attempt
to bring together concerns that usually are divorced: a commitment to
personal autonomy and a commitment to collective action. Of greater
interest, perhaps, is the fact that Winstanley's effort to establish "a community of earth and spirit" led him to develop an explicitly political
dimension to his radicalism. As a digger, Winstanley theorized and enacted a radical politics that fused the spiritual and psychological concerns of the saint, the social interests of the poor, and the vocabulary
and commitments of the citizen.

1

The digger colony was defeated in the spring of 1650, a year after its inception. Winstanley's concerns, language, and alternatives were buried then and still are discredited by the institutions and discourse whose emergence he opposed. His radicalism therefore marks a direction that might have been chosen but was not, a road not taken. Since Winstanley was present at one of the major turning points in the movement toward modernity, his theory reveals the roots of ideas and institutions that now dominate our world. Even more important, the road not taken still exists, in certain dimensions, as a set of concerns and commitments that remain fugitive unless given voice, that remain haunting ghosts unless acknowledged.

I focus on Winstanley, first, because of his analysis of Puritan radicalism. In a way unrivaled by any commentator since, Winstanley diagnosed its psychological, social, and political character, unfolded the meaning of its spiritual, scriptural, and political language, and sought a way to heal the tragic flaws he had identified in its ideas and practices. My interpretation of Winstanley will follow the stages of his own development as he worked through, criticized, and transformed the key concepts of Puritan radicalism.

Winstanley's earliest pamphlets, written in the spring and fall of 1648, represent a psychological moment that is the concern of Part I. In an introspective effort to come to terms with his own suffering as a diligent Puritan, Winstanley analyzed the inner life reflected in Puritan religiosity. He deepened the Puritans' language about the pride and sin of "fallen Adam" in order to diagnose the core aspects of Puritanism that he found troubling: a punitive conscience and asceticism toward the body, the anxious accumulation of commodities in the market, doctrinal orthodoxy, and the willful refusal to grant religious liberty to poor men and women. The Puritan effort to link piety toward god to self-control and worldly effort, Winstanley argued, produced a self-defeating and punishing kind of autonomy and an exclusive and intolerant culture. By reworking Puritan ideas of rebirth and regeneration, however, he also developed an alternative. Intended as diagnosis and cure, Winstanley's initial theory represents a profound argument about the inner life, the fashioning of moral autonomy, and the creation of culture.

In the spring of 1649, after what he declared was a revelation, Winstanley suddenly enlarged his focus and began to criticize the Puritans' exclusion of the poor not from god's grace but from the earth. Winstanley now linked his analysis of "the inner kingdom" to newly developed insights about property, wage labor, and the state. In this "social moment," the focus of Part II, Winstanley redefined the Puritans' language of "calling" as he criticized their view of self-determination in matters not only of spirit but also of labor and worldly power. At the moment King Charles was executed, Winstanley argued that Puritan rebels were merely acting out, in mystified and murderous ways, their psychological conflicts and propertied social interests. As a result, he contended, rebels were likely to betray their promises to establish a community that restored liberty and fulfilled Christ's gospel. Committed to those promises, Winstanley argued that piety and liberty required common property, shared production, and religious toleration.

Winstanley's integrated theories of what he called the "kingdom within" and the "kingdom without" became the basis for his "political moment," the concern of Part III. Late in the spring of 1649, shortly before Parliament declared England a republic, Winstanley joined with dispossessed poor people to establish communal production on commons land that had not been enclosed yet. By refusing to work for wages and by sharing the earth as "a common treasury of livelihood for all," Winstanley argued, poor people could retard the expansion of "cursed propriety of mine and thine" and thereby initiate "the beginnings of public freedom to the whole land."

As the diggers planted the first furrows of public freedom, however, they faced violent harassment. Winstanley responded with a stream of pamphlets that addressed all the key actors and groups of the time. He propounded a theory that radically reinterpreted the Exodus narrative of the Old Testament as well as the New Testament prophecy of Christ's Second Coming, which the Puritans had invoked to justify both their struggle for self-determination against church and king and their denial of rights and power to the poor and women. Since Winstanley's colony of diggers suffered that denial in a brutal way, he questioned the Puritans' commitment to the family and property, which excluded propertyless men and all women from public life, and he criticized their commitment to the vanguard politics of an "elect," which generated violence and precluded dialogue.

At the same time, by joining the Old Testament promise of an earthly inheritance to the land to the New Testament promise of a regenerated "kingdom within," he included the poor as agents in a redemptive history that authorized them to overthrow not only church and king but also the emerging market, the social power of propertied Puritans, and the limited democracy defined by Puritan election. By the time the digger colony was crushed, Winstanley had articulated a radical republicanism that joined "freedom in the earth" to the activities of citizenship.

But we recover Winstanley for much more than the interconnections he articulated theoretically and enacted politically. That very accomplishment bespeaks the particular importance of two interrelated qualities central to his radicalism and my argument about it. One is linked to his religiosity, drawn from the Puritans he tried to instruct but given a character all his own. The other is his richly metaphoric language, which he created out of Puritan idioms in his effort to move beyond Puritan orthodoxy. Each quality provides reason enough to return to his landmark, for each signifies what is of enduring worth in his radicalism.

What made Winstanley radical, and his radicalism special, is a vision that roots human beings quite literally in the personal life of bodily experience and in the shared experience of life in a social body. Thus, his thought developed as an explication of how humans are *creatures*, shaped and parented by the experiences, relationships, and history they embody, carry, bear, and witness. Because of his radical grasp of the ways in which humans are rooted, needy, and limited creatures—what he called "created beings"—Winstanley reconceptualized how humans should conceive of their capacity for choice and change, assert their freedom, and realize their potential as *creators*.

At the heart of his vision of humans as creatures and creators is a critique of pride, which he believed was the source of what he called "inner and outer bondage," and a defense of a kind of piety we will call *reverence*, which he believed was the source of "inner and outer freedom." His radicalism and my argument hinge on his unfolding sense of the psychological, social, and political meaning of pride and the bondage it causes and his ongoing effort to define a reverence that frees.

At each of his "moments," Winstanley attacked what he called "the evil, masculine powers of pride," which he attributed to "the back part" or "the dunghill within" each person, and which he believed were leading Puritans to fashion identity, seek worldly autonomy, and reshape society in ways that oppressed others and enslaved themselves. Winstanley used gendered and excremental language to reveal his insights about the fantasies and impulses he analyzed through the concept of pride. To him, pride arises from inner conflicts about bodily limitation, need, and dependence; it is fueled by fantasies of willful or unconditioned action; and it is manifested as an impulse to dominate and control that does not acknowledge limits of action, grounds of being, or bonds of interdependence. As pride makes a person inwardly divided, anxious about control, ascetic toward the body, and acquisitive of objects, so pride's worldly emblems are the power of fathers and aggression against nature, clerical rule and ideological language, property and the exploitation of labor, elitist politics and violence. Because Puritans created "inner bondage" to pride, he believed, their worldly endeavors yielded not freedom but the denials of mutuality that signify "bondage without."

In response, Winstanley developed a theory of "freedom within and without" that was linked to an idea of piety radically different from the Puritans'. Initially he argued that human freedom depends on establishing the right relation toward the inner authority he called god. This "Father within" offered each soul "breasts of love" that provided a "sincere milk" Winstanley described as "the spirit of reason and love." Inward receptivity or piety toward this nurturant part of the self, he contended, delivered the self from anxious acquisitiveness and the punitive conscience, generating instead self-respect, inner direction, and worldly independence.

This inner piety led Winstanley back to the world in a new way. He came to argue that human freedom also depends on abolishing property in order to establish the right relationship to the earth, "our Common Mother," with which humans necessarily must "subsist." As he had theorized that respect for "the Father within" each person encouraged moral autonomy and mutual respect, so he reasoned that respect for the common source of physical nourishment for all would generate recognition of the bodily need of each and, thereby, social relations of "mutual preservation" among men and women, whom he termed "fellow creatures."

Winstanley had retained the Puritans' commitment to the idea that piety is essential to freedom, but in order to fulfill their promises of self-determination and justice, he redefined their piety and thereby radicalized the entire Puritan project. Because he insisted that god's "spirit of love and reason" animated nature and each person, Winstanley developed a politics that was radical in its demand for the abolition of property and hierarchy, the inclusion of the poor and women, and attention to earthly needs and spiritual equality. Because he valued reciprocal social bonds, language rooted in "experienced speech," and individual choice based on "experimental knowledge," his politics repudiated violence and demanded a commitment to toleration and dialogue.

Thus, Winstanley defined need and understood freedom by articulating a distinctive relationship to the soul and the body, to god and the earth, and to the needs and capacities of others. That relationship is characterized not by the alienation, distance, and denial he associated with pride but rather by the attitude of reconciliation and reciprocity he associated with true piety, or reverence. We use that word to connote deep respect, tinged with awe, and he manifested this attitude toward the spiritual and physical needs that define and bind created beings, toward the sources of nourishment on which he believed humans must depend, and toward the values and truths appropriate to "created beings" and therefore god's spirit in them.

Winstanley argued that creatures embedded in the body, nature, and history can achieve freedom only if they act in ways that "bear witness" to the needs and values that animate and limit them and to the sources of nourishment that parent and feed them. Thus, the word *reverence* describes Winstanley's radicalism not only because of the religiosity that was its premise but also because it suggests the way in which Winstanley theorized a *conditioned* and *conditional* freedom from which there is much to learn.

Central to Winstanley's idea of reverence is a second quality that also makes his radicalism special: his theoretical insights and political innovations depended on a seriousness about language rarely rivaled in the tradition of political thought. Only by way of a profound meditation on the meaning of common Puritan idioms could Winstanley have developed his own innovative and critical reading of pride and piety; only by taking seriously the meaning of Puritans' own metaphoric prose could Winstanley have created the bodily, sexual, parental, and gendered metaphors that literally embodied the connections he theorized between the inner life and worldly action. Through images of "the Father within," god's "breasts of love," "sincere milk," "teats of creatures," "the dunghill within," and "the back part," he exemplified in graphic terms the origin of pride and the meaning of reverence.

Whereas modern commentators often unmask or devalue language to reveal the class interests and unconscious motives underlying beliefs and practices, Winstanley used the meaning of common idioms both to disclose the capacity for free action in people and to identify the causes of their behavior in psychological and social forces. Therefore, he also could *address* others, speaking as one living creature and actor to another. In an irreducible and vividly authentic voice, he passionately and indignantly prodded his contemporaries to reexamine the meaning of what they said, so they could act in a way that was faithful to their own words. In this sense his theory yielded a practice that was profoundly "political," for he analyzed power and engaged in dialogue about intentions and choices. As a result, his words made—and still make—visceral sense of what people feel, see, and know in their own lives. Indeed, Winstanley's vision of self-fashioning and collective action invites a reexamination of more modern conceptions of selfhood, social life, and radical politics.

In part, I will situate and assess the continuing significance of Winstanley's arguments by contrasting him with the Puritan radicalism that was his legacy and adversary. But a full appreciation of Winstanley's accomplishment as a theorist also depends on contrasting his reverent radicalism and the theory of Thomas Hobbes. It is a significant coincidence that after his defeat in 1650 Winstanley completed his last book in November 1651, the same month and year as Hobbes published his famous *Leviathan*. For it is not Winstanley but Hobbes who towers over that era in the modern imagination. Because he established a discourse still dominant in many ways, Hobbes has defined the modern view of Puritan politics and thus of critics like Winstanley who were twinned with it. As Winstanley helps us reexamine concerns and commitments buried by Hobbes's text and devalued by the world it foretold, however, so Hobbes helps us understand the troubling consequences of Winstanley's effort to avoid the sin of pride.

In part, Hobbes sharpens the significance of Winstanley because each criticized Puritan radicalism in contrasting terms and with opposed purposes. Both were concerned with the problem of pride, and each synthesized theories of the body and selfhood, the market and society, the state and history in efforts to articulate an alternative to Puritan radicalism. But Winstanley was bound to the Puritanism he criticized, taking seriously its core concepts, whereas Hobbes was an enemy, intent on subverting any aspect of Puritanism that fostered rebellion. Thus, Winstanley used the language of the Puritans to question their allegiance to the market and paternal power in order to extend the Revolution they began. In contrast, Hobbes introduced the language of science into the study of politics to depoliticize Puritan rebels and thereby to provide a more secure basis for the market and patriarchy. By discrediting the Puritan idea of god and the rebellion it spawned, Hobbes exposed the anxieties and interests Winstanley had tried to transform, and thereby undermined the Puritans' effort to restore the king's power to the body of society.

Such radically diverging arguments arose from a fundamental difference. Winstanley posited a "Father within," a god whose reason ordered nature and whose inner authority sanctioned worldly rebellion; therefore, Winstanley criticized the Puritans for not being radical enough. In contrast, Hobbes deprived nature and the body of spirit, and on this basis he theorized the transition from kingship to a state sovereignty that enjoined only obedience. Winstanley's god sponsored rebellion and cultural heterodoxy; Hobbes's "mortal god" subverted politics by generating cultural conformity and confining human action to private life.

As this analysis suggests, Hobbes is a valuable foil to Winstanley because he is the first and perhaps greatest "modernizer." He justified the emerging market, but more important, he defended the process of *state building* regardless of social relations and in conjunction with a new faith in science. In this effort Hobbes developed a view of human conventionality that was extraordinarily prescient in its understanding of the *estrangement* that has seemed to attend all modern forms of collective action and state building, whether liberal, nationalist, or Leninist.

Puritans used the idea of redemptive history to attack the church and the monarchy: Attributing "bondage" to prideful invention, they tried to define and establish a contrasting self-determination based on piety toward god and justified by the claim to know and fulfill his purposes. The flaws and limitations of their struggle led Winstanley beyond their orthodoxy. He sought a politics untainted by pride, and therefore he rebelled. In contrast, Hobbes exposed pride in order to prevent rebellion. By showing how the idea of redemptive history dissimulated the Puritans' pride and inventiveness, he tried to teach men that they are, and must be, the prideful creators of the authority they live by. In this way, however, he argued that men become humbled creatures who must, and will, piously submit to their own prideful invention. Thus, Winstanley's significance emerges by contrast with the politics Hobbes aptly foreshadowed in the myth of Prometheus and the image of Leviathan.

In 1642, at the outset of the Civil War, Hobbes used the myth of Prometheus in *De Cive* to argue that Puritan language about God had masked the full conventionality, and thus the radical inventiveness, of the Puritan effort at collective self-fashioning. Hobbes depicted the Puritans not as pious saints and instruments of god but as rebels without sanction, predicting that parricide would create fratricide as their revolt generated anxiety and anarchy.[1]

When *Leviathan* appeared in 1651, however, the monarchy was already in ashes, and not surprisingly, Hobbes's description of Prometheus had changed. Anxiety and anarchy became the natural basis of all society at all times, as if there never had been fathers, kings, god—and rebels. Human problems appear to result not from prideful revolt but from the natural character of desire and imagination and from the natural absence of binding authority. Thus, Prometheus the rebel was replaced by a new Prometheus, one who anxiously suffers not as a punishment for rebellion, but by his very nature.[2]

Politically, the problem had become not preventing rebellion against a still-extant authority but creating an authority that prevented any further rebellion. Thus, Hobbes had become much more sophisticated theoretically, for sovereignty appeared as an abstraction and invention necessary for any effective form of order, of which kingship was merely one, albeit preferable, version. While Prometheus in *De Cive* signified invention in a pejorative sense, Hobbes now had recognized the saving power of the right sort of invention, while still condemning the inventions of "private men."

---

1. In *De Cive* Hobbes contended:

It seems that the ancients, who made the fable of Prometheus, pointed at this. They say that Prometheus, having stolen fire from the sun, formed a man out of clay, and for this deed he was tortured by Jupiter with a perpetual gnawing at his liver. Which is, that by human invention, which is signified by Prometheus, laws and justice were by imitation taken from monarchy; by virtue thereof, as by fire removed from its orb, the multitude, as the dirt and dregs of men, was as it were quickened and formed into a civil person, which is termed aristocracy or democracy. But the author and abhetor being found, who might have securely and quietly lived under the natural jurisdiction of kings, do thus smart for it; that being exposed still to alterations, they are tormented with perpetual cares, suspicions, and dissensions. (Thomas Hobbes, *De Cive*, in *Man and Citizen*, ed. Bernard Gert [Garden City, N.Y.: Anchor, 1972], p. 224)

2. As Hobbes said in *Leviathan*:

For being assured that there be causes of all things that have hitherto arrived, or shall arrive hereafter; it is impossible for a man, who continually endeavoreth to secure himself against the evil he fears and procure the good he desireth, not to be in a perpetual state of solicitude of the time to come; so that every man, especially those that are overprovident, are in a state like that of Prometheus. For as Prometheus, which interpreted is the *prudent man*, was bound to the hill Caucasus, a place of large prospect, where an eagle feeding on his liver devoureth in the day as much as was repaired at night; so that man, which looks too far before him in care of future time, hath his heart all the day long gnawed on by fear of death, poverty, or other calamity, and has not repose nor pause of his anxiety, but in sleep. (Thomas Hobbes, *Leviathan*, ed. Michael Oakeshott [New York: Collier, 1962], pp. 87–88)

Thus, as Hobbes himself became the teacher of the new science, he tacitly replaced the rebellious Prometheus. For now he had stolen fire from the gods on behalf of mankind, whom his science would teach to *invent* precisely the "civil person" or "artificial man" whose creation he once condemned as a dangerous act of pride. The solution to the problem of naturally orphaned creatures was to invent a god who would throw them on the rock if they ever rebelled. Prudent Promethean men must create a sovereign to which they transfer their right to define, judge, and act; only obedience to an invented sovereign power can save them from the unfortunate consequences of their natural temptation to be political actors, while providing them with the secure property and abundance and the peace and moral certainty they really need.

Hobbes moved from a history of rebellion to a concept of nature in order to expose the Puritans' pride and bury their radicalism; then by moving from nature to sovereignty, Hobbes used pride to build a state on the grave of Puritan rebellion, which now appeared as the emblem of uncontrolled nature. As he changed the significance of Prometheus, Hobbes did not rescue people from nature but rather used the state of nature and the science "apt" to it to rescue people from politics, represented by Puritan radicalism. As Hobbes shifted from condemning the Prometheus who signifies invention to inventing a sovereign that saves the Prometheus who signifies prudence, we see the burial of Puritan radicalism and the birth of modern politics. Behind Prometheus the creator lies Prometheus the defeated rebel.

Deeply ambivalent about the pride he had exposed in the religious claims of Puritan rebels, Hobbes conceived of a science and a state that would transform the pride rebels had disowned into the creator's pious regard for his own creation. Hobbes used Prometheus to signify the insight into conventionality provided by his science, to suggest the benefits of that science, and to endorse the pride that is always essential to creating civilization. Yet the book is titled *Leviathan* because, as only a Promethean would, Hobbes had taken on god's challenge to Job and with "his own right arm" pridefully created a man-made Leviathan to "humble the children of pride."

By linking the pride that worships only what is humanly invented to the estranging power of those inventions, Hobbes originates the question that modern politics has forced many later theorists to ask: can people shape themselves in ways that neither require them to act as gods nor compel them to become the submissive creatures of their creations? It is this question that animated each "moment" in Winstanley's thought and action as he tried to articulate an alternative to Puritan radicalism.

Accordingly, Winstanley appears as a ghost from the grave of the Puritanism Hobbes buried, as one of its orphaned progeny, but therefore also as a founding voice in a countertradition that has been opposed to the forms of thought and action that Hobbes typified.[3]

What was at stake in Winstanley's and Hobbes's time to a great extent is also at stake now. For this reason I also will explore how Winstanley's reverence addressed dilemmas that still animate the psychoanalytic language of self-understanding, Marxist arguments about social relations and collective action, and the republican vision of citizenship. To be sure, Winstanley's religiosity differs considerably from these later, secular traditions. But in the context of parallel concerns, these differences are especially instructive. Thus, my argument traces the stages of Winstanley's development, at each moment rooting his thought and action in the Puritanism he transformed, situating his radicalism in relation to Hobbes, and directing his perspective toward more modern traditions of theorizing.

Part IV concludes this study with Winstanley's defeat, his final book, and his subsequent respectability in the very county of his rebellion. These disclose what was problematic in his radicalism all along and illustrate in a poignant way how Hobbes would foreshadow the road taken; for Winstanley's disavowal of pride—including his own—distorted his radicalism, contaminated his last book, and finally drove him into the arms of worldly authority.

Unlike Hobbes's Prometheus, this dutiful rebel emulated Christ, acting not in the name of what he self-consciously imagined and invented but for the sake of overthrowing precisely such prideful "ways and works." Thus, Winstanley disowned the aspects of himself he associated with pride, with humans as creators. He disavowed the very rebelliousness that was inextricable from his reverence, portraying himself as the wholly innocent lamb of god. In this way, his very claim to reverence was his own form of pride, an ideal of an unreal purity by which he devalued, and sought to purify, the imagination and anger, the invention and willfulness, that he found in the Puritans but insisted were not intrinsically part of "created being."

While he claimed that his reverence authorized him "to turn the

---

3. For a full argument about Hobbes, see George Shulman, "Hobbes, Puritans, and Promethean Politics," *Political Theory* 16, no. 3 (August 1988): 426–44, and "Metaphor and Modernization in the Political Thought of Thomas Hobbes," *Political Theory*, forthcoming.

world upside down" and obligated him to engage in a politics of revolt, we also see how the denial of his own rebelliousness was the central premise of his rebellion. As he claimed complicity in the victory over Charles, reckoned with the conventionality of his ideas, and took responsibility for the suffering of the diggers, his political action implicated him precisely in what he meant to purify from the world and himself. But Winstanley could not grant that the transgression he abhorred was central to the reverence he idealized. As he suffered on this cross, so his defeat at the hands of a far superior force reflected his own inner pressure toward an act of expiating self-sacrifice. Still seeking to deny his pride and find an authority to revere, he then created an imaginary orthodoxy in *Law of Freedom,* and finally he submitted to the real authorities he once attacked.

Winstanley was not defeated because he had tried to avoid the sin of pride; nor does his defeat prove Hobbes "right" about life and politics. But the issue of pride is Hobbes's way into the politics of his time. Pride is the truth that Hobbes always will remind us of, so that the issue becomes one of facing pride without becoming a victim of Hobbes's logic. Hence, Winstanley is not a hero to be resurrected or emulated literally. Rather, the specific story he told about Puritanism and revolution yields a parable about being a rebel and a creator: he appears as a character shaped by the very narrative he dramatized and subject to the very dilemmas and prideful creativity he diagnosed in others. Attending to the tale and not only to the teller suggests what is problematic about Winstanley's reverence: his refusal, in spite of his revolutionary project, to "own" his pride and see himself as other than god's obedient son. In this way, Winstanley reveals an important cautionary tale, inextricable from what he explicitly tried to teach about reverently shaping the self and world.

Thus, this study is not strictly a historical inquiry or intellectual history but rather an effort to build bridges between, on the one hand, Winstanley's language, theory, and action and, on the other, issues that still are troubling and controversial. It is constructed as a conversation across time in an effort to clarify what Winstanley, defeated by history, offers a modern reader.[4]

4. Accordingly, this study does not situate Winstanley's thought in all the various traditions on which it draws, and is not, except in footnotes, situated in the academic literature about him. It focuses on the significance of his thought, not on its derivation or originality, and the validity of my interpretation rests on his language, not on arguments with other commentators.

PART I

The Psychological Moment

In most books, the *I*, or first person, is omitted; in this it will
be retained; that, in respect of egotism, is the main difference.
We commonly do not remember that it is, after all, always
the first person that is speaking. I should not talk so much
about myself if there were any body else whom I knew as
well. Unfortunately, I am confined to this theme by the
narrowness of my experience. Moreover, I, on my side,
require of every writer, first or last, a simple and sincere
account of his own life, and not merely what he has heard of
other men's lives; some such account as he would send to his
kindred from a distant land; for if he has lived sincerely, it
must have been in a distant land to me.

> —*Thoreau*, Walden

As a tradesman in London, Winstanley sold the cloth produced by his
father. But the financial difficulties that followed the death of his father
in 1639, exacerbated by the Civil War, which began in 1641, led to his
bankruptcy in 1643. He left London, and for the next five years he and
his wife lived in the countryside of his childhood, supported by the gen-
erosity of her friends and by his day labor as a tender of cows. In the
spring of 1648, not long before his fortieth birthday, he announced himself in his first pamphlet, *The Mystery of God:*

> To my beloved country men of the county of Lancaster: Do not be surprised
> to see my name here, for God does not always choose the learned in whom to
> manifest himself. If anything in this book seems strange, do not brand it as
> error, for I myself could not at first bear many truths of God in which I now
> see beauty. (81)[1]

1. *The Collected Works of Gerard Winstanley*, ed. George H. Sabine (Ithaca: Cornell
University Press, 1941). All page numbers in parentheses after quoted passages are from
this edition. Sabine collected only the "abstracts" of the earliest works, however; refer-

After describing what the Puritans called a "wilderness condition" of anxiety and despair, inner conflict and "barrenness," Winstanley declared that he had been reborn as god's humble instrument and good son:

> I have writ nothing but what was given me of my Father; and at the first beholding of this mystery, it appeared to me so high above my reach that I was confounded and lost in my spirit; but God, who I believe is my teacher, for I have joy and rest in him, left me not in bondage, but set me at liberty, and caused me to see much glory in these following truths. (MG, preface)

His first four books elaborate that experience and those truths, and they constitute a spiritual autobiography and a portrait of his time.

Although the countryside was being devastated by war, famine, and the enclosure movement, all of which later became the focus of his concern, these early writings are not explicitly political or social. Winstanley looks at the storm raging around him with the detachment of the Christian who is "free within." Professing to be nourished and guided by the inner authority he calls "the reason and love of the Father," he says he is able to "rest quietly in the midst of these national hurley-burlies," though he lacks "food, riches, clothing, and even the communion of good people" (94). Yet this appearance of religious withdrawal or noninvolvement is deceptive: Winstanley feels sure that what he describes in terms of his experience of God can resolve the worldly troubles of his time.

Winstanley diagnoses the causes and consequences of pride in order to instruct his readers how to overcome the "inner bondage" that he believes has caused the worldly conflicts currently overwhelming them. Like the Puritans, he argues that the way human beings shape personal desire, identity, and autonomy is externalized in their worldly relations. But he turns against the Puritans their own diagnosis of the inner disorders that people act out in self-defeating and destructive ways.[2]

---

ences to them are noted by abbreviations of their titles followed by the page number of the copies in the rare-book room of the Columbia University Library: MG (*Mystery of God*), BSG (*Breaking of the Day of God*), and SP (*Saints Paradice*). Passages from the preface to the collection Winstanley issued in 1650 are noted by the word "preface" in parentheses and can be found in *Law of Freedom in a Platform and Other Works*, ed. Christopher Hill (Cambridge: Cambridge University Press, 1982). Finally, G. E. Aylmer discovered a pamphlet authored by Winstanley, entitled *England's Spirit Unfolded; or, An Encouragement to Take the Engagement*. The pamphlet, noted here as ESU, was published in *Past and Present* 40 (July 1968).

2. In doing so, Winstanley lumps together all Puritans, as if they shared a common orthodoxy, whereas the most recent historical scholarship focuses on their baffling variety. Like the greatest interpreters of Puritanism, however, Winstanley emphasizes the parame-

Winstanley opposes the core beliefs and practices he associates with pride precisely because he has taken seriously but transformed the Puritan belief that a pious relation to god is central to human freedom. By working through Puritan ideas about god, Winstanley believes he has "discovered" that god is neither transcendent nor angry but rather a "spirit of love" that "dwells in the body" (95). As a result, and contrary to mainstream Puritanism, he contends that Christ's resurrection and kingdom is to be "enjoyed" by the "material life of the five senses" while in "this body of flesh":

> The Father is that universal power that hath spread himself in the whole globe; the son is that same power drawn into man . . . making that person subject to the Spirit . . . that dwells everywhere. There is not a person or creature within the compass of the globe but he is a son of the Father, or the breakings forth of that power in one body. . . . Man living in the light of the Father is the well-beloved son because that one power of righteousness dwells bodily in him, and the whole creation is drawn up into that one center, man. (168)

Although an inner and even bodily experience, the Father within is not private or subjective in the modern sense. To Winstanley, god is the "power," the "reason," the "righteousness," and the "love" that animates all creation, and therefore god is an inner authority one discovers and lives by, but does not fabricate:

> When thou art made to see him rule and govern not only in thee, but in the whole creation, . . . thou mayest call him God warrantably, for thou knowest . . . that the government of the whole creation is on the shoulders of that spirit to which thou art made experimentally subject. (108)

Experimental knowledge of this god, he believes, enables people to transform the punitive conscience Puritans confuse with god's presence; to still the anxious desire they confuse with nature; to disenchant the objects they mistakenly sanctify in their pursuit of a hidden god's love; and to accept their equality with those they had defined as reprobate. Moreover, Winstanley has learned that piety toward the inner reason he calls "the word of power" has enabled him "to speak my own experienced words." Freed from clerical authority and theological dogma, he feels authorized to enter history as a "witness," "testifying" to his re-

---

ters within which variations occur: piety for a transcendent god and an ascetic relationship to the body; commitment to the "visible signs" of god's grace, which were linked to ritual observance and worldly endeavor in the market; and concern with legal forms and social control, typified by the politics of covenant theology.

birth in order to disclose to others their own capacity for inner change, authentic speech, and independent action. In this way, he prophesies the appearance of a new kind of community, one that arises from the "inward freedom" engendered by the right relationship to god.

Obviously, this is a psychological approach toward Winstanley's initial pamphlets. But as William Haller says of the Puritans, they were "physicians to the soul," administering to the "troubles, call them spiritual or psychological, by which men of their time were actually beset." One could say that Haller psychologizes Puritanism, making a theology into a therapy, but it would be truer to say that he has disclosed, in fact, the relationship between the religious discourse of the past and the secular and psychoanalytic thought of the present. What Haller suggests about the Puritans, and others have argued about Luther, can be suggested about Winstanley. Indeed, Winstanley's initial theory reveals him as one of the great psychological theorists in the Western tradition. He appears as the first great "analyst" of what might be called the religious neurosis, the diagnosis of which involves a theory of cure.[3]

Winstanley's religiosity does not make him alien to psychological thought because his spirituality is foremost an emotional and even bodily experience. His religious language builds on his awareness that humans are mortal and needy, desiring and angry creatures. His metaphors evoke the meanings, images, and experience of maternal and paternal authority, of oral feeding and excremental purging, of the unconscious and the way it is projected onto people and objects. He intentionally uses theological concepts and scriptural metaphor to analyze unconscious feelings about the body and food, dependence and authority, sexuality and power, need and autonomy.

Indeed, his language seems as if it were lifted from a psychoanalytic textbook. "Fallen Adam" is described as a creature ruled by "the masculine power of pride," which arises from "the bottomless pit," his "back part," and the "stinking dunghill within." Because of his pride, Adam is confused about nourishment, resentful of authority, and deceived by his fantasies of autonomy. Adam can gain inner direction and nourishment, however, by "sucking sincere milk from the Father's own breasts of

3. William Haller, *The Rise of Puritanism* (Philadelphia: University of Pennsylvania Press, 1972), pp. 27, 33.

love" (140), which "weans" him from dependence on the "invented teats" of worldly authorities and the "waste words" of preachers (232).

Such metaphors enable Winstanley to give voice to realities otherwise addressed only by psychoanalysis. Moreover, Winstanley's understanding of the relationship between Adam and Christ represents a developmental theory of the human psyche and a standard of health by which to define truly adult autonomy. By instructing adults about pride and true piety, Winstanley wants to develop in them the capacity to "digest" consciously what has shaped them so they can fashion the autonomy appropriate to them.

Accordingly, just as Luther's language inspired Norman O. Brown's psychoanalytic speculations in *Life Against Death,* so Luther's heirs— Winstanley and the Puritans he criticizes—work within a discourse that prompts the use of psychoanalysis here. There are parallel genealogies, as it were, that link Winstanley's interpretation of Puritanism to the Christian, especially the Protestant, tradition and join my interpretation to a psychoanalytical tradition. The goal is to establish a conversation about the inner life between theorists in two different, but mutually illuminating, *interpretative* traditions, each of which is rich, speculative, and "experimental," to use Winstanley's word.[4]

To explicate Winstanley's theory in terms of pride and reverence is to emphasize not only its basis in religiosity but also its secular meaning as a psychological approach to autonomy and culture. Such an approach is surely controversial. Ironically, Winstanley's anticipation that some of

4. Perhaps I should emphasize that I am not presuming a dogmatic truth about either discourse, nor striving to prove with methodological rigor the truth of either, but rather I juxtapose what are, after all, two traditions of interpretation, neither one monolithic or fixed. Thus, the use of psychoanalysis does not devalue Winstanley's language about god; but to understand his metaphoric language, one cannot "privilege" his faith, either. Finally, that metaphoric language can yield many possible readings; this reading attends to the psychological. Accordingly, the following two chapters are deeply indebted to, but also comment on, the arguments in Norman O. Brown, *Life Against Death* (Middletown, Conn.: Wesleyan University Press, 1959); Erik Erikson, *Young Man Luther* (New York: Norton, 1958); Susan Griffin, *Pornography and Silence* (New York: Harper and Row, 1981); and Dorothy Dinnerstein, *The Mermaid and the Minotaur* (New York: Harper and Row, 1976). Essays by Jessica Benjamin have had a profound impact on my understanding of Winstanley's insights and value: "The Oedipal Riddle," in *The Problem of Authority in America,* ed. Mark E. Kann (Philadelphia: Temple University Press, 1981); "The End of Internalization: Adorno's Social Psychology," *Telos* 32 (Summer 1977): 42–64; "Authority and the Family Revisited: Or, A World Without Fathers?" *New German Critique* 13 (Winter 1978): 35–58; and "A Desire of One's Own," in *Feminist Studies/Critical Studies,* ed. Teresa de Laurentis (Bloomington: Indiana University Press, 1986), pp. 78–101. Her arguments now are woven together in *The Bonds of Love* (Pantheon, 1988).

his readers would find his language "strange" is more appropriate now, when metaphoric speech often is deemed, as Hobbes put it, "absurd."[5] Nonetheless, modern readers can recognize the truths in Winstanley's language if we follow his advice to his contemporaries about reading the Bible, namely, look within yourself:

> Adam and Christ . . . are to be seen within your heart. . . . Travelling and drudging in the wilderness and coming to rest on the seventh day is to be seen within you. . . . Christ lying in the grave . . . and Christ rising up . . . is to be seen within you. And the stone that lies at the mouth of the sepulchre, your unbelief, and the removing of that stone, setting you at liberty, are to be seen within you. (215)

When read in this way, Winstanley appears not only as a stranger from a "distant" land but also as a "kindred," awakening people to the common experience that makes them "neighbors."

5. Winstanley's early works were the equivalents of best-sellers, and he believed his theory of "the kingdom within" was central to his later theories and activities. Indeed, nine months after he began digging, he reissued his early works in a single book with a new preface. But the early writings are hardly read and have not been republished since then, perhaps because Winstanley's religiosity and his metaphoric language seem so foreign, even impenetrable, to the modern reader.

Certain modern writers, however, have attended to Winstanley's early works. Christopher Hill, especially, shows a certain sensitivity toward them and toward their relationship to what follows, but his edition of Winstanley's writings excludes them. His interpretation, however, is available in "The Religion of Gerrard Winstanley," *Past and Present* Supplement 5 (1978), and *The World Turned Upside Down* (New York: Viking, 1972). Also sensitive to the connections between Winstanley's early texts and his later politics is T. Wilson Hayes, *Winstanley the Digger* (Cambridge: Cambridge University Press, 1979). Neither author, however, really explores the theoretical significance of Winstanley's early writings, and neither attends to the *problematic* legacy they provide for Winstanley's later, more social and political theorizing.

CHAPTER I

The Fall of Adam

I have travelled a good deal in Concord; and every where, in
shops, and offices, and fields, the inhabitants have appeared
to me to be doing penance in a thousand remarkable ways. . . .
But men labor under a mistake. . . . By a seeming fate,
commonly called necessity, they are employed, as it says in
an old book, laying up treasures which moth and rust will
corrupt and thieves break through and steal.

—*Thoreau*, Walden

As Erik Erikson said about Luther, so commentators as diverse as Perry
Miller and William Haller, Michael Walzer and Christopher Hill, have
asserted about Puritanism: the effort to define for oneself one's own relation to god, and thus to the beliefs by which one conscientiously lives,
was the birth of the modern and individualized ego, a self that shapes its
own destiny or salvation. At the same time, the idea of moral autonomy
spurred Puritans to seek self-determination in other matters, and ultimately led to revolutionary action against worldly authorities.

These writers also witness, however, that what Erikson called the
"ego revolution" was rooted not in an attack on all authority but in the
discovery of a god whose inner authority was felt to be empowering. It
was submission to this authority that enabled men and women to feel
justified in their speech and action and therefore entitled to rebel against
worldly authorities. Accordingly, prideful defiance of god and pious
submission to god's word were central to the Puritans' theory: freedom
is possible only for those who overcome pride, as pride is the refusal
to acknowledge human limitation and the need to live by god's word
and law.

In the acuity of their diagnosis of pride, and in the psychological ambition of their transformative idea of individual moral agency, lies one
key to what made the Puritans radical. The psychological premise of
their religiosity and politics, however, was gendered in a problematic
way. For Puritans, maternal authority and images, represented by the
Catholic church, make men helpless and dependent, and correspond-

ingly, the "carnal" desire for love is inherently dangerous to freedom. Since love diminishes the capacity for freedom by eliciting the desire for dependence, autonomy can be achieved only by way of what separates people from maternal authority and from the infantilizing need for love. Since love is problematic, and what nurtures us can enslave us, autonomy is conceived by way of voluntary subjection to the discipline and law associated internally and externally with paternal authority.[1]

In contrast to idolatrous rituals and physical images, therefore, Puritans believed that voluntary subjection—to inner paternal authority, the ascetic demands of labor in a "calling," and the laws of a sanctified "covenant"—constituted their freedom, not only *from* childish dependence, but also *for* systematic action to build a New Jerusalem. In these terms Puritans linked inner piety to worldly activity and authority. Accordingly, Puritan preachers repeatedly returned to the story of the golden calf. They believed that Aaron loved the people too much when he let them make and worship the golden calf; or at least, he acted like a stereotypical mother, concerned more with their happiness and physical well-being than their freedom. Rather than say that Aaron left the Hebrews free to choose the calf, as god left them free to choose sin, the Puritans defended Moses' coercion as the proper paternal exercise of authority.

Unlike Christ, but like Moses, Puritan fathers felt entitled by their god to punish those they characterized as the "wives and children" subject to them. Their sense was that only a certain kind of father can establish separateness and self-control; only external discipline and a certain asceticism can fortify the self against feminine snares. More generally in the tradition of political theory, autonomy and political freedom have been associated with gender: a deep ambivalence about maternal authority, real women, and desire appears in the repeated assertion that autonomy is generated only by the right sort of paternal authority.[2]

Hobbes also used fear of feminine nature and maternal power, but to subvert Puritan revolt and defend "the rights of kings." Hobbes discredited the idea of an empowering paternal spirit, while defending submission to an invented, visible, and coercive power that is constructed as

1. See Jessica Benjamin, *The Bonds of Love* (New York: Pantheon, 1988), from whose work this formulation is derived.
2. For the role of gendered images in the Old Testament itself, see Herbert Schneidau, *Sacred Discontent* (Berkeley and Los Angeles: University of California Press, 1976), who links the project of the exodus liberation specifically to a struggle against matriarchal religion, associated with the idea of slavery in Egypt. On Machiavelli, for example, see Hanna Fenichel Pitkin, *Fortune Is a Woman* (Berkeley and Los Angeles: University of California Press, 1981).

artifice but understood in paternal terms. As the metaphor of Prometheus suggests, Hobbes used prideful male invention self-consciously to secularize the Puritans' attempt to achieve autonomy by controlling what they represented as feminine and maternal, natural and chaotic.[3]

In contrast to the Puritans and Hobbes, Winstanley discovered "by experience" that god "is to be felt in the body" as a loving, partly maternal authority with "breasts of love." He therefore argues that the key to a prideful understanding of autonomy is the divorce of love and freedom, bodily need and human autonomy. Thus, Winstanley uses his metaphors to diagnose the pride animating worldly asceticism: because of a pride they do not understand, he argues, Puritans create bondage rather than freedom. In these terms, he also subverts the logic of Hobbes's *Leviathan*.

THE PSYCHOLOGY OF ADAM: AMBIVALENCE AND PRIDE

Winstanley begins his account of the Fall with the following argument: "When God made Adam, there was two beings, different from one another, that is, God himself that was uncreated Being, and the human nature that was created Being" (MG/1). God made a garden for Adam, but Adam himself was a garden wherein god meant to dwell: those qualities that Winstanley deems god's creation are the "herbs and flowers" in the garden of Adam. Yet because Adam is a "distinct creature" as well as a "created being," there arises the "weed" of pride in the garden of Adam's created qualities. Pride is the desire "to be as a God, or to be a being of itself, equal and distinct from God" (MG/1). This "spirit of self-love" makes Adam "discontent with being as God made him" and promotes the aspiration "of the creature to be an absolute being like God." (81).

This desire to be the creator of himself, instead of a created being, is

3. Hobbes's state of nature includes literal references to women and signifies a symbolic reading of nature. On the one hand, the earth is a mother whose indifference promotes anxiety and power seeking and whose availability promotes contention and bloodshed. On the other hand, children (usually described as male) are in the actual mother's power, partly because "where there are no matrimonial laws it cannot be known who is the father" (L/152) and partly because "he who is newly born is in the mother's power before any others" (DC/212). Like the earth, however, actual mothers are either indifferent, malevolent, or incapable of nourishing. In Hobbes's picture of our natural condition, those subject to mother love are likely to be "invaded" or killed by marauders, or "alienated," "sacrificed," "pawned," or "sold" by mothers. Thus, Hobbes's Prometheus lives in the absence of actual fathers and therefore is exposed to mother nature and by actual mothers. It is in this context that Prometheus must learn to build an "artificial man," as if to say he literally must parent himself by inventing a father.

"the fruit or invention of the creature after he was made; God did not make it" (MG/1). Thus, Winstanley affirms that "sin is properly man's own work," as if to say that the prideful desire to be self-generating is a self-generated pride. And this pride becomes fertile and powerful: "All the faculties and powers of that living created being, Adam, are now become absolutely rebellious, and enmity itself, against the being of God" (MG/5).

Winstanley is here describing a conflict *within* Adam, who represents both men and women, about the fact that he is a created being. As Winstanley frames it, Adam's struggle takes the form of choosing what shall parent and rule him: Adam is choosing whether to honor god or his pride, which suggests Adam's prideful ambivalence about being wholly a creature. To depict his understanding of choice and inner authority, Winstanley turns psychic life into a political drama:

> And truly here lies the chiefest knowledge of a man, to know those two powers that strive for government in him, and to see and know them distinctly . . . , that he may be able to say: This is the name and power of the flesh; and this is the name and power of the Lord. (173)

Winstanley's language suggests that "created being" is a wholly passive part of himself—the senses, which Winstanley calls "the living earth," and the receptive qualities of his emotional being, which he calls "the living soul." Rendered as the "feminine part" of Adam, created being is formed and fed by the inner "government" or "power" of pride, or by god. By depicting how Adam pursues spiritual nourishment and thus fashions his identity, Winstanley's internal drama represents adult choices about achieving inward direction and autonomy (477–80).

In Winstanley's language, if Adam defies the inner authority of the Father, he makes "the feminine part" into a "bondswoman" of the "evil masculine power of pride" (SP/47–50). If Adam becomes the "disobedient son," a "first" or "fallen Adam," then the garden of his created being becomes a grave, for when "the first man of flesh governs the kingdom, thy body, in unrighteousness," then Christ, "the son of freedom, . . . lies buried in this earthly tabernacle, under those cursed powers, in thy enslaved body" (173). Winstanley is saying that if adults consent to their pride and deny their dependence on god, they cannot satisfy truly the needs of created being or achieve genuine autonomy.[4]

More broadly, Winstanley's internalization of theological argument

4. By and large, Winstanley's references to the Fall do not distinguish between Adam and Eve and do not "blame" Eve. But see *The Collected Works*, p. 203.

can be rendered as follows: how we become and behave as adults depends on the relationship we establish toward the god within and toward the physical and spiritual needs of our created being. Winstanley highlights what is receptive, needy, and sentient in humans as creatures, but also he emphasizes that humans choose the values and commitments, or authority, by which they nourish themselves and fashion an identity. He believes that adult autonomy depends on choosing and honoring the right sort of inner government, and it is with that concern in mind that we should understand his analysis of pride.

Thus, the Father within is not a literal parent, but Winstanley's account of Adam also points to what will be troubling in his argument about pride. The inner drama of Adam reveals Winstanley's dream of being purely a created being, wholly god's garden. He would cultivate in himself only those qualities he says god has "planted" in him, by uprooting, as "weeds of pride," precisely what he defines as originating only with himself. Feeling obliged to create a perfect inner harmony by wholly submitting himself to the Father within, Winstanley disowns as "not me" what he calls pride, namely, those aspects of himself that interfere with the constitutive marriage between an active, nurturing God and a passive, feminine soul (446).

Every child is ambivalent about its real parents, but for Winstanley only those who are *not* ambivalent about the god within can become "good sons and daughters" and therefore, he means, truly adult. This relationship between, on the one hand, adult choices about spiritual nourishment and inner authority and, on the other, childhood conflicts about real nourishment and parental authority suggests two obvious questions. What does Winstanley mean by calling pride a "devil within" and an "evil masculine power"? How do those ruled by this "selfish power" fashion their autonomy and culture?

PRIDE AND NOURISHMENT

To answer both questions, we must begin with Winstanley's understanding of "the flesh," a concept that refers to how we desire and what we desire when we are ruled by pride. The flesh is not the physical body but fantasies, usually unconscious, about nourishment and, thus, power. "Fleshly desire" is acquisitive, possessive, and merely self-regarding, or what Winstanley calls "covetous." Human desire takes this form, or becomes fleshly, when it is animated by what Puritans call the "fleshly imagination," a term that Winstanley uses to describe fantasies of abandonment and hunger and, thus, compensatory fantasies of omnipotence, of the exclusive control of what a person defines as nourishment.

In Winstanley's account, therefore, the prideful desire "to be as a God" is manifested in covetous desire because the dream of self-sufficiency is closely associated with anxiety about nourishment. Indeed, Winstanley makes pride the flip side of an inner emptiness about which people are unconscious:

> If you look for hell or sorrows in any other place than what shall be made manifest within the bottomless pit, your very fleshly self, you are deceived; and you shall find that when this bottomless pit is opened to your view, it will be a torment sufficient, for hence doth the curse spread and all the misery you are or may be capable of is but the breakings forth of that stinking dunghill that is seated within you, that power of darkness that rules within the creation, your body. (216)

The images of inner emptiness and of being filled with the stinking dunghill suggest that Adam's pride is related to the hunger of one lacking god's nourishment and is manifested specifically in the fantasy of self-sufficiency, of filling himself up not with god's milk but with his own excrement, that is, with his own creations and accomplishments (133).

Because of pride, Adam will seek to gain from external objects the spiritual nourishment he lacks and rejects:

> Every man and woman that lives upon the objects of creation and not upon the spirit that made the creation, is a son or daughter of the first man . . . : so that we may see Adam every day before our eyes, walking up and down the street. (120)

Instead of seeking the love of the Father within, fallen Adam "imagines a content and happiness to himself" and seeks it from objects outside him. Thus, "the apple that Adam the first man eats is not a single fruit . . . but it is the objects of creation . . . upon which the powers of the flesh feed to delight himself" (177). Such objects or creatures are "wife, friends, riches, places of dominion" as well as "sermons, prayers, studies, church fellowship, and outward forms and customs of divine worship" (226). Adam tries to feed himself rather than be fed by god; he feeds on external objects rather than internal love (117):

> God bids the heart trust in him by inward whisperings; the heart, not knowing God, looks after the creature, thinking it cannot live without money, lands, help of men, and creatures. This is the devil that tempts. (SP/21)

The phrase "the devil that tempts," is ambiguous, however, because Winstanley tries to account both for the inward compulsion that fuels acquisitiveness and for the danger to self-control posed by the objects Puritans accumulate. From one point of view, Adam's complicity in his Fall originates in the covetous imagination. Rather than acknowledge his need for god and, thus, his weakness, Adam "will fain be a God and calls his weakness strength" (378). Rather than live within himself by admitting he needs to be nourished by god, Adam "strives with greediness after outward content." As "content" implies that a person is not seeking happiness through physical satisfaction but is trying to fill a void, so "when thou beginst to imagine a content and happiness to thyself by thy hypocritical self-inventions, then thou art tormented or will be" (378).

Mistaking the nourishment he needs, Adam is drawn into an unsatisfying dependence on external objects: he is "led away like a bear by the nose, by every object before his eyes, which the flesh lusts after to enjoy, and places contentment in" (136). His desire is insatiable not only because of his "bottomless" hunger, but also because the failure of objects truly to satisfy him binds him to pursue them ever more desperately. Thus, objects are not powerful in themselves: it is Adam who places too great a burden on externals too weak to "work true peace."

Yet Winstanley also attributes great power to objects themselves, whose "promises of delight" seduce people away from the love within. This romance with objects powerful in themselves *opens* a bottomless pit in Adam, depriving him of real nourishment and therefore self-control. Adam becomes the natural man of Calvin and Hobbes—compulsive, aggrandizing, overwhelmed by the desires and fantasies objects elicit, a "prisoner to his lusts and in bondage within himself" (483).

Because Adam consents to "imaginary covetousness within" and "objects without," this would-be god actually becomes less than fully human:

> He indeed goes in the shape of a man, but properly he is a beast of such and such a ravenous principle. And this now is the curse, man is gone out of his Maker to live upon objects. . . . The branches of mankind have acted like the beasts or swine and though they have called one another men and women, yet they have been but the shadows of men and women. (156–57)

Becoming a beast means, first, "those objects which are for the preservation and delight of mankind, he immoderately uses, and by his excess destroys himself and them too" (483). Second, Adam becomes incapable of mutuality: a victim of inner hunger and imagination will victimize others because "imagination begets covetousness after pleasure, honor, and riches; covetousness begets fears, lest others should cross him in his design" (379). Indeed, because of Adam's need for a respect and recognition he lacks within, "he endeavors to make himself a lord over his fellow creatures" (158).

Hobbes draws a comparable picture of human "vainglory," as well as of its relationship to "fancy" and the "restless pursuit of desire after desire." Both theorists question the Puritan pursuit of earthly recognition and worldly goods, which Puritans claim is a saintly choice to pursue visible signs of god's grace. But the actions that Hobbes reduces to *natural* desire and fancy Winstanley attributes to *choice*, for Adam falls only through consent to the rule of "evil masculine powers" in him. It is not the saint within Adam that desires these objects, but neither is it nature. Rather, "his inward power is not suitable to his outward profession" because he is a "saint without and a devil within" (378). Moreover, since the objects he pursues can work no true peace, they are not signs of god, but neither are they all we have, for god's inner love really would satisfy.

By claiming that the bottomless pit is also a stinking dunghill that Adam "spreads abroad," and by calling Adam's loved objects "dung," Winstanley gives a specific, bodily meaning to the devil in Adam, to the motives and fantasies that professed Puritan saints bring to objects and action. Winstanley's excremental language is not illustrative or invective, but essential: these metaphors actually embody the deeply personal and physical meaning of the choices Hobbes suppresses through his version of nature.

In this regard, the parallel between Winstanley's analysis and the psychoanalytic study of child development is truly remarkable. Of course, Winstanley speaks of an internal relationship to god, and psychoanalysis speaks of a child's relationship to the mother. What matters at this point, however, is that Winstanley's language about nourishment, separation, excrement, and objects evokes the childhood experience that psychoanalysis describes. What Winstanley identifies as the pride of adult Adam and finds "ruling" Adam's relationship with objects are the impulses and fantasies that psychoanalysis seeks to identify in adults who have failed to digest the childhood experience of separating from the mother. The flesh (or prideful son) ruling Adam is like the child (or childhood legacy) ruling an adult; Adam ruled by his pride is an adult ruled by ambivalences unresolved since childhood. And Winstanley, like psychoanalytic theorists, diagnoses those ambivalences through an argument about the meaning of milk and excrement.

As Winstanley depicts Adam's ambivalence about being a "created being" dependent on an authority that provides "sincere milk" (128), so psychoanalysis depicts the ambivalence of the oral stage of infantile dependence on the mother. In its dependence the child feels receptive, loved, and grateful as well as hungry, aggrandizing, and resentful. Because of its ambivalence the child internalizes two different images of the mother, one a dangerous, devouring, ungiving "bad" mother, and the other an unconditionally loving "good" mother. At the same time, the child's ambivalence shapes its initial view of itself, which is split into aspects to love and hate. This is much like Winstanley's account of first Adam, who suffers inner division and who, like the Puritan saint, expresses contradictory feelings about himself and god.

Just as Winstanley's images of excrement are meant to describe how ambivalence about dependence on god shapes Adam's relationship to separateness and objects, so psychoanalysis depicts an anal stage of development, in which the child's ambivalence about the mother and separate selfhood is worked out through objects, specifically the excrement that is the child's first "creation." Since the self-mastery of the sphincter muscles is the first step toward autonomy, excrement becomes symbolically the first gift to the mother, a proof of self-control, and an offering of gratitude to an authority that wants it to learn self-control. Such is still the meaning evoked by the colloquial expression "to have one's shit together." But excrement also becomes something the child can withhold stubbornly, or "spread abroad" in angry protest against the mother. That power remains in the excremental expletives we fling at each other when angered.

According to psychoanalytic theory, the child's ambivalence about the mother, separation, and excrement is sublimated into a love for its possessions and creations. Like its own excrement, its possessions are loaded with meaning. By its love for objects the child declares its often angry self-sufficiency: the emerging self says, I can nurture myself, I don't need mother and milk. In this sense, the objects Puritans sanctify as visible signs of god's grace are to Winstanley the dung by which they try to replace god's milk. By calling objects dung, Winstanley points to what they are unconsciously for saints, suggesting that saints, despite their protestations of pious dependence on god, have inverted the nature and location of nourishment in their effort to declare their autonomy.

As Winstanley argues concerning Adam, so psychoanalysis argues concerning the child: although each wants to supplant the milk of an authority, neither has given up the longing for that authority's love. Each still tries to recapture that love by way of the objects that symbolize it. The fantasy Winstanley calls prideful is that these objects, unlike god or the mother, are a form of nourishment that can be created alone and therefore controlled completely. Thus, says Winstanley, adults deny their need and loss, which appear indirectly in the covetous attachment to possessions.

Rather than admit his need and dependence, Adam tries to live by his own products. For Winstanley and psychoanalysis, ambivalence about separation and dependence creates this pride, which each associates with "the back part," whose products become emblematic of the effort to live by one's own creations as if one were utterly self-generating. Following what Perry Miller calls the Augustinian piety, Winstanley contends that sin is separation from god, and pride is turning to other, false gods or idols. As Adam tries to make a god of himself, he chooses the pride that constitutes the Fall. In psychoanalytic language, Adam is trying to parent himself through his own creations: those suffering from "separation anxiety" will create an empire of objects, a second womb of culture, to regain a love they will not admit they have lost. As with all idols, however, their creators become enslaved to them (117):

> The devil, or the powers of the flesh in every man and woman, brings misery to everybody and corrupts the whole creation . . . (1) by drawing them into unreasonable ways, which ways and works (2) become the creatures own tormenters, . . . for all mens' sorrows are but the rising up of their own works against themselves. (219)

But Puritans themselves use excremental language to condemn the idols or inventions of Catholicism, from which people mistakenly seek nourishment and on which they therefore become childishly dependent. To achieve the worldly independence that Puritans believe god really requires, they develop what Max Weber called a worldly asceticism. By accumulating visible signs of grace in a worldly calling, they profess to honor god's wish that they should be autonomous while acknowledging their ultimate dependence on his grace. At the same time, they deny themselves enjoyment of the objects they accumulate in order to emphasize their own self-control and the carnal character of objects: the point of accumulation is neither prideful assertion and idolatry nor fleshly enjoyment and childish remission. As a result, they believe, these objects are the emblems of god's grace and their autonomy.

When analyzing the acquisitiveness that is part of worldly asceticism, Weber focused on anxiety about salvation. Diligent labor and self-denial was meant to give men confidence in the love of a distant, transcendent god. Winstanley goes beyond Weber's analysis by considering the bodily meaning of that anxiety, as well as of labor and self-denial. He uses the Puritans' own excremental language to reopen the question of the right relationship to god and, thus, to nourishment, objects, and autonomy. Winstanley is not criticizing the Puritans for literally creating, and then "feeding" on, objects: like psychoanalysis and the Puritans themselves, Winstanley believes that worldly endeavor and real nourishment are essential to autonomy. However, his language of "the back part" is meant to suggest that the Puritans are not aware of what motivates their acquisitiveness and, thus, of the unconscious meaning they give to objects.

When one loves objects covetously, it is because of anger and insecurity; such love is a weakness calling itself strength, a way to enact compensatory fantasies of self-sufficiency. Accordingly, to pursue Winstanley's argument, whatever Puritans may say, they still are ruled by the ambivalences associated with the dunghill within, and the objects they pursue are that dung externalized. As a result, they manifest merely the "signs" of autonomy or grace, for they are enslaved to unconscious desire and to the objects on which they anxiously and mistakenly depend for their identity. Thus, Winstanley is not condemning the literal enjoyment of objects but rather is explaining why Puritans abjure taking pleasure in the objects they compulsively accumulate. When objects are unconsciously excremental, they will be "loved" in a profoundly ambivalent way, for what they represent rather than for what they are.[5]

Winstanley's argument is that if Puritans discovered that god were present in their bodies and that they themselves embodied god's love, what had been a bottomless pit would be filled with real spiritual nourishment. The discovery that god's milk is internally available would free adults from acquisitiveness by freeing them from anxiety about god's love and their own worth. No longer compelled to prove their worth,

---

5. Covenant theologians promoted accumulation, but as if they were aware of its bodily basis, they also forbade enjoyment of the fruits of labor. By exposing the "back part" as the bodily basis of "works," Winstanley would remove the taint that requires asceticism. As Norman O. Brown argues in *Life Against Death:*

> A new stage in the history of the money complex begins in modern times with the Reformation and the rise of capitalism. On the one hand, definitive sublimation (of anality) is attained at last by a final repression of the awareness of the anal-erotic sources of the complex; up till then, the pursuit of money appears to have been inhibited by the knowledge that lucre is filthy. And on the other hand, there is a turn against the sublimation, a withdrawal of libido because the aim has become accumulation rather than enjoyment. (302–3)

they would not spread abroad the dunghill within. Then objects could be enjoyed without anxiety or guilt, and in moderation, for they would not embody the ambivalent meanings signified by the Puritans' own excremental language.

Thus, Winstanley's excremental vision attributes anxious acquisitiveness and worldly asceticism to the denial of the god that dwells in the body. In other words, Puritans anxiously try to prove their autonomy by accumulating signs of a divine love they believe is otherwise disembodied and external, invisible and uncertain. Their anxiety about god's love is inextricable from what is prideful and unsatisfying about their worldly endeavors. Consequently, Winstanley asks, why do Puritans imagine a god outside their bodies and outside creation itself?

IMAGINATION, IDEAS, AND AUTONOMY

Like the Puritans and Hobbes, Winstanley considers imagination a profoundly problematic human capacity: it means invention rather than image, distortion rather than reflection. Most important, imagination reflects desire rather than reality. The basis for this shared view, widespread in the seventeenth century, is a profound anxiety about knowing the world, arising from the awareness that pride entails a capacity for delusion. People are inclined to make over the world to suit their fancy rather than honor what binds and limits them. This is a kind of idolatry: as people worship their ideas (about themselves, objects, and reality), they collapse the potential difference between fiction and truth, ideas and reality. By taking what they imagine as the truth, people try to become like gods; such confusion is the fruit of pride and a failure of self-knowledge. On all this, Puritans, Hobbes, and Winstanley agree, and they all claim to define a right relationship to the faculty of imagination and to ideas and reality. But they make their arguments in contrasting ways.

Puritans contend that god is a transcendent spirit not literally embodied in nature but potentially manifested as the conscience. This spirit helps overcome the bodily particularity and the vain fancy they associate with "self," by teaching the difference between truth and the fantasies they associate with idolatry and the flesh. In the name of god's truth, however, Puritans feel entitled to act against what they consider the illusions that animate Catholicism, tradition, and monarchy.

In contrast, Winstanley *returns* god to nature. He restores the spirit to the body and finds truth in felt experience:

> To know the secrets of nature is to know the works of God; and to know the works of God within creation is to know God himself, for God dwells in every visible work or body. And indeed, if you would know spiritual things, it is to know how the spirit, or power causing motion and growth, dwells within and governs both the several bodies of the stars and planets . . . and the several bodies of the earth below. (565)

Embedded in a nature that god animates, human beings are also bodies in which god dwells (81). Thus, declares Winstanley, "no man or woman can say that the Father doth not dwell in him, for He is everywhere" (93). Accordingly, Winstanley argues that the soul is mortal and that a person can know god only in life, through felt experience of what he or she embodies (109).

As a result, it is the endeavor of abstraction that Winstanley associates with the faculty of imagination and calls fleshly and prideful; it is the reliance on abstractions divorced from experience that he considers idolatry. Only because of imagination do people believe that god is outside their bodies and creation, depriving their bodies of spirit, and god of embodiment. The imagination of disobedient man deceives him, "for he either looks abroad for a god and so doth imagine and fancy a God to be in some particular place of glory beyond the skies, or somewhere that cannot be known until the body is laid in the dust" (93). To those who live by "imaginary inventions" Winstanley therefore declares:

> Go read all the books in your university, that tell you what hath formerly been, and though you make speeches of a day long from these readings, yet you shall . . . increase your sorrow until your eyes return to yourselves, and . . . read in your own book, your heart. (213)

What is special in Winstanley's argument appears in his attempt to provide a bodily and psychological explanation for why people disembody knowledge or look for god elsewhere than "that line or station wherein you stand." According to Winstanley, Adam imagines that god is "abroad" because he lacks experience of the spirit within. He lacks that experience and feels devoid of spirit because in fact he is separated from god and ruled instead by the dark power, the dunghill within. Adam abstracts ideas from experience, spirit from the body, and god from nature, as if to escape what he feels is contaminated. That sense of contamination discloses the legacy of his separation from god while shaping his response to it. Believing that spirit could not possibly dwell in the body, or truth be found through sensed experience, fallen Adam imagines an "outward God," and righteously professes to be a "spiritual man" who has "risen above the low and carnal things" (566).

If Adam is still ruled by the back part, however, how can he speak about god at all? "The word God signifies a governor, and it may as well be attributed to the devil as to the law of righteousness" (168). But if Adam calls by the name of god whatever in fact rules him, are there criteria by which to distinguish between true knowledge of god—or god rightly understood—and merely imaginary ideas? The dunghill within shapes Adam's ideas and his relation to them in identifiable ways.

Winstanley's most important criterion is whether people imagine the divorce of spirit and body, which signifies the rule of the dunghill within. Therefore, the dunghill also can be recognized by the angry conscience that accuses one of sin. Lacking the inward power to justify his "outward professions," a saint who is really still a devil within is tormented by the contradiction. Of course, he will imagine that his torment originates from outside himself:

> For he that hath a troubled conscience . . . sees fearful shapes without, but they arise from the anguish of his tormenting conscience within, for they be the shapes and apparitions of his own cursed flesh that is presented to him, which comes from out of the bottomless pit. . . . For certainly, unrighteous flesh presented to its own view is the torments of hell. . . . For a man suffers by no other but the work of his own hands. (218)

The dunghill from which he would rise follows him upward, so to speak, tormenting him with the face of his own flesh. The saint's idea of spirit presumes, but cannot heal, the inner division that characterizes those ruled by the flesh.

The way people create and possess their ideas is another criterion for identifying those ruled by the dunghill. The "imaginary man" does not live according to a god he feels, but feeds on words and ideas he either invents or learns from others (459). As Winstanley says of himself in London:

> I myself have known nothing but what I received by tradition from the mouths and pens of others: I worshipped a God, but I neither knew who he was or where he was, so that I lived in the dark, being blinded by the imagination of my flesh, and by the imagination of such as stood up to teach . . . and yet had no knowledge of the Lord themselves. (SP/preface)

Thus, the imaginary man can be known because of his reliance on the external objects—in this case the words of others—from which he hopes to gain the nourishment of truth (210).

As with desire and objects, so with imagination and ideas: the dunghill is revealed whenever people give power to ideas because they are driven from within to feed on externals. Because they "live by other mens' words" or "by other mens' eyes," they live according to ideas they have invested with inappropriate, even magical, importance (469). Yet "outward preachers" and "humane learning" are also objects powerful in themselves, which "bewitch and delude mankind in spiritual things." Ideas and teachers "draw men from knowing the spirit, to own bare letters, words, and histories," seducing them into "captivity" (214).

From either point of view for Winstanley, ideas about god become objects that serve as the coveted basis of identity and worth. Since "the power that rules in the bodies of your flesh" is the "particular, confining, and selfish power, which is the devil," Puritans claim to possess an exclusive truth, are incapable of tolerance, and imagine a god whose blessings are limited to the few (172). Indeed, Puritans will kill: the flesh that "leads men to imagine God in a place of glory beyond the skies" also "leads men to kill those that disagree with them" (93).

Winstanley's understanding of ideas and imagination once again suggests a remarkable psychoanalytic parallel. As the anal stage unfolds, psychoanalytic theorists argue, the child resents the bodily needs that make it dependent but also resents the bodily particularity that enforces separateness. Thus, the child fantasizes being free of a body that is enslaving (in its need), limiting (in its particularity), and tainted (by rage). On the cross of its ambivalence about the body, the child, like fallen Adam, imagines it is split into excremental (bodily) and nonexcremental (spiritual) aspects. In this way, psychoanalysis suggests, religion expresses the child's yearning to transcend the excremental and mortal body. Inwardly divided adults imagine that piety for a paternal god will separate the spirit from the flesh and free the self from contamination. The yearning for god's love spiritualizes, and thus safely displaces, the ambivalent and dangerous physical desire for the mother. Indeed, in the name of love for god, men strive to conquer that fleshly desire and its power.[6]

Like psychoanalytic theorists, Winstanley diagnoses the religious

6. Joel Kovel, in *White Racism: A Psychohistory* (New York: Random House, 1970), writes:

> Excremental symbolism will become manifested in those situations where a heightened ambivalence persists over the conflicts of separation. . . . The whole cleavage between body and spirit—which is at the root of the cleavage between a stage of maternal fusion and a stage of separateness—begins at the anal stage, and uses the split between the excremental self and non-excremental self as its symbolic cornerstone. Accordingly, the body becomes identified with the excremental self, and the spirit is the non-excremental self. (268)

idea of a disembodied paternal spirit saving an immortal soul because he knows there is no such salvation from a body felt to be contaminated. Accordingly, he also criticizes the power of abstraction as a flight from what is experienced in the self as limiting and dirty. Through such abstraction, which appears to transcend the body, adults fashion an autonomy that denies the feelings he associates with the dunghill within. Further, he is concerned that ideas then become an armor against anxiety and a weapon of unconscious rage. By returning the soul to the body, therefore, he teaches adults to confront the ambivalences they would escape through their dream of spirit.

Winstanley's critique of ascetic religiosity also suggests what shapes Hobbes's effort to secularize Puritanism into the ascetic discipline of science. Hobbes carries to a scientific conclusion the Puritan contention about god's transcendence: he refers to god as an abstract first cause, outside a creation of dead matter in motion. As a result, he deprives the body of spirit altogether and discredits the Puritan view that conscience is the voice of god. By exposing Puritan religious ideas as fictions, he further deprives Puritans of the authority (or spirit) that entitled them to speak and act. Yet Hobbes's iconoclastic science, like the Puritan god, abstracts from particular bodily experience in order to control a deeply mistrusted body and imagination. As a rigorous method based on a language of abstract definitions, Hobbes's science also promises to establish control over nature and freedom from the dependencies on tradition and superstition that he calls childish.

To be sure, Winstanley's effort to return god to the body and nature is a "pagan fancy" according to Hobbes's science. Yet Winstanley's excremental vision suggests the bodily basis of that science and of the culture that extolls it. Whereas a religious thinker like Luther turned his back on human enterprises irremediably tainted by pride, however, Winstanley still endorses an "experimental" approach toward the understanding of nature, and he would regenerate, rather than reject, culture.

THE CULTURE OF FALLEN ADAM

Winstanley contends that Puritans externalize their inner lives as worldly practices and common beliefs, which in turn shape the inner struggles he is trying to diagnose. As he argues about particular objects and ideas, so he argues about institutions: Puritans seek "content" from worldly inventions because they are ruled by pride, not god. Just as they give the name of god to the evil masculine power that rules them, so they claim god's sanction for their own rule in the body of society. And like the pride and imagination within, their worldly magistracy and ministry draw men and women away from true spiritual nourishment.

Because of their pride, ministers "will not believe that God will now give his spirit to tradesmen as formerly he gave it to fishermen, but believe that only those who have human ordination may teach" (89). Associating the elect with spirit and the poor with the flesh, they exercise their authority in a way that deprives others of the right to speak. As pride makes the living soul a "bondswoman," so their worldly idols hold captive the women and unlearned poor in society, in whom Christ could become manifest. Indeed, just as Puritans imagine a depraved nature they would control through their imaginary inventions, so they would control those they call "wives and children." Thus, the clergy "get magistrates to make ecclesiastical laws, compelling all men to conformity with outward forms of worship" (89).

To prove the fraudulence of these "false prophets" (127) in a way that also explains why they deem him heretical, Winstanley must show how their culture is ruled by the "dark power" rather than god. His case unfolds as he links Puritan religious practices and cultural politics to the acquisitive desire and ascetic imagination by which he identifies the dunghill within. Most simply, Winstanley argues that Puritan religious conventions reflect anxious covetousness about earthly objects: Puritans make use of the ministry for worldly gain, not truth. Like Hobbes, Winstanley avers: "They that stand up . . . teach for gain and preach for hire" in order to "engrosse the earth into their hands":

> A man must not take a wife, but the priest must give her him. If he have a child, the priest must give the name. If any die, the priest must see him laid in the earth. If any man want knowledge and comfort, they teach him to go to the priest. And what is the end of all this, but to get money. (187)

Winstanley also connects the desire to "engrosse" the earth and the corruption of language. He argues that "divines" have "gotten hold of" the apostolic accounts of Christ and turned these into income-producing property. They "engrosse other mens' spiritual teachings to themselves" by treating the spirit exclusively in terms of the letter of the gospels (474–75). Then they declare that only those men "bred up in humane learning" are qualified to interpret the letter and, thus, the spirit as well (100–101, 144).

In this way, the letter of the gospels, which others once spoke and wrote by experience, becomes a commodity the clergy control to sell for a living. "The learned scholars . . . hold to the letter, getting their living by telling people the meanings of those tradesmens' words and writings" (239). To protect their monopoly, the clergy "press upon the powers of the earth to make laws to hold under bondage . . . lay people, tradesmen and such as are not bred in the school" (239). Winstanley therefore accuses the clergy of being "witches and deceivers" who "pick purses extremely by this divination and sorcery, . . . selling words for money to the blind people [they] have deceived" (242)[7]

Winstanley, however, does not see the Puritan clergy simply as manipulative spiritual entrepreneurs: they deceive their audience about spiritual food because they are deceived themselves. Lacking the experience of god, "the university public ministry runs before he be sent; he takes up another man's message and carries abroad other mens' words (like parrots)" (208). "Full of waste words, they speak they know not what" (232), and "by their multitude of false expositions and interpretations" they "mightily corrupt" the gospel's meaning (239):

> You persecute the gospel itself, which is the Lord of spirit within you, and you tear in pieces the declarations of the gospel, which is the scriptures, by your various expositions. And so all you do is trouble the children and throw dirt on their food. (144)

Ministers throw dirt rather than light on the gospels because what they call "their light is but a candle stolen from the apostles' and prophets' writings; it is not their own light, but hearsay" (241).

Similarly, Winstanley argues that not only do preachers earn a living by "worshipping of God in types, ceremonies, forms and customs," but also these are the inventions from which they seek the justification they lack inwardly:

> Ashamed and afraid to own the spirit within, . . . you presently run and hide yourselves from Him . . . and run preaching and praying and sheltering yourself in a congregation . . . and so doth sew the figleaves of your own observing forms, to hide your soul from the face of displeasure, that you may not see yourself, for the sight of yourselves is your hell. (211)

The anxiety of Puritans about worldly objects bespeaks a separation from god that also leads them to mistake their inventions and waste words for spiritual food.

---

7. The unintended irony in these passages is that Winstanley condemns those who "trade" in words, yet defends "tradesmen" deprived by ministers of the right to speak. Although he is hostile to acquisitiveness and analyzes its psychology, he still makes tradesmen his heros. He has not linked his account of acquisitiveness to the social relations of trade (or of property and wage labor). But this is precisely what he will do soon, condemning tradesmen as he condemns ministers.

As Winstanley uses and transforms the Puritans' metaphors, he exposes what is wrong with all religious institutions and in a way that literally embodies the connections between childhood struggles for autonomy and the adult effort to fashion culture. A male power, arising from the bottomless pit in the body and appearing in people as the flesh, leads them to pridefully create "Babylon," which is "the multitude of fleshly inventions arising from the spirit of self-love; or the multitude of people in whom the flesh works powerfully, or both joined in one body" (BDG/46).

This conjunction of the flesh within and its outward inventions takes on specific shape as "the Beast of Ecclesiastical Power." This androgynous and "bastardly" Beast is produced by the illegitimate marriage of state and church, the fornication of "magistracy out of joint," and the "spirit of whoredom pretending to love God" (BDG/114). On the one hand, the Beast is a male power that proclaims:

> He can perfectly discern what is truth and what is error, and takes upon him by his usurping power to punish error. . . . Does he not thereby declare himself to be as a god in knowledge . . . and as God likewise in magistracy, by punishing anyone who opposes his beastly being? And he declares himself to be an absolute infallible prophet to teach men, a king to rule and punish them, and a priest to save men from death by his skill and operation. (BDG/107)

At the same time, the Beast "hath reigned and lived in pomp like a delicate whore [who] first killed and then trod the witnesses [of spirit] under her feet, for now she doth what she will, she sits like a Queen, and knows no sorrows; for she hath a power from the kings of the earth" (BDG/63).

The meaning of these male and female images becomes clear when related to Winstanley's bodily metaphors. Fallen men, he says, "suck content and delight" from "the teats of creatures," which he also calls "the teats of their own self-inventions" (226). This image suggests that men try to provide nourishment to themselves and others; but unlike god, these inventions do not provide sincere milk. The milk of culture is insincere because it is man-made; it is neither authentic nor nourishing. In fact, the dung of externals and the waste words of imagination pour forth from these teats (226). Rather than become true adults by sucking the sincere milk of the god within, fallen Adams become like children who mistake dung for food. Ruled by the prideful fantasy of creating and controlling their own nourishment, they succumb to an endlessly unsatisfying dependence on the "formula" of their invented culture.

It is male authority that offers men and women these teats, as many ministers take from Exodus the image of the "nursing father" to sanction and soften their authority. The maternal authority they attack returns under their control; but their paternal power cannot feed and free anyone, for it does not provide real love or genuine nourishment. For Winstanley, bondage arises as adults, separated from god's sincere milk, create substitutes in the excremental products of the invented teats of fake fathers. Bondage does not arise from the need for love as such or from a truly loving authority; adults are trapped specifically by a *lack* of love, both within the self and in the world. The need for love, if directed toward that which truly would satisfy it, is not a threat to freedom but its very basis.[8]

Accordingly, Winstanley contends that the Puritan effort to build a New Jerusalem is vain, in the sense of futile or self-defeating. As long as people live by unnourishing inventions rather than god's love, they will find neither freedom nor peace:

> And while it is thus, poor creatures, they are in bondage within, for they know not what to do; the way to Zion is not yet clear and they are filled with sighing and secret mournings, to see themselves in confusion and loss, . . . stuck in the mire but [unable to] come out. (230)

Yet ministers declare that their inventions are sanctioned by god; indeed, the Puritan fathers proceed to usurp magistracy precisely in order to remake society in their image:

> Men fancy that their present troubles would disappear if the worshipping of God in spirit could be beaten down and if all men could be forced to practice one lazy, outward, formal, customary and tithe-oppressing way of pretended divine worship. (90)

Here Winstanley evokes another sense of vanity—the prideful infatuation with one's own inventions, which leads ministers to act self-righteously and intolerantly. "By calling anything blasphemy unless they approve of it, tying the spirit to themselves," the ministers turn outward what they call god's anger so as to punish others they call fleshly (475). Rather than acknowledge their own pride and hunger, ministers suppress the devouring flesh they profess to see in the devilish heretics who torment them.

Not long before, in New England, John Winthrop made the typical Puritan claim that it was necessary for fathers, husbands, and ministers to rule over children, wives, and poor people, all defined as unregenerate. Ann Hutchinson challenged this monopoly of spirit and worldly power. As an independent woman and midwife subverting paternal

---

8. For the psychoanalytic underpinnings of this formulation, see the work of Jessica Benjamin; see also Carolyn Walker Bynum, *Jesus as Mother* (Berkeley and Los Angeles: University of California Press, 1982), for an account of the male appropriation of female and nurturant imagery in Catholicism.

spiritual power, she literally embodied what the fathers feared. Winthrop attacked her, charging that her antinomian revolt of the spirit was really a revolt of the flesh: her belief that each person embodied god would destroy all order by sanctioning anarchy; she would release the unsublimated desires and unbridled imagination that make men the captives of powerful feminine forces.

Like Ann Hutchinson, Winstanley condemns the orthodox covenant that deprives most men and all women of the right to speak and act. He is treated as an Ishmael, just as Hutchinson is banished as a Hagar. But just as the ministers' own flesh appears as a devil, so too those they call Hagar and Ishmael have been turned into mirrors of the flesh the fathers have not exorcized in themselves.

Thus, paternal power punishes precisely those who, because they are nourished by the god within, are not bewitched by paternal inventions. Critics of the fathers do not embody the flesh but expose the "masculine powers" ruling the fathers and their law. They do not counsel regression but disclose what is regressive in the orthodox New Jerusalem. They do not return people to Egypt but represent a truer liberation, a culture that really would feed and free men as well as women because of the power of love they embody.

This inversion of perspective is accomplished, Winstanley says, by discovering the god within, whose breasts of love provide sincere milk for the soul. Therefore, he continues, as a result of gaining god's milk, he knows the dunghill that shapes human inventions. "Anyone who has lain under the bondage of the selfish power and is in any measure delivered [can] from that experience declare what the power of darkness is in mankind" (235). Thus, he can declare what rules in the ministers: "I look upon them with the eye of pity and love, seeing them as yet to lie under those strong delusions and powers of darkness which I myself did lie under" (243). He even turns their accusations against them:

> By molding scriptures into their own language, walking according to their inferences and conjectures . . . and by holding forth God and Christ to be at a distance from them, they are the men that deny God and Christ. (104)

Winstanley models himself on Christ, for Christ taught that "the Father will have all men look to him for teaching, to acknowledge no other teacher and ruler but himself" (206). Having discovered the teacher and ruler within, he knows "the spirit is not so scanty that a dozen or twenty pairs of eyes shall serve the whole world, but every son or daughter, as they are called children of light, have light within themselves" (127).

Thus, Winstanley accuses the ministers of being pharisees who reenact the crucifixion of Christ (238). The ministers "turn upside down the scriptures that testify to Christ" and "carry sinners back again to a ceremonial, Jewish, and legal way of worship, to seek salvation not by faith only but (as it were) by works of the law" (BDG/90). These modern pharisees would "kill and suppress not men and women simply, but the manifest appearance of God in them" (BDG/114).[9]

Like Hobbes, Winstanley unmasks the motives and interests that shape Puritanism. Both theorists attack what each calls a "kingdom of darkness" in the name of an "experimental knowledge" of nature, desire, and truth. But Hobbes devalues the idea that piety for an inner authority can transform desire or entitle people to speak and act independently of worldly authority. He would replace the fictional, delusional, and dangerous god of the Puritans with a mortal god of human construction, the better to define truth and enforce order. He would supplant inner authority with the sovereign's voice, and historical action with regulated motion.

In contrast, Winstanley professes to have experienced a god that "dwells" in the body. As a result, he insists that choices shape the covetous desire Hobbes teaches is natural. "This law of darkness in the members is not a state of nature, for nature or the living soul is in bondage to it and groans under it, waiting for deliverance" (493). Accordingly, Winstanley undermines Puritans' fraudulent authority in order to establish what he calls "true ministry," whose goal is

> to find out this darkness and cast it out, and to worship the Father in spirit and truth, and so to advance the blessing, or the son in whom the Father is well-pleased. That so mankind might cease speaking and acting from thoughts and imagination, and come to speak and act purely as the truth was in Jesus. (457)

Unlike Hobbes, then, Winstanley attacks the clergy in the name of an authority earned by experience, manifested in authentic speech, and dedicated to teaching others to become agents in their own right (165–66).

Winstanley has learned that teachers can take others only where they themselves have been: only those who have found the inner authority

9. Winstanley is, in certain important ways, unfair to the Puritans and does not acknowledge his debt to them. He never grants that he has taken their own "covenant of grace" and turned it against their idea of a "covenant of works." Accordingly, he denies the ambivalence about externals that Puritans did express as they struggled to differentiate themselves from Catholics. Indeed, his obvious sense of betrayal suggests that he feels they have betrayed their own claims, which they taught him to take seriously. It is as if he uses ideas he knows they all agree about to expose their hypocrisy. But his anger leads him virtually to caricature them.

that overcomes bondage can liberate other people blind to their own bondage. Only teachers who "know what they speak" are able to direct their listeners to the experience that would yield "an experimental persuasion, grounded upon sight and hearing" (83), of the god dwelling within each created body. Thus, good teachers are "true prophets," who make themselves unnecessary by helping others to become sons and daughters "taught by the Father." Empowered to speak and act, such adults can reappropriate the power misplaced onto fathers and externals. In this way, Winstanley's critique of the clergy specifically embraces the idea of tolerance by rooting truth in the unfolding of experience and, thus, of history.

Having been a believing Puritan, Winstanley comes to argue that a true ministry is meant to sponsor a movement beyond Puritan orthodoxy, and he teaches the meaning of that change. By testifying, however, to personal knowledge of god and to an inner rebirth that regenerates desire, he commits precisely the prideful and vain errors by which Hobbes identifies the Kingdom of Darkness and twins Puritans with their antinomian critics. Such claims, Hobbes believes, enable these erstwhile enemies to deny in themselves the pride they attack in others, thereby justifying their own action to remake culture.

Accordingly, Hobbes's concern about the conventionality of ideas of god, and the rebellious purposes to which such ideas are put, suggests the two key questions animating the next chapter, about Winstanley's effort to find an alternative to Puritanism. First, what does Winstanley's idea of god mean? Is it a credible idea, and does it involve a genuine transformation of the desire Hobbes teaches is natural? Second, how does Winstanley's animus against his own pride shape his effort to remake self and culture? Is his rebellion not animated by the pride he condemns in others?

CHAPTER II

The Rebirth of Adam

But ye are forgers of lies, ye are all physicians of no
value. . . . Miserable comforters are ye all . . . Hold your
peace, . . . that I may speak. . . . I will say unto God, . . . Is
it good unto thee that thou shouldest oppress, that thou
shouldest despise the work of thine hands, and shine upon
the counsel of the wicked? . . . Though he slay me, yet will
I . . . maintain my own ways before him . . . Call thou and I
answer; or let me speak, and answer thou me. How many are
mine iniquities and sins? make me to know my transgression
and my sin. Wherefore hidest thou thy face, and holdest
me for thine enemy? . . . Oh that I knew where I might find
him! . . . I would order my cause before him, and fill my
mouth with arguments. . . . When he hath tried me, I shall
come forth as gold. . . . [For] I have esteemed the words of
his mouth more than my necessary food. . . . Oh that my
words were now written! . . . For I know that my redeemer
liveth, and . . . in my flesh shall I see God: Whom I shall see
for myself.

—Job

Whom shall he teach knowledge? and whom shall he make
to understand doctrine? Them that are weaned from the
milk, and drawn from the breasts.

—Isaiah 28

Wherefore laying aside all malice, and all guile,
and hypocrisies, and envies, and all evil speakings.
    As newborn babies, desire the sincere milk of the
word, that ye may grow thereby.

—I Peter 2

In his first four pamphlets Winstanley can analyze how pride shapes Puritanism because he has learned how pride shaped his own life as a

Puritan and still takes seriously Puritan insights into the causes and consequences of pride. But Winstanley moves *beyond* Puritan orthodoxy
because he transforms the Puritan idea of god. He feels freed from what
characterized his old self and former life because he had internalized as
a loving power the god that the Puritans consider angry and distant. As
a result, Winstanley believes that everyone might enjoy, in this life, the
redemption that Puritans reserve only for an elect, and only after death:

> O you hearsay preachers, do not deceive the people any longer by telling
> them that this glory shall not be known and seen til the body be laid in the
> dust. I tell you, this great mystery is begun to appear, and it must be seen by
> the material eyes of the flesh; and those five senses that is in man, shall par-
> take of this glory. (170)

Because Winstanley locates god in nature and the body, he is unlike
the many theorists who begin the world with a dangerous, devouring,
chaotic nature, often depicted as female, which will consume men if
they do not oppose or subdue it. From this point of view, human freedom is constituted by willfully giving form to what otherwise is an overwhelming chaos of external forces and internal passions. It is in this
spirit that Puritans develop a formative notion of redemptive paternal
grace and that Hobbes devises an "artificial man" and Promethean
science.

I am interested not in exploring the genealogy of this powerful strain
in the Western tradition of religious and political thought, but rather in
examining how Winstanley is a lost voice in the chorus of opposition to
it. He in part originates, and surely illuminates, a different tradition of
theorists, who are committed to finding an alternative to the prideful
shaping of self and culture. That alternative is well represented in the
(contrasting) arguments of psychoanalytic and feminist theorists. Common to them and Winstanley is the search for a relationship to the body,
nature, and others that is characterized by integration, mutuality, and
reparation, or "reverence"—a sense of piety toward the interconnections humans do not invent literally but on which their life depends *and
through which their freedom must develop*.

Norman O. Brown is perhaps the modern founder of this countertradition. He turns inside out the classic defense of prideful self-fashioning: assimilating the religious argument, he contends that Western
culture is the curse into which human beings fall when they act as
"Faustian men," creators committed to erecting monuments to their rationality and power. When adults try to "father themselves," as he puts
it, they alienate themselves from the nature and the erotic instincts they

would dominate, and they become captive to their own lifeless creations. Since money and rationality create a death-in-life characterized by repression, he contends, the death of this culture would be the rebirth of life.

Like the tradition he would invert, Brown says that giving up the works of culture would return people to a formless, Dionysian nature. But for Brown, such an immersion would bring a "Dionysian Christianity" that restores adults to an erotic union of the body, others, and nature. In an ironic way, he jettisons the ego, abandons the idea of form-giving, and dismisses the idea that culture is saving; only then, he appears to argue, can adults recover the being and body that culture has repressed, the wholeness that pride has divided.

Many feminist theorists affirm Brown's rejection of a culture that engages in a prideful war with nature. But thinkers such as Dorothy Dinnerstein, Nancy Chodorow, Susan Griffin, and Jessica Benjamin attend explicitly to the issue of gender and the significance of the mother. As a result, they argue that the desire to dominate what is perceived as a natural chaos and the dream of mystic union with a nature perceived as wholly benign appear as reflections of male ambivalence about the mother.

The struggle of culture, by which Brown says that humans would "father" themselves, appears then as an overcoming not of god and actual fathers but of the mother, whose power over nourishment once humbled the child. To this vengeful struggle for a fantasized self-sufficiency feminists have not responded by following Brown and dissolving the ego in a Dionysian sea. Human beings need not choose between autonomy and the bonds of nature and love because dependence on the mother's love helps the child to separate. Thus, autonomy appears not through repudiation and denial but as the gift of loving reciprocity. Correspondingly, human culture is best developed by acknowledging our bonds with, and not only our separateness from, nature and other people. By reevaluating the meaning of the mother, feminist theorists articulate an idea of freedom opposed to the "Promethean" tradition originating explicitly with Hobbes.

This cryptic summary is meant to introduce modern examples of the countertradition in which to situate Winstanley. At the same time, however, Winstanley represents the difficulties in conceiving an alternative to pride. Those who challenge a Promethean view of autonomy and culture often deny in the self and nature whatever disrupts the harmony they seek. They tend to devalue and stigmatize the rage, ambivalence, and imaginative striving that psychoanalytic thinkers associate with separation from the mother and that Winstanley, like other religious thinkers, associates with pride.

Thus, the quest for an alternative to pride can appear as a dream of "curing" pride and therefore as an unreal ideal of purity. Paradoxically, then, critics of pride can define a valuable concept of conditional freedom yet construe it in a way that—pridefully—denies basic aspects of our "created being." This is the case with the reverence of Winstanley and with some modern feminist theorists.

JOB AND CHRIST: MOVING BEYOND ORTHODOXY

As the previous chapter attests, the Puritans' angry and distant god, their punitive conscience, and their worldly asceticism exemplify to Winstanley precisely the fleshly desire and worldly servitude that Christ actually challenged. The first question to address, then, is how Winstanley accounts for his new perspective, which has moved him beyond the core beliefs and practices of Puritanism.

Winstanley professes to have moved from subjection to pride to deliverance through reverence, from subjection to an angry and distant god to deliverance by a god of love, and thus from the Old Testament to the New Testament. In struggling to describe this change, he recurrently refers to the story of Job. Job's sufferings signify Winstanley's tribulations as a Puritan; Job's god symbolizes the judgment and wrath from which Winstanley found no refuge; Job's friends represent the Puritan preachers, "physicians of no value," whose doctrines provide only "false comfort"; but Job's humbling by god also foreshadows the redemptive promise manifested in Christ. Job becomes Winstanley's emblem for himself as a Puritan struggling with Puritan orthodoxy, whereas Christ represents his movement beyond it.

Let us first summarize the Biblical story of Job, which begins when god allows the devil to afflict Job in order to prove that Job's piety cannot be shaken. As Job is robbed of his family, wealth, and health, he finds the world inscrutable, beyond human comprehension, and out of joint with the desires and ethics of humankind. Job does not curse god or doubt His excellence, but his piety is shot through with anger, resistance, and protestation. He "contends" with god because god's creatures are subject to evil, death, and innocent suffering, and he wants to know why. If he is suffering for a reason, then he wants to know his transgressions so that he can repent; he is willing to humble himself only to an authority that gives an account of its actions.

In the course of the parable, Job's friends try to offer him comfort by declaring the meaning or purpose in his suffering. They appear as "false comforters," however, for they either condemn Job or argue away the validity of his grievances. They say that Job is suffering because he deserves it, which justifies god by blaming Job; or they proclaim that "in the end" Job's innocence will be rewarded because god always blesses the righteous and punishes the wicked. Either way, the friends deny the contradiction between god and man that prompts Job's complaint, plea, and demand for a hearing.

After rancorous and poignant arguments between Job and the comforters, the ultimate author of Job's torments appears "out of the whirlwind." God simply asserts his power, however, as if it transcends any human claim or right; he displays his great monster Leviathan as proof of his singular ability to "humble the children of pride." We witness a tragic conflict: humans are limited, sentient, mortal creatures, who therefore are not to expect fulfillment or certainty; their efforts to make the universe conform to their desires and ethics is punished as a pride inappropriate to a limited being.

Yet god specifically vindicates Job, "who says the things that are right," as if to affirm the truth of Job's complaints. Moreover, by restoring all Job's wealth and authority, god implies that man is justified to contend piously, to assert human innocence, and to maintain human standards of justice in this life. Accordingly, god condemns the comforters, whose desire for solace means avoidance of the contradiction to which god and Job both testify.

Indeed, the Book of Job can be read as the most profound Biblical attack on the prophetic strain that increasingly characterizes the Old Testament: defeated and ridiculed are those who pretend to know god's purposes in history and thus the meaning of suffering. The parable suggests that true piety must abjure such final explanations, for the solace they provide disguises the prideful desire of the creature to know god's will and purpose. A mature relationship to god and history must be constituted by humility in the face of human mortality and finitude, by acknowledgment of human responsibility, and therefore also by contention for the sake of justice.

Winstanley, however, reads the text of Job and his own experience from the prophetic point of view that animates the comforters and leads from Isaiah to Christ. Anxious to justify god and find a purpose in the

sufferings Job exemplifies, Winstanley interprets them as the necessary basis of the redemption promised by god and symbolized by
Christ. Winstanley reads the parable as an internal drama foreshadow-
ing Christ's resurrection in each person, and he thereby turns the story
virtually inside out.

He insists that (the pride in) man, and not god, is the author of Job's
torments, and he argues that recognition of this fact makes possible a
complete reconciliation between man and god. In this way, Winstanley
offers a powerful argument about coming to understand his complicity
in his own sufferings, and this "experimental knowledge" did move him
beyond orthodoxy. Yet he also embraces the false comforters' theodicy,
for he tries once and for all to "answer" or resolve the conflicts that the
story attests are irreconcilable.

When he was a tradesman in London, says Winstanley, he was a
"strict goer to Church, as they call it. . . . I was counted by some of the
priests a good Christian and a godly man" (243). He sees in retrospect,
however, that "I was a stranger to God," for his bankruptcy led to anxiety and despair (243). He describes his anguish as a dispossessed sinner,
echoing Job's lament:

> He sees nothing fulfilled to him, he feels no power from God. . . . Let him
> look to creatures about him and there is no help, all hath forsaken him and
> stand aloof; Let him look within himself and he sees nothing but slavish fear
> and unbelief, questioning the power of God: how can such things be? (461)

Like Job, Winstanley declares, "Oh that this body had never been
born . . . and had died in the womb" (461), and like Job, he imagines
that an angry god afflicted him with "tormenting devils": "I could ap-
prehend from God nothing but anger, for as long as I looked upon God
as angry, I could not look upon him and live" (SP/31).

As this comment suggests, however, Winstanley has come to believe
that he suffered not because god was arbitrary or angry, but because he
"looked upon" god as angry and arbitrary (95). Indeed, he now considers his bankruptcy a saving opportunity, arguing that only by way of
such losses can a fallen Adam discover god's redemptive and loving purpose. He reads Job in the light of the Puritan narrative that leads to salvation only by way of a fortunate fall into sin and suffering; but for him,
that narrative includes an unsatisfying and restless movement through
the "works" of Puritanism:

> The Father is driving his people through all the ways and forms and customs
> and reformations and governments of the Beast, to weary them out in all;

so that they may find rest for the soles of their feet nowhere, in no outward form of worship, til they come . . . to worship the Father in spirit and truth. (230)

Thus, Job's sufferings represent not an ontological condition but the transitional "wilderness condition" that engenders a new relationship to god. Therefore, says Winstanley:

> Think it not strange to see many of the Saints of God at a stand in the wilderness, and at a loss, and so waiting upon God to discover himself to them; many are like the tide at full sea, standing a little before the water runs either way: Assure yourselves, I know what I speak, you must be dead to your customs before you can run into the sea of truth or the river of the water of life. (82)

By coming to understand his suffering in this wilderness, Winstanley believes he has learned the answers to Job's questions about human transgression and divine purpose.

Winstanley answers Job (and justifies god) by arguing that human suffering is the result of pride, not god's anger or inscrutable ways, and that pride is a sin because it is a choice. Regardless of his intention to be righteous and his conscientious performance of religious practices, Winstanley believes he suffered because he lived by fleshly desires and fantasies. These made him subject to "the rigor of the law," the moral injunctions of his conscience, or "God's flaming sword":

> For the creature strives to be wise, and the law proves him a fool; he fain would be righteous and the light of the law shows him he is a wicked hypocrite; he would fain have faith and holiness and the law shows him he is an unbelieving sinner. (SP/39)

Winstanley accepts that he is the author of his own torments, which he mistakenly had attributed to an angry god. He believes it is this insight that begins to take him beyond Job's suffering and Puritan orthodoxy: it is when adults project and displace their own rage that they imagine a distant and angry god and suffer internally from a punitive, alien conscience. Because they project their anger onto god, they can profess, like Job, to be righteous and innocent victims of god's anger.

The realization about his own anger drives Winstanley at first to despair, for he then feels himself to be entirely "a devil." But confronting his own pride yields the most important insight of all, which he associates with Christ. Having realized that "the law is a light that lets man see himself to be a devil," he then discovers that he is not merely a devil and that god is not only the implacable judge whose law is a "righteous dispensation of wrath."

Having become "dead to all his own wisdom, strength, memory, learning, and actings," Winstanley for the first time becomes alive to his "living soul," whose voice and needs he now acknowledges. Quoting from the Song of Solomon, Winstanley describes his soul's helpless need for love and guidance, frustrated by separation from god: "longing to see Him, mourning His absence, for the soul hath no sensible manifestation yet. . . . She waits, she breathes after Him, Oh when shall I see my God?" (BDG/54–58). In the wilderness condition, then, Winstanley is neither left with mere particularity nor overwhelmed by something like pure id. Instead, he finds the living soul held captive by the flesh, "in the earth," buried under the dunghill within.

At the same time, the yearning of his soul does not go unanswered but calls forth god's love in response. Since "it is the *flesh* which presents god as angry when he is loving, yea, love itself to the poor sinner," admitting his own need cuts through the pride that made god seem angry. Then "the creature looks on God not as an angry God, but as a God of love." By facing in himself the anger he had split off and disavowed, Winstanley discovers his own need, god's love, and his own capacity to embody it (165).

Once crucified by an ambivalence he did not understand, Winstanley now feels reborn: by owning the pride he once dissimulated and acknowledging the need he once denied, he is able to perceive a love he never knew was in him (233). Opening himself to that love, he overcomes the distance and silence of which Job complained; embracing a power he believes can give him all he really needs, he discovers "the mystery and work of God," which is "to heal the creature" (BDG/53). Thus does Christ exemplify submission to the loving Father, which promises to release mankind from Job's sufferings (BDG/13). Therefore:

> If you truly own Christ, you will cheerfully hold forth the restoring spirit in your actions; Christ the annointing spirit doth not enslave any but comes to set all free; he comes not to destroy but to save; he comes not to put sackcloth and mourning weeds on mankind, but to pull them off and wipe away all the tears. (447)

Winstanley uses Christ to fashion the parable of Job into a powerful account of the insights he gained from his sufferings: piety for Winstanley is an "experimental knowledge" one can learn only by experiencing what he believes are the consequences of pride. Only by way of blindness, transgression, and loss do human beings learn about their condition and needs as creatures; only subjection to sin and mortality drives them to admit their need for god's love and guidance. Since the "wise and covetous flesh thinks himself to be a god or angel of light," only by allowing him "his will to act his principles" can that conceit be shaken. For only "after a man hath had trial of his own wisdom and power of the flesh, and finds it a devil, and that there is no blessing in it" will he be "without excuse" and ready to "lie down in the wisdom and power of the King of Righteousness" (220).

Winstanley has gone from being an angry and afflicted Job, righteously contending with a god whose will appeared arbitrary if not malevolent, to being a witness of Christ's example of wholehearted service to that will: "Father, do what thy will with my estate, body, and life" (SP/14–29). Thus, Winstanley's argument is a theodicy, as he wills the fall he once resentfully denied and exonerates god of evil intent:

> Many men live in their innocency longer than others, some are tempted sooner than others, but all must be tempted and tried by the evil one, that some way may be made for Christ to show his power. . . . Therefore, temptations and falling from innocency must be, so that man may be drawn up into the life and strength of the righteous God or ruler from whom we shall never fall again.[1] (481)

That god appears to Job and restores all his earthly treasures and authority suggests to Winstanley this narrative of god's love, manifested more fully in the life of Christ. Indeed, there will be salvation in historical time because "God will dwell in every man and woman without exception, as he did dwell in Jesus Christ" (81). To bring god back inside, as Christ counsels, forces a confrontation with the rage Puritans split off and disavow, which yields the possibility of integration and reparation, of moving beyond the inner punitiveness they associate with their Cal-

---

1. Winstanley imagines being asked, "Is there any evil in the city and the Lord hath not done it?" He answers:

> God suffers man to take his own course and act his own will, and to follow his own lusts, letting him alone and permitting him a time to do what he will . . . that when the time comes that he shall be made to see himself and his works, he may be left without excuse. . . . When all flesh hath corrupted his ways, then the Sun of Righteousness arises up and lets man in His light see himself to be a devil. The King lays no hand upon him, but lets him see himself and the man's own works become the devils that torment him. (220)

Put simply, god has created a creature who is free and therefore lets the creature "have his will to act his principles." Indeed, god—the spirit of reason and love in humans—is subjected to the flesh and suffers for the sake of that freedom:

> For the devil desired a liberty to try Job, and the righteous power Reason gave him leave; only telling him, he should not touch [Job's life]; and then the devil . . . burns his house and kills his children. Who was it that the Devil did afflict? Not an enemy to the King of Righteousness, but a body in whom he dwelt. Yea, the Father did suffer himself to be persecuted by the devil, in that humane body Job, that at last, that power of darkness, which is the accuser of brethren and the bondage of creation, might be made manifest . . . and so cast out justly. (222)

vinist god. That movement, promised by Christ, is to Winstanley the very narrative of history, which he invokes to explain his own transformation and to authorize his rebellion against Puritanism. Thus, that he himself was "driven by the Father" away from the "forms and customs" of Puritanism is not merely a personal experience but also a manifestation of Christ's Second Coming.

Deepening the Puritans' own argument about God in history, Winstanley becomes a witness to the historically emerging covenant between a loving god and "created beings" satisfied fully by their reverence. Associating Calvinist Puritans, who deny universal grace, with the pharisees who persecuted Christ, Winstanley rebels in the name of a reverence they call heretical but which he contends is Christ's teaching and the basis of human freedom.

He becomes a particular sort of rebel, however: reverence for god sponsors his rebellion against the "evil masculine powers of pride" but also pressures him toward an unreal purity. He discovers a loving god and beneficent nature, but he purifies them of the contradictions to which Job testifies. Winstanley denies the possibility of innocent suffering by insisting that "all misery is from the creature"; he rationalizes evil by imputing to god the redemptive purpose of "bringing good out of suffering"; he eliminates the conflict between god and man by imagining that pious submission to god provides all that men and women really need. Correspondingly, he feels called on to purify himself of what he associates with pride: only the wholly submissive creature is entitled to god's deliverance, which will restore the intended harmony of creation (132).

Thus, Winstanley feels compelled to disavow not only Adam's works of pride but even Job's contending, for he believes that both transgress the perfect inner harmony to which he would "testify." By answering the Book of Job with the Book of Revelation, Winstanley not only lays the foundation of his rebellion but also subverts the very tensions that made the Job story tragic. Indeed, the tragedy in his alternative to Puritanism arises from his denial of tragedy, of the conflicts and dilemmas that in fact are exemplified by Job.[2]

---

2. In *The New England Mind* Perry Miller says that Puritans were "cosmic optimists" seeking "those perspectives of vision in which evil becomes resolved in the design of the whole, like shadows in a picture." The Puritans' antinomian children rebelled by giving this optimism its fullest expression in the idea of a "universal grace" to be enjoyed in the present. Thus, Miller's judgment of this optimism applies to Winstanley:

So far was the Puritan spirit from being itself tragic that it was actually incapable of perceiving tragedy. This deficiency is by rights the accusation which ought to be lev-

In contrast to Winstanley, Hobbes seems to honor that sense of tragedy. By entitling his book *Leviathan,* Hobbes suggests his allegiance to the Old Testament Jehovah and proceeds to attack the Puritans and their critics as so many providers of "false comfort." He insists on the utter transcendence of god and therefore ridicules their prophetic claim to know and enact god's purposes, in order to deprive them of the authority to act. But Hobbes does not embrace the tragic tensions in the Book of Job because he does not vindicate Job: by building a Leviathan he calls a mortal god, he tries to prevent anyone from contending, even piously, with authority. Thus, he embraces the idolatry—and the bondage—condemned by Old Testament and New Testament alike.

Hobbes's questions about the idea of redemption manifest a common skepticism. By challenging the redemption that human invention is supposed to bring, however, Winstanley manifests a different kind of skepticism, which needs to be explored before we return to the problematic purity entailed by his theodicy.

WINSTANLEY'S THEORY OF REVERENCE AND FREEDOM

To understand Winstanley's idea of freedom, we must explore his understanding of Christ's submission to god. In secular terms, Winstanley's god is an inner authority: what truths does it represent, and how does piety for it bring freedom? These questions can be answered by attending to the two central metaphors that Winstanley uses to describe god, the piety exemplified by Christ, and freedom.

The first metaphor depicts the "living soul" as a child, and the Father within as having "breasts of love" that nourish the soul with "sincere milk." The soul is the hungry and receptive part of the self, something like the child every adult once was, but exclusively innocent, an "estate of plainheartedness that hath the life of the five senses only" (478). This living soul becomes the captive of the "masculine" power of pride when a person enters the world of culture, seeking nourishment and identity from its invented teats and dung.

In the wilderness condition, however, the soul is "weaned" from these unsatisfying inventions and brought into a "condition of sensible barrenness." That happens because

---

elled against it, and constitutes a much more telling charge than that of being over-gloomy or dismal. . . . The tragedy of Puritanism may be that it could not always retain a vivid sense of the fall of man, but certainly while Puritans did have such a sense, they could not look upon life itself as tragic. (38)

God never manifests himself to a soul until he hath first emptied her. . . . The creature's teats are to be dried up, that the soul can suck no refreshing milk from them, before the Lord teach it knowledge. God says, Whom shall I give understanding to? And to whom shall I teach doctrine? To them that are drawn off from the milk, and are weaned from the teats of mans own self-conceits and from sucking contentment from mens learning or invention. (quoted in Hayes, *Winstanley the Digger*, p. 57)

Unlike Hobbes's state of nature, whose dangers promote anxiety and whose insufficiencies require human invention, Winstanley's wilderness is actually a "very safe condition," where "the soul is under God's protection from the face of the serpent [and] wherein the soul is fed and nourished by God and not by any creature" (quoted in Hayes, p. 31). In Winstanley's wilderness, the "wearied soul" can "suck sincere milk from the Father's two breasts of love" (93, 140). To enjoy this milk "brings mankind back to that plainhearted state of simplicity . . . and makes him humble, meek, flexible, loving . . . like the state of a little child" (480). Indeed, says Winstanley, only if the soul "waits upon the Father with a meek and obedient spirit" will God "teach us and feed us with sincere milk" (128).

What are we to make of these images? By speaking of the soul as a child and by representing the Father as two breasts of love, it seems as if Winstanley is telling people to become children again and dependent on a mother's nourishment. He does urge people to give up the compulsive insistence on mastery that has constituted their adulthood. Only then can they face directly the inner conflicts he associates with the flesh and discern as well the child's need for love, which they have "trod under foot."

Thus, Winstanley actually seeks a truer and more honest adulthood. This is confirmed by the crucial fact that he locates childhood feelings about love and nourishment *within* the self, in relation to another part of the self, a power he calls "the God within." This inner parent is not the same as a real parent, but is what Winstanley is discovering now to be an essential part of his self, a parent to his child. To be nourished by what once seemed, as he put it, "beyond my reach" suggests the process of digesting what has been an unknown, alien, and even punitive part of himself. As he feeds, he is integrating what had been separated and antagonistic.

That the Father within has breasts means that this internal authority includes the real or fantasized mother's love: Winstanley here reexperiences and fulfills primitive needs by contacting and enjoying what is maternal in this internal father. Thus, the spirit ruling Winstanley also reaches back to, and embodies, the lost love of maternal authority. Because that love is now internal, however, it provides a way for adults not to return literally to the mother and infancy but to separate truly. Closeness to the Father within resolves ambivalences originating in separation from actual mothers because it establishes basic trust in a loving power inside the self: experiencing this internal love stills the anxieties and rage Winstanley associates with the rule of the back part and separation from god. Unlike the Puritan fathers and Hobbes, he does not equate nurturance and bondage: god's milk, like the mother's love, helps promote his self-respect and independence.

Yet it is as if Winstanley is aware that the mother's love does not suffice to make children free, for it is a father who has breasts. Here he suggests the real (or perhaps ideal) father, whose love and teaching help children establish their separateness from the mother. The idea of sincere milk is not about natural birth and infantile dependence on a mother, nor is it simply about the ways the mother's love, taken inside, can free adults from anxiety. The Father's milk is also about the "birth" of a distinct self, achieved partly through the support of a nurturant father.

By calling the Father's milk sincere, Winstanley distinguishes internal milk from both the actual milk of a real mother (which, however sincerely offered, must be withheld by her and relinquished by children if they are to mature) and the ersatz milk of culture. By acknowledging the basic spiritual needs from which they cannot escape, people can find what they need internally. Indeed, they must find an inner source of "milk" if they are to become autonomous in the world. For Winstanley, this is what Christ exemplified: a true adult is always the pious child of the god within.[3]

But how does Winstanley justify his claims about god and rebirth? Most simply, he declares that he feels transformed. "To be made experimentally subject to the spirit in creation," he says, "gives a feeling experience to the heart that can never be forgot. This alone overcomes the

---

3. Strictly speaking, a "true" god would have to be androgynous because what humans consider sacred in and to themselves must reach back to the earliest and most basic aspects of the self (the living soul and the need for love), as well as forward to more advanced capacities, such as reason. To be sure, Winstanley still reflects the Christian view of god as a paternal sponsor of rebirth, but he knows that a strictly paternal god, abstracted from the body and associated with the punitive conscience, reflects the very ambivalences he would heal. Only the love of an authority to be felt in the body and associated with the mother can heal those inner divisions. (I am indebted to Hanna Pitkin for help in clarifying these claims.)

self-conceit and evil inclinations of the flesh" (93). Inwardly, Winstanley no longer feels captive to the hungers, fantasies, and anxieties that turn human desire into "the flesh." It is in this sense that Winstanley says the power of love makes him "a new creature, in whom the old lusts are passed away and every power is a new power" (176).[4]

As a result, he believes, enjoying a sincere milk also transforms his relationship to "the kingdom without" and "creature objects." Experiencing a new sense of detachment and moderation, Winstanley says of himself:

> Though objects be tendered to me, I reject them and so I fall not; and now Satan or the tempter, which are outward objects, finds nothing in me. . . . And thus it was said of Jesus . . . that there was nothing in him that consented to the temptation without; he made use of outward objects in moderation, for the safety and peace of his body, but desired nothing in excess of immoderately. (494)

What Winstanley calls "freedom within" is the inner fulfillment or strength that makes possible the moderate use of objects. "He that is free within is moved to excess or unrational action by no outward objects. He that is not free within, is moved to excess by every object" (495). Because there is no inappropriate hunger driving a person to control and possess objects, "nothing within consents to temptation without"; because he does not seek "content" or identity from objects and people, he sees them for what they are. The dutiful son of god, sucking sincere milk, is overwhelmed neither by the pressure of anxious desire nor by the attractive power of objects.

Winstanley appears to suggest the stereotypical passivity and otherworldliness of "Christian freedom," but a second metaphor represents another aspect of god's authority, which generates a freedom profoundly implicated in the world. In this metaphor, the earth is Adam's sentient bodily senses; the Father within is "the sun" or "the power of reason." When oriented by the sun, an adult develops "the seed of Christ" and becomes "the son of freedom." By describing the Father

4. Psychoanalyst Herbert Fingarette's argument about mystics helps explain what Winstanley may mean. Mystics seek release, he says, from the "inner compulsiveness" that is "a characteristic symptom of anxieties originating in the primal separation." Thus, the "self" that the mystic seeks to "lose" is the "neurotic, driven, anxious self, and not the self that is essential to the practical carrying on of one's activities, nor is it the ego in the psychoanalytic sense. . . . It is self-consciousness colored by intra-psychic conflict and anxiety." Accordingly, Fingarette contends, the "selflessness" of the mystic is associated with what psychoanalysts call ego strength. See Herbert Fingarette, "The Ego and Mystic Selflessness," in *Identity and Anxiety,* ed. Maurice Stein, Arthur Vidich, and David White (New York: The Free Press, 1960).

within as an Apollonian sun, Winstanley suggests that freedom is a seed developed by the capacity to reason and by the choice to live according to the light it sheds. Thus, freedom does not blossom automatically, but only as a person is oriented consciously by the sun of reason within. But what does the "sun" teach the "son," and why does its light bring him freedom?

By using his reason to examine his experience, Winstanley claims to have discovered "experimentally" the truth about creation, which he describes as a body composed of interdependent bodies. He describes, in effect, an ecology:

> The clouds send down rain, and there is great undeniable reason in it, for otherwise the earth could not bring forth grass and fruit. The earth sends forth grass, or else cattle could not be preserved. The cattle feed on the grass, and there is reason in it, for else man could not be preserved. The sun gives light and heat, or else the creation could not subsist. So that the mighty power Reason hath made these to give life and preservation one to another. (109)

Thus, Winstanley sees "mind" in nature, such that there is a reason to all things, in all things, and for all things:

> Reason is that living power of light that is in all things. . . . It hath a regard to the whole creation, and knits every creature together into a oneness, making every creature to be an upholder of his fellows, so everyone is an assistant to preserve the whole. (105)

Accordingly, human beings embody the spirit of god:

> Every creature in its place and stature is a son to the Father; because every single creature does demonstrate his maker to the view of his fellow creatures, everyone being a candlestick holding forth the Father by the light that is in itself. For indeed, the light that is in it is the Father himself, and the Father shows himself to the creature by every particular parcel of creation.[5] (131)

---

5. According to Winstanley, the experience of god's reason in creation is transforming specifically because it includes the creature in the love he or she sees:

> When the Father shines and rules in him bodily, then he can declare the Father by all his senses to the creation . . . because he sees and hears, feels and smells and tastes that He who is the spirit . . . uniting all together in love . . . does govern the whole creation . . . subjecting all flesh under him, and making it servicable. (131)

The "reason in creation" can be known, but only through the senses combined with reason. Although god is neither transcendent nor irrational, however, human knowledge will be limited because we are mortal, finite creatures: "The soul shall ever be learning what God is" (SP/2).

Humans are endowed with the capacity to reason that Winstanley associates with the righteousness of god's spirit, which "governs" by intentionally giving everything its due "according to its nature and necessity." Therefore, humans can know, and enact by choice, the righteousness that other creatures manifest only as objects. When Winstanley imagines an interlocutor asking about the "testimony" of the spirit Reason in humans, he replies:

> Justice and judgment are the two witnesses or the manifest appearance of the spirit, or the pure light of reason, teaching a man both to know what is righteous and to do righteously. And when these two rule in a man, then is the flesh made subject to the spirit. (122–23)

Justice and judgment manifest god's presence: the exercise of these capacities is "the reasonings of the heart" that Winstanley calls "prayer" (136).[6]

Humans testify to god's spirit of reason in them by becoming "assistants to preserve the whole, and the nearer man's reasoning comes to this, the more spiritual they are" (105). The "reason" for the human capacity to reason is that humans need to know and uphold the interdependence that is as constitutive a fact about human life as it is about nature. As Winstanley declares: "Reason makes a man to live moderately and peaceably with all. He makes a man just and righteous in all his actings. . . . Wherein is the reason? Because this man stands in need of others, and others stand in need of him; and therefore makes a man do as he would be done unto" (109).

But how does the presence of reason, and the insight into interdependence that it provides, generate human freedom? It is not only the passive reception of god's love but also the conscious effort to honor god's reason within that enable humans to achieve self-mastery and moderation. Reason also frees adults from dangerous dependence on worldly authorities. Since "every single man, male and female, is a perfect creature . . . subject to reason his maker, and hath him to be his teacher and ruler," no one needs to "run abroad after any teacher or ruler without him" (251). Partly because of this self-respect, Winstanley manifests a sense of personal authority: "What I hear another speak is nothing to me until I find the same experience in myself; the testimony of others is

6. Partly, the "reason" within humans is the *idea* of giving each creature its due, a rule of justice "given" in human nature, which people do not and cannot invent. Rather, people become conscious of this rule within them and learn to apply it, as it were, deductively. At the same time, however, the idea of righteousness is learned and developed only as people proceed inductively, by consciously reasoning about their experience.

known to be true by the testimony of the same experience within myself" (96).

God represents a power of love and reason; piety for god therefore
offers what he calls "inner freedom," in the sense of transformed desire
and self respect, and "outer freedom," in the sense of independence
from worldly authorities. Yet for Winstanley, freedom *from* anxious
desire and dependence also entails freedom *for* a new kind of worldly
agency. The metaphors of milk and the sun enable him to describe the
proper way not only to fashion a self internally but also to conceive of
its worldly freedom.

REVERENCE IN ACTION

Although Puritans provide "waste words" and "invented teats" to
others, Winstanley believes that worldly action can offer real nurturance
and therefore real autonomy. That endeavor is exemplified for him by
Christ's "true ministry," which represents the way he initially links inner
piety to an idea of legitimate worldly freedom.

Winstanley says that god's love and reason is experienced as a "word
of power speaking in and to your hearts, causing your hearts to open to
His voice." In turn, he believes, piety toward god's word empowers and
entitles him to "speak my own experienced words." Thus, Winstanley
believes that he must embody god's voice in his own speech: as a mouthpiece, he would declare "in pure speech" the words arising from within;
as a candle, he would "hold forth the light" that now illuminates his
experience (131). As he tries to become a witness whose testimony discloses to others the voice that is within them, he moves from inward
piety to engagement with others.

But what does he mean by "witness"? Winstanley "bears witness" to
his experience and to the meaning of his words. A witness is responsible
first to his experience, which he must "own" in the sense of understanding, digesting, and making his own. But a witness also is responsible for
conveying the truth of his experience, through the words that are his
testimony to others. Therefore, a witness must attend honestly to his
experience so that he can own the words by which he declares it; but he
also must attend faithfully to the meaning of words so that his speech
testifies truly to his experience. A witness bears an experience pregnant
with words; responsible for what he embodies, he is committed to
"bringing forth" its truth.

As a result, Winstanley's account suggests, a witness is imbued with authority. To deserve and retain that authority, however, a person must promise to speak only what he or she knows and only in words that clarify rather than conceal. That authority is jeopardized, then, when a witness gives "false testimony," which mystifies the truth of an experience or the meaning of words. The language of a true witness is illuminating, and therefore authoritative, because it is earned and true to the meaning of words.

Feeling authorized to "speak my own experienced words," Winstanley reenacts Christ's example of being called to a true ministry in the world (93). That ministry is devoted to teaching people to discover the roots and authority of language so that they can judge and digest others' testimony and become witnesses in their own right. In addition, the witness becomes a prophet, calling people back to "the word of power" that declares the truths, values, and commitments they merely profess but have not earned and do not own in action. Thus, Winstanley is led into an engagement with his peers through the sanctified endeavor of speaking with others.[7]

Winstanley feels called to be a witness, yet

> since it pleased the Father to reveal his son in me and caused me to speak what I know from an inward light and power of life within, now both priests and the professors they have deceived . . . call me a blasphemer and a man of errors and look upon me as a man of another world. (243)

As Winstanley testifies that the once crucified Christ is rising within him, he finds himself persecuted, like Christ, by proud people calling him the heretical inventor of "another world." But he feels compelled to testify; he cannot do otherwise:

> The power of that everlasting annointing [hath] taken hold on me, and I have been made another man immediately, and my heart hath been opened as if a man should open a door and carry a lighted candle into a dark room; and the power of love . . . hath so overpowered me that I could not forbear but must speak and write again. . . . And by such experiences I learned to wait upon the spirit and to deliver that to the creation which he revealed in me; and I have a settled peace by that obedience. (Preface)

His settled peace also arises because he believes he is not alone, even though he is a pariah. The Father in him is moving others to bear witness

---

7. I am indebted to Peter Schwartz for his clarification of the relationship between Christ rising, the power of speech, and Winstanley's view of history. It was Hanna Pitkin, in a talk about George Orwell's view of language, who alerted me to the idea of witness, which led me back to the Old Testament idea of prophecy.

to the meaning of Christ's gospel, reanimating a social body rendered
mute and passive by the clergy:

> I have persuasions in me from experimental grounds of God's own work-
> ing, that within a few years will come . . . plentiful manifestations of God in
> his saints. And the great men will be filled with anger at seeing inferior
> people raised up to speak the deep things of God. Tradesmen will speak by
> experience the things they have seen in God, and the learned clergy will be
> slighted. (90)

Because they are learning to speak in their own right, the poor are enter-
ing history, taking for themselves the language and rights expropriated
by the clergy. Here is the final way, for Winstanley, in which inner piety
sponsors freedom: self-mastery, personal authority, and the power of
speech are expressed in the fashioning of a new community.

Saints not only bear witness in their speech but also "own" their
words by acting. In contrast to those ruled by the flesh, those who are
"free within" can enact as well as profess Christ's gospel. A community
of "sons and daughters" is revealed as men and women use the reason
within to discover the needs and limits that are appropriate to their "nature and necessity" as created beings; that community is made manifest
as people exercise "justice and judgment" to develop real mutuality.
Living according to reason, says Winstanley, means

> living in all acts of love to his fellow creatures; feeding the hungry, clothing
> the naked, relieving the oppressed, seeking the preservation of others as well
> as himself; looking upon himself as a fellow creature to all other creatures of
> all kinds. (111)

As men and women become conscious of the god within, they learn to
gain the autonomy that worldly fathers did not and could not sponsor;
as they become children of god, they are delivered from the household
of the fathers.

EVALUATING THE REVERENCE:
JOB AND CHRIST

Winstanley's argument about freedom can be evaluated by situating
it in terms of his theodicy. For Winstanley believes that his movement
from pride to freedom, associated with Christ, has provided an "experimental knowledge" that offers definitive answers to the questions Job
asked god. Those answers suggest terms of evaluation.

First, in answer to Job's question about why there is suffering,

Winstanley argues that human suffering is not something natural, or a curse by which innocent people are malevolently afflicted, but rather the ineluctable consequence of pridefully living by inventions that violate what defines humans as creatures. To be sure, people suffer because they live with the consequences of past choices, personally and historically, but as Stanley Cavell writes:

> The reason consequences furiously hunt us down is not merely that we are half-blind and unfortunate, but that we go on doing the thing that produced those consequences in the first place. What we need is not rebirth or salvation, but the courage, or plain prudence, to see and stop. But what do we need in order to do that? It would be salvation.[8]

Cavell captures the theological and existential elements in Winstanley's answer to Job's second question: why does god allow human suffering? Because god is committed to the freedom of his creatures, to their ability to choose whether to honor him. To put this theological view existentially, humans learn about freedom only by suffering the bondage caused by what they *call* freedom. One feels outrage at Job's suffering, but Winstanley affirms it as the basis of salvation: only through the disillusioned admission of insufficiency and failure is one brought to "see and stop," to confront more soberly one's true nature and necessity.

In this way, Winstanley answers Job's third question: what is the right relation to establish with god? One might squirm at Job's final humbling by god, but the key to Winstanley's insights lies in getting beyond this discomfort, which is prideful. By internalizing Job's drama, Winstanley sees that he can achieve freedom within, as well as worldly autonomy, only by admitting his need for love and guidance. Once Winstanley recognizes this need, he does not have to squirm anymore, but rather submits voluntarily to the inner authority he now characterizes as a spirit of reason and love.

Accordingly, Winstanley's reverence for a god he professes to embody does not entitle him to do just anything, as Hobbes argued it would. On the contrary, his idea of reverence for god means that humans cannot do certain things and must do others if they are to be autonomous. In Cavell's terms, Winstanley develops prudence by learning to trust the reason that tells him what choices and commitments produce inner harmony; he develops courage by learning to trust the love within and

---

8. Stanley Cavell, *Must We Mean What We Say?* (Cambridge: Cambridge University Press, 1976), p. 309.

abjure false substitutes to its nourishment. As a result, he fashions a freedom that is deeply conditioned and bound, situated in terms of the values and commitments represented by the inner authority of the Father.

Thus, Winstanley grounds human identity, language, and community in the reason and needs he believes humans cannot and do not create: human capacities yield freedom only if exercised in reverence for the "fountain of life" in each person and the interdependence of all people. Hence he no longer tries to prove his autonomy by fleeing his personal body and the body of nature, or by rising over others through the accumulation of commodities on earth. Rather, he addresses his spiritual needs in a way that acknowledges the carnal reality of mutual need, and addresses his material needs in a way that acknowledges his spiritual relationship with others and nature.

As his account of the movement from Job to Christ suggests, however, Winstanley's idea of a reverent freedom involves a problematic ideal of purity. Believing that he follows Christ, Winstanley argues that pride must be "cast out" and "cleansed" completely if humans are to enjoy god's redemptive promise. For the heart to "be made a fit temple for the spirit to dwell bodily in," Winstanley insists there must be "no opposite power remaining" (170) to contend with god and subvert his sovereignty: "There is no quiet peace in a man until the Kingdom of Darkness be conquered and the Serpent cast out" (171). Accordingly, Winstanley's language of love and healing is invariably accompanied by violent images of purification.

At the outset of his transformation "the sun shines and the dunghill casts up its stinking smell" (222). But Winstanley is not satisfied with shedding the light of reason on what struggles for rule in him. Knowing the flesh, or even choosing not to feed on its imaginary food, does not suffice: Winstanley wants the flesh to be removed entirely. Thus, he also describes the sun as a purifying fire that, by burning away pride, transforms "dross into gold":

> Know this, that the body of sin and the created flesh [are] so nearly wrapped in each other that before the spirit hath parted them, thou shalt roar in bitterness and wish thou hadst never been born, and the more familiarity thou hast had with thy cursed lust, the sharper thy torments will be. The Founder cannot turn away the dross but must burn the gold too in the fire. (132–33)

Although Winstanley acknowledges here that pain is involved in the process of separating from his old self, he also has granted, in effect, that Job is not entirely wrong about god's anger. God's anger is elicited by the creature's pride, which "won't let the Father appear. Therefore, saith the Father, this sin or curse shall never be pardoned: that is, the Father will never reconcile that wicked one to Him; the Father and the serpent will never become one" (132). In this way, Winstanley clarifies the nature of the anger he feels in himself: "the Father . . . is not angry with his creature, but with this sin or curse in the creature, with which the creature has made a covenant . . . and so fights against its maker" (SP/84–85). God's anger is directed not against the body as such but against the impulses and fantasies Winstanley associates with pride:

> A man is not counted a man from the bulk of his body of flesh, but the power that dwells in that body of flesh is the man, either the righteous man or the wicked. And if the wicked power rule in the body of the flesh, this is he that must be burned up, subdued, destroyed, and never enter into rest. This is Christ's enemy. (171)

The good son, then, identifies not only with the loving breasts that feed the soul but also with the "dispensation of wrath" that "destroys" the flesh "until the creature is redeemed from the power and bondage of it" (SP/84–85). As a result, Winstanley says that the rising of Christ within him "doth kill and crucify the first Adam daily, with all his lusts, and frees me from that slavery" (173). In moving from Job to Christ, he embraces a revenge Job never would seek:

> As soon as Christ is rose up in a man, the first thing he doth, he takes revenge of the pride, lust, envy, covetousness, which ruled within the flesh, and casts out that serpent and dragon out of heaven . . . and makes a man to . . . hate and abhor his cursed lusts, which held him captive. He makes a man to look abroad with pity and compassion to his fellow creatures, but to look with hatred and loathing upon the serpent, his unclean lusts, desiring nothing so much as the death of the body of sin within. (227)

Winstanley has seen through the unconscious fantasies that render the body excremental. But he also feels that he must disown and purify what he associates consciously with the "back part," which he contends is not really himself. Thus, he rejects the Puritan quest for a spirit uncontaminated by the body but seeks the spirit in a body uncontaminated by excrement, by what he associates consciously with covetousness, the prideful "disposition of every creature to promote itself." He no longer imagines a temple in heaven but thinks that he must purify himself to build one on earth (472). He manifests the fiery will to purity, the splitting of the creature into excremental and nonexcremental selves, that he criticizes in the Puritans. His, like theirs, is a sign of the dunghill within, of anger directed against something in the self that is considered unclean.[9]

Like many other theorists, Winstanley confronts problems that are stronger than his insight into a cure. Winstanley's arguments about the inner kingdom parallel certain features of psychoanalytic theory, however, which can clarify how his piety is shaped by the very ambivalences it is meant to heal.

Dorothy Dinnerstein, in *The Mermaid and the Minotaur*, argues that mothers are enormously powerful relative to their infants, whose helpless dependence inevitably engenders rage. That rage becomes a valuable spur to separation, for children mature partly because of the angry desire to stand alone, and not only because of the loving sponsorship of a parent. But full maturity requires that the child integrate its loving and angry feelings and its contradictory images of the mother. Unless the child learns that anger will destroy neither the loved mother nor itself, it will disown its anger; unless it learns that its loving feelings will not render it helpless, it will disown its love. Thus, maturity means relinquishing the fantasy of unambivalent union between a wholly loving child and a wholly loving mother, as well as the fantasy of an utterly unbound independence from an utterly malevolent force. Only by accepting their own ambivalence toward the mother, the argument goes, can adults establish an identity that denies neither the bonds of love nor the anger that denotes separateness.

Winstanley's religious language follows the standard Puritan practice of marking the childlike soul as feminine and thereby reverses the situation of early childhood: the male child has become the feminine soul, and the powerful mother has become the internal father. Because feelings about the mother are represented internally toward god, the desire to separate is stigmatized rather than affirmed, just as the need to "contend" with god is suppressed. Given the way Winstanley conceives and internalizes god, it is difficult for him to recognize that this "pride" is an inevitable and valuable aspect of his created being. Here, then, is one crucial difference between his religious language and the discourse of psychoanalysis: Winstanley's god devalues as pride the angry particularity that psychoanalysis to some extent must affirm.

9. As with Luther, so perhaps with Winstanley. In *Young Man Luther* Erikson says that Luther's excremental language directs outward his rage at parts of himself. In *Life Against Death* Brown says that Luther's excremental language reveals a problem that is in the world: Luther locates and exposes the anal sources of emerging capitalism. In certain ways they are both right.

This difference is not necessarily required by any religiosity. In part, I have intentionally emphasized Winstanley's use of the story of Job, for in trying to move beyond it, Winstanley leaves behind the image of a god who accepts Job's ambivalence and the legitimacy of Job's contending. One could also say that his ambivalence about his own anger shapes this shift, for he declares that perfect union between the soul and the Father would be possible were it not for his pride, and that god would provide all he needs if only he were wholly submissive. Accordingly, he conceives of an inner piety that deprives him of the right to contend angrily with what is sacred in and to him, as if love and anger were mutually exclusive.

But the anger Winstanley disowns returns as god's anger, with which he identifies. Full of shame, he punishes whatever prevents him from being the wholly receptive and dutiful child of the Father within. Calling down on himself an anger whose roots remain unconscious, he seeks a purity that bespeaks an unacknowledged resentment of what once made him a separate, and not only a created, being.

As a result, his reverence yields a radical critique of the pride in the Puritan fathers; but it also sponsors a rebellion that is premised on Winstanley's denial of himself as a creator. As he deepens the Puritans' own ambivalence about pride, he insists that speech and action are legitimate only if "undefiled" by anger, imagination, or invention. After all, if he were to be the creator of the values and truths in the name of which he rebels, he would be like the Puritans, an Adam or Job ruled by pride. Accordingly, Winstanley feels authorized to speak and act only if he is a "pure instrument" of the god within and therefore wholly unlike those he criticizes.

Thus, Winstanley feels obliged to be motivated solely by love. Obviously he is angry, not only at his own fleshly weakness and pride, but also at the flesh ruling others, which leads them to persecute him. Hypothetically, he could accept the legitimacy of this anger: like god, he could love the creature in his enemies even as he angrily condemns their covenant with the pride that holds them captive; he could empathize with their weakness even as he angrily insists that no one (including himself) has the right to commit evil. But for Winstanley, love must preclude anger because love precludes ambivalence: "I have many times thought that love, being crossed, grows angry; but I see by experience that it is improper, for love cannot be angry, it beareth all things" (SP/83). Anger connotes lack of love, especially for god: the good son must say without rancor, "Thy will be done."

Correspondingly, Winstanley also believes that he must purge imagination from his testimony as a saintly rebel. Since he believes that imagination is merely a self-regarding capacity that mystifies "the nature and necessity of every body," he is not permitted to maintain that his understanding of texts, god, reality, and righteousness is (in certain defensible ways) a better interpretation than the "conjectures" of the Puritans. His testimony is legitimate only because he utters the Father's truth, not merely his own interpretation. Given to all by the Father's reason within each, truth ends the need to interpret and, thus, ends conflicts about interpretation (224–26). Truth precludes interpretation because, for Winstanley, it precludes ambiguity (142–45).

Thus, Winstanley is a rebel who turns against his own anger and disavows the imagination that so strikingly animates his thought and rebellion. He disowns both anger and imagination as signs of the fleshly particularity he wishes to cast out. As a result, he rebels in the name of a vision of culture that is deeply unpolitical.

EVALUATING THE RADICALISM: CHRIST AND PROMETHEUS

Since Winstanley's religious language expresses the problems that Dinnerstein identifies in modern critics of pride, her argument also helps situate his cultural politics. She is another voice in the tradition that runs counter to Promethean history making, yet she also defends the human project of making history against those critics of pride who reject it totally.

Dinnerstein emphasizes the prolonged dependency of the child, which suggests the way in which humans are unfinished and therefore unnatural: unlike other animals, humans are creatures completed only by culture, which is a second womb they themselves must create. In addition, Dinnerstein emphasizes the inequality in the relationship between the powerful parent and the dependent child. As a result, autonomy not only is the fruit of loving reciprocity, as some feminists contend, but also requires the rage those theorists disown. Indeed, it is partly because of rage about dependence, limitation, and mortality that children become adults and that humans become historical creators, fashioning and reshaping their world.

For Dinnerstein, then, the task of human beings is to acknowledge and sublimate the unavoidable rage that is now unconscious and misdirected so that they can express their capacities as creators, consciously building a culture based on reciprocity with nature and sensitivity toward their deepest needs as creatures. But there is no final cure for pride, no perfect reconciliation with nature, and no refuge from history. In fact, only because of the human capacity to create, and only through large-scale collective action, can humans develop an alternative to what she calls "the mad megamachine."

This account suggests that Winstanley misconceives the enterprise of culture because he completely disowns in himself the pride he diagnoses in others. Even as he demonstrates a legitimate form of action, the idea of community to which he "testifies" is shaped by his shameful denial of the anger and imagination that signify prideful particularity. The premise of the "community of one heart and one mind" is not simply god's promise to appear in each person but also the promise of each to purify the self of whatever makes god distant: "Let every man and woman cleanse himself of the wicked masculine powers that rule him, and there will speedily be a harmony of love in the creation, even among all creatures" (quoted in Hayes, p. 69).

Winstanley believes that as the covetousness that particularizes interpretations is purged, conflict about reality and conventions will yield to "sweet harmony":

> Let all men cease spending constructions upon the Scriptures and leave the pure Scriptures to shine in their own luster, not mixing imaginary inferences with them. . . . And let us leave the pure teachings of the Father in every man to conjoin themselves with those Scriptures, and then there will be no jarring but a sweet harmony between the experience of every man and these Scriptures. (144–45)

Even his own "true ministry . . . must cease," for "silence shall be man's rest and liberty, it is . . . the soul's receiving time, it is the forerunner of pure language" (224).

Thus, the fire of Winstanley's millennial dream specifically consumes the clergy and the artifice of culture. Just as he would overcome the flesh he blames for ambivalence about righteousness within, so too he would cast out the clergy he blames for conflict and error about righteousness in the kingdom without: "It is the misery of this age that men try to uphold a usurped ecclesiastical power. They are even so mad that they deny magistracy, contrary to God's ordinance, unless it is upheld by ecclesiastical power" (90). As he attacks the imaginary flesh in the name of god's inner sovereignty, so he attacks the clergy while advocating "pure civil magistracy." Once clerical power is destroyed, he says, "magistrates shall love the people and be nursing fathers to them, . . . and the people shall love and cheerfully obey the commands of magistrates" (BDG/preface).

It seems clear that Winstanley is unable to accept the legitimacy of "contending" about the authority that rules a community because he is unable to accept personal ambivalence about what rules him. As a result, neither his mention of magistracy nor his challenge to the worldly authority of priests makes his glad tidings political. Winstanley's saints do act: "Let your chief endeavor be to act according to your creation; that is, to do as you would be done unto" (125). But those who engage in this "practice of love" abjure actual politics or intentionally collective action as they "wait on the Father" to transform each person individually and internally, thereby transforming society from the inside out.[10]

The saint's attitude toward politics, in fact, is noninvolvement. Political struggles are part of the dark kingdom from which Winstanley feels freed and protected: "God can make an outside professing service book man kill an outside professing Presbyterian, or he can permit the latter to kill a hypocritical Independent, while sincere-hearted ones look on and are preserved" (94). To be sure, Winstanley does give voice to his involvement by writing—and indignantly and passionately at that. But notice his stance:

> Though my words may seem sharp to some, yet I do not write them out of envy to any man, but out of love to all, . . . speaking the truth as it is in Jesus; that is, speaking my own words, what I see and feel in my own experience, from that light of Christ within. (244)

Attributing all pride and anger to his adversaries—that is, projecting it outward—Winstanley depicts himself as the wholly impartial and innocent saint who loves them in spite of *their* selfish anger.[11]

Here we see the deeper senses in which Winstanley's early pamphlets are not political. I do not refer simply to his moralism but to what lies

---

10. Winstanley declares:

In effecting this great work, God shakes and will shake Kings, Parliaments, Armies, Counties, Kingdoms, Universities, humane learning, yea, rich men and poor men. . . . For as all outward abominations in mens practices came from the indwelling of the Beast in every mans heart, so when God first shakes down and crafts the Beast out of mens hearts, the outward abominations and unjust practices in Church and State shake together and fall presently. (BDG/124)

11. That Winstanley has undergone a conversion that fills him with great feelings of love and with new insights that could liberate others, and that he then is punished and stigmatized for expressing these insights, becomes the paradigmatic experience for him. The claim of innocent good intentions, and indignation at those who treat him as if he were crazy or sinful, sets the tone for all his later theoretical and political work.

behind it: the presumption that conjecture and conflict are the emblems of pride, the badges of sin. This premise is the flip side of the redemptive dream that completely reconciles humans, god, and nature. As pride is cast out and community becomes a literal mirror of the spirit ordering nature, there will be perfect harmony between people sharing a fixed and god-given end. In god's true household, in which every member is a son and daughter, there will be no ambivalence and anger, no ambiguity and interpretation. Indeed, as reality becomes transparent and all differences are "swallowed in love," politics will cease, for humans will be released from the cross of history (87).

Therefore, Winstanley is especially vulnerable to Hobbes's critique of the Puritans, for Winstanley also dissimulates his anger and imagination and denies that culture must be conventional. Hobbes's version of Job does expose the "false comfort" in the assumption animating the rebellion of Winstanley and the Puritans: he discredits their belief in a ground for speech and action that is beyond or beneath culture. As a result, it is Hobbes, and not Winstanley, who asserts the primal political insight that any authority is always invented and who thereby teaches about the formative power of a culture that must be invented.

In this way, Hobbes "humbles" the rebels he considers "children of pride"; but he also appropriates the pride Puritans dissimulate and externalizes the god he says they merely imagine. By making conscious and explicit what he maintains all cultures have accomplished unconsciously and therefore ineffectively, he turns Puritan saints into Promethean modernizers: they will shape themselves consciously, by submitting to the dictates of the mortal god they create.

As a result, one could say that Hobbes teaches the primacy of prideful creation and, correspondingly, devalues the nature that creators control and order. Moreover, he reads politics as an eruption of that nature and therefore uses his political insights to suppress actual politics, the appearance of men and women in public speaking and acting on their own. Paradoxically, then, his vision of conventionality turns him against the very historicity of culture, for the unregulated agency of its members appears as a threat to order.

Thus, Winstanley and Hobbes develop contrasting responses to the pride they diagnose in Puritanism. As a witness to Christ, as a purely submissive creature animated by reverence for what he does not invent, Winstanley authorizes rebellion against worldly authority, but he premises that rebellion on the denial of his pride and of the conventionality of culture. Hobbes, as a Promethean, a being for himself animated by reverence for his own inventions, calls for the creation of a consciously conventional culture, but he believes this mortal god must suppress ongoing human agency.

Accordingly, Winstanley exposes the conventionality of what Hobbes teaches is nature; and by instructing us about the bondage required by Hobbes's inventions, he suggests an alternative to Hobbes's view of politics and culture. But Hobbes exposes the pride Winstanley would purge from himself and the world; and by instructing us about the conventionality in Winstanley's idea of authority, he suggests the contingency of the truth on which Winstanley would build culture. In Dinnerstein's terms, Hobbes exemplifies the truth of culture and the freedom, even heroism, of the prideful creator, and yet he therefore builds a mad megamachine. In contrast, Winstanley exemplifies the truth of nature and the freedom that comes from reverent reciprocity with it, and yet he therefore disowns the human enterprise of creating culture.

But there is also a strange symmetry in their efforts to move beyond Puritanism. Both theorists seek a profound transformation that each symbolizes through the imagery of fire; both use fire to overcome what they consider shameful and dangerous, although rage at maternal nature fuels the "visible power" of Hobbes's sovereign sun, whereas rage at masculine pride fuels the "fiery orb" to which Winstanley's saints submit themselves (132). Since each is at war with essential aspects of life, each is engaged in a project impossible to complete. As Winstanley says, "the fire never ceases so long as there is fuel," and existence forever will stoke the contrasting flames they revere.

To be sure, Prometheus would emulate and therefore displace god, stealing fire from god in order to form men in his own image, whereas Winstanley would emulate Christ, submitting to god's fire in order to conform himself to god's image. But the idea of perfectly conforming to an image suggests the pride that animates Winstanley's reverence as well as Hobbes's invention. As Winstanley says:

> Christ, or the spreading power of light, is drawing the knowledge of himself as he lies in all things into the clear experience of man, . . . and he, the Son of Righteousness, will not only shine but fix himself in everyone. So that perfect man shall be no other but God manifest in the flesh. (166)

The idea of people perfectly conforming to an image, however, also suggests that it is not only Winstanley who is a theorist of reverence. For Hobbes also seeks a pious relationship to authority, invokes Job's final submission to depict it, and virtually sacralizes it as "public worship."

In his prideful effort to overcome pride, Hobbes dreams of creating a man-made Eden in which men and women reverently revolve around the orthodoxy of their invented sun. Although Hobbes's adults will obey an external sovereign they pridefully invent, and Winstanley's adults will submit to an internal sovereign they do not invent, both theorists desire to establish reverence toward an indisputable authority. In this way, both hope to conquer what each calls "the kingdom of darkness." Perfect allegiance to god, or to a mortal god, could overcome the doubt and contending, the ambiguity and interpretative conflict, the imagination and political invention, which each theorist associates with Puritanism, politics, and pride.

Winstanley and Hobbes conceive of a sovereign authority that leaves "no opposite power" (170). But Winstanley's loving authority, dwelling in each body, is a sovereign that sponsors the kind of autonomy, and therefore the rebellion, that Hobbes' sovereign is designed to humble. To Hobbes, of course, those who profess to act as god's instruments are either victims of demonic possession or diabolical con artists advancing a narrow self-interest. Winstanley's claim to embody the "word of power," however, does not make him crazy or mercenary: he is trying to articulate the authority that entitles him to speak and the grounds that make his or any action legitimate. He does deny the anger and imagination that shape his rebellion and even a reborn community. Indeed, he believes he has announced the emergence of a community whose harmony is based on universal and internal reverence toward truths beyond dispute. These truths do not appear as externally imposed orthodoxy, however, for they are an "experimental knowledge" developed only through dialogue among people bearing witness to their experience. For this reason, Winstanley's submission to the sovereignty of god, despite the self-denial it involves, illustrates precisely what is empowering in his piety and, thus, why Hobbes would subvert it.

Winstanley's reverence liberates his personal voice, entitles him to question authority, and enables him to conceptualize shared grounds for revolt. Moreover, by trusting in the human capacity to embody god's love and reason, he opens up the historical process to interventions he himself cannot anticipate. In fact, the god within him soon leads him to claim his freedom by engaging in the more explicitly political act of digging.

PART TWO

The Social Moment

Who built Thebes of the seven gates?
In the books you will find the names of kings.
Did the kings haul up the lumps of rock?
And Babylon, many times demolished
Who raised it up so many times? . . . Great Rome
is full of triumphal arches. Who erected them?
Over whom did the Caesars triumph? . . .
The young Alexander conquered India.
Was he alone?
Caesar beat the Gauls.
Did he not even have a cook with him?
Phillip of Spain wept when his armada
Went down. Was he the only one to weep? . . .
Frederick the Second won the Seven Years' War.
Who else won it?
Every page a victory.
Who cooked the feast for the victors?
Every ten years a great man.
Who paid the bill?
So many reports.
So many questions.

—Brecht, "Questions from a Worker
Who Reads"

The Father within does not leave the dutiful son quietly resting in the kingdom within. "Being quiet at my work" of tending cows, Winstanley tells us in his next book, *The New Law of Righteousness,* "my heart was filled with sweet thoughts and many things were revealed to me which I never read in books nor heard from the mouth of any flesh" (315). Those revelations, which he professed to experience in a trance, animate this book, dedicated on January 26, 1649, four days before the execution of Charles I. Winstanley describes them thus:

73

I heard these words, "Work together. Eat bread together; declare all this abroad." Likewise I heard these words, "Whosoever labors the earth for any person or persons that lift themselves up as lords and rulers over others, and doth not look upon themselves as equals to others in the creation, the hand of the Lord shall be upon that laborer: I the Lord have spoke it and I will do it; Declare this all abroad." (190)

Now Winstanley calls landlords, freeholders, and gentry "you great Adams of the earth," who in turn call "the earth yours and look upon others as servants and slaves to you, as if the earth were only for you to live at ease and honor upon it, while others starve for want of bread at your feet and under your oppressing government" (195). By "selling the earth from one particular hand to another, saying this is mine," he argues, "you uphold this particular propriety by a law of government of your own making, thereby restraining other fellow creatures from seeking nourishment from their mother earth" (158). As pride once deprived the living soul of god's nourishment, now "elder brothers" deprive "younger brothers" of the earth and its fruits. As covetousness once created an inner conflict he called "the torment of hell," now it turns the "living earth of mankind" into a hell "wherein one torments another" (253).

To rich and poor alike, Winstanley insists, "Every man is an equal to every man, not a lord over any, for all men looked at in the bulk are but the Creation, the living earth" (192). Common membership in the body of mankind means that "every part of creation should lend a mutual help of love in action to preserve the whole" (192). As people become aware of this membership and their mutual need, "the King of Righteousness shall be governor in every man, none shall work for hire, neither shall [any] give hire; but every one shall work in love, with and for another, and eat bread together as members of one household" (191). In this household adults honor "the Spirit Reason" within each, and they honor the earth itself as a "common mother" that exists to nourish *all* her children (265, 271, 283).

Winstanley says that having "obeyed the command of the spirit, that did bid me declare this all abroad, . . . my mind was not at rest because nothing was acted, and thoughts run in me that words and writings are nothing and must die, for action is the life of all, and if thou dost not act, thou dost nothing" (315). He makes the following promise:

And when the Lord doth show unto me the place and manner how he will have us that are called common people to manure and work upon the common lands, I will then go forth . . . to eat my bread with the sweat of my brows, without either giving or taking hire, looking upon the land as freely mine as others. . . . I have an inward persuasion that the spirit of the poor shall be drawn forth ere long to act materially this Law of Righteousness. (194)

The development of the seed of freedom depends now on planting real seeds in the earth; the vision of January will bear fruit in April as he organizes a group of activists who call themselves "diggers" or "True Levellers." Part Two, therefore, is restricted to Winstanley's vision of social bondage and historical transformation, which provides the theoretical basis for the action examined in Part Three. First, however, let us consider what has happened to Winstanley.

WINSTANLEY'S SECOND WILDERNESS
EXPERIENCE

What accounts for Winstanley's shift in emphasis, from sincere milk to earth, from speech to labor, from the poor as stigmatized and silenced saints to the poor as an exploited, laboring class—thus, for the shift in the way he defines his adversaries from the clergy to the landlords? What do these changes signify about his experience and learning? Something like a revelation did befall him, and his language yields some inferences about it.[1]

---

1. These are difficult questions, and responses often reveal more about the respondents than about Winstanley. Those analysts committed to seeing Winstanley as a religious thinker tend to see digging as a purely symbolic act, not literally meant to feed people or change society (see W. S. Hudson, "Economic and Social Thought of Gerrard Winstanley," *Journal of Modern History* 17 (1946): 1–21; and L. Mulligan, J. K. Graham, and J. Richards, "Winstanley: A Case for the Man As He Said He Was," *Journal of Ecclesiastical History* 27 (1977): 57–75). Those analysts who value Winstanley especially as an activist critic of private property, and thus as a forerunner of Marx, tend to view digging as an example of a welcome secularization of his thought, a move away from religious "idealism" and toward social realism, materialism, and worldly commitment (see George Juretic, "Digger No Millenarian: The Revolutionizing of Gerrard Winstanley," *Journal of the History of Ideas* 36 (1975): 268–80). Both views suggest an either-or relationship between religious vision and social analysis, as if they were really incompatible. A more fruitful view, however, must see Winstanley's revelation and digging in the context of his early writings, for Winstanley does call digging a "true religion," and yet such a view also must account for the new meaning and scope he gives to, or finds in, religion.

Those who try to show the relationship between Winstanley's religion and his social thought and activism include Christopher Hill, who disputes both the above positions in *The World Turned Upside Down* and "The Religion of Gerrard Winstanley," *Past and Present* (Supplement 5), 1978. Others include David Petergorsky, *Left-Wing Democracy in the English Civil War* (London: Victor Gollanz, 1940); Perez Zagorin, *A History of the Political Thought in the English Revolution* (London: Routledge and Kegan Paul, 1945); George Sabine, in his introduction to Gerrard Winstanley, *The Collected Works;* and T. Wilson Hayes, *Winstanley the Digger* (Cambridge: Harvard University Press, 1979).

Consider first Winstanley's position after his initial wilderness condition. Having discovered sincere milk, Winstanley enjoyed the "kingdom of God in man." Unlike many mystics, however, he located spirit in the body and in relation to its needs and worldly power. But Winstanley did not address directly either real food and labor or exploitive social relations; he imagined being "preserved" regardless of bodily necessity; and he professed to be free in spite of the actual social relations in which he found himself. Thus, while he experienced the way god's inner nourishment transformed his desire, he was ambivalent about a body that still needed earthly food: to some extent, he fantasized that sincere milk could free him from dependence on worldly objects.

Witnessing the enclosure movement and famine, however, Winstanley saw people crucified by the contradiction between a Christian morality that requires then to be good and the acts that hunger could compel. At the least, numerous passages in his texts indicate his outrage that good men and women were forced by hunger to steal and then were hanged as thieves (388). This painful contradiction, whether witnessed or experienced, one can infer, drove him into a second and social wilderness condition. He began to consider the needs not only of the spirit in the body but of the mortal body that must be preserved if the spirit is to live, let alone flourish. Hunger may have taught him about the inadequacy of inner milk and the necessity of earthly food: no longer could he rest content with inner freedom because the Father's milk does not physically preserve people. But it was precisely sincere milk that enabled him to address bodily need and nourishment in a new way.

As his initial imagery of milk suggests, those issues are associated symbolically with real mothers. Now, however, mother's milk is not described in paternal terms and fed to a feminine soul. Rather, the source of nourishment is overtly female and external, and those needing nourishment are men (as well as women) (265). Thus, Winstanley must have reconceptualized necessity and morality: by reconceiving how people do and should feed themselves, he was led to propose a way to save both the body and morality and thereby to achieve a personal auton-

---

These writers work from the materialist pantheism of Winstanley's spirituality to infer the grounds of his development into a digger. That is surely the right approach, but I hope to make clear that the logic of his change not only is an extension of his earlier views but also arises from his attempt to resolve certain crucial contradictions in his initial religiosity. Moreover, the extension and contradiction that shapes his development can be understood best through his new understanding of Scripture, which no commentator has adequately addressed.

omy rooted in a "community of the earth." Feeling that he had experienced a revelation, he unfolded his new insights in *The New Law of Righteousness*.

The first element of his revelation is that "all men seek the earth, their common mother," who in turn "loves all her children" (158). Correspondingly, he grants an unabashed legitimacy to his body and its needs: "Better not to have a body, than not to have food and rayment for it" (371). Since Winstanley enjoys god's love within, he is able to see the mother earth as a loving source of nourishment and, hence, his body as worthy of being fed. Thus, it now appears wholly understandable and legitimate that people seek material preservation: "Do not all strive to enjoy the land? The gentry strive for land, the clergy strive for land, the common people strive for land" (373). Nourishment has become literal, and perishable outer objects are no longer a danger to be abjured, but it is still sinful to deny nourishment and recognition to others: as Winstanley says in a later work:

> What are the greatest sins in the world? I answer these two: First, for a man to lock up the treasure of the earth in chests and houses and suffer it to rust and molder while others starve for want. . . . The second is . . . to take the earth by the power of the murdering sword from others, and then by the law of their own making, to hang or put to death any who take the fruits of the earth to supply his necessaries from places or persons where there is more than can be made use of. (496)

Yet this insight about the earth's love and his need is not reflected only in consumption and a morality of sharing. His second basic insight addresses the fact that gaining earthly fruits requires work, so that the capacity to gain nurturance still is linked to freedom, but now by work in addition speech. Like the Puritans, Winstanley believes that working to feed oneself is a person's moral responsibility and a sign of individual autonomy. In contrast with the tradesmen with whom he once identified, however, Winstanley insists that work is by nature collective: since no one feeds oneself alone, moral autonomy depends not only on work as such but on the circumstances in which people work *together*. Just as he specifies when speech enslaves and deceives, so now he specifies what sort of labor establishes the right relation to the body, the earth, and other people.

Winstanley's view of the legitimate way to labor is at first sight startling: "True religion and undefiled is to let everyone quietly have earth to manure, that they may live in freedom by their labors, for it is the earth that everyone seeks after that they may live in peace, let them say what they will" (428). He articulates the meaning of work and the right relations of labor through repeated and vivid stress on "manuring the earth" with cow dung, which he considers an act of love and religious sacrament.

But what does Winstanley mean? A psychoanalytic vocabulary might help, for according to psychoanalytic theory, the child offers its excrement to its mother as a gift that proves autonomy and self-control. In an act of love, the child reciprocates for the fact that the mother provides nourishment, while expiating its guilt and anger over the separation symbolized by that self-control. By offering the mother its excremental gifts, the child exercises its newly won self-control, reassures itself of the mother's love during this anxious separation, and thereby feels justified in its continuing liberty. The risky achievement of autonomy is aided by the mother's love but also is furthered by the child's autonomous yet reverent acts toward what still is its source of sustenance.

This theory, broadly construed, suggests how Winstanley deepens his sense of what it means to establish worldly autonomy in the right sort of way. He locates his freedom, and not only his survival, in his capacity to feed himself, for the Father within enjoins work and separateness. But the act of autonomy also entails anger at separation, fear of abandonment, and therefore potential rivalry with others. Accordingly, the Father within teaches both that the mother earth is abundantly loving but in need of her children's love and that individual need necessarily involves others. Thus, Winstanley links human autonomy to a kind of work that honors one's need for, and bond to, the earth and others.

As a result, Winstanley comes to understand fallen Adam in a crucially different way. He now attacks Puritan clergy: "Examine yourself . . . and you shall find that the enjoyment of the earth below, which you call a low and carnal knowledge, is that which you . . . (as well as men of the world, as you call them) strive and seek after" (566). Professing to live "spiritual" lives "above low and carnal things," the clergy "tell poor people that they must be content with their poverty and shall have their heaven hereafter." But the clergy "require their heaven in this world, too," and "grumble mightily against the people that will not give them a large temporal maintenance" (409).

The clergy are not wrong to seek the earth and its pleasures, but they are wrong to deny they are doing so and hence to deny the same need and right in others: "But why may we not have our heaven here (that is, comfortable livelihood in the earth)? . . . Therefore, we say while we have bodies that must be fed and clothed, let us have earth to plant"

(409). Winstanley anticipates their likely response: "But if you say, that this is only old Adam's condition, to look after the earth, but the new Adam, Christ, looks after heaven above and minds not the earth, . . . why then we say, you make old Adam, that brings in the curse, to be more rational and tender to our bodies than the second Adam, Christ" (409). But why do ministers use the name of Christ to guiltily disclaim their own need and hypocritically deny it in others?

Initially, Winstanley had declared that covetousness is the result of not enjoying the sincere milk of the Father, which leads one to confusion about independence and nourishment. Now he suggests that those who lack the Father's sincere milk are ambivalent about the separateness and need signified by the mortal body and their dependence on the earth. On the one hand, Puritans are guilty about the earthly needs they stigmatize as enslaving and fantasize a spiritual self-sufficiency that proudly denies their need for the earth. At the same time, they are ambivalent about this maternal source of life and anxiously seek exclusive control of its nourishment, which they do not trust will be forthcoming. Thus, the Puritans' asceticism and acquisitiveness are inextricable from social conflict.

In contrast, Winstanley has discovered that the mother earth loves and can preserve all her children, that the body is not shameful, and that autonomy through labor involves reciprocity. As a result, he now sees that excrement is not bad or dirty when used rightly. Whereas before, objects appeared as the dung Puritans mistook for signs of god's sincere milk, now he says that earthly milk, so to speak, can be gained only by labor that manures the earth. Manuring the earth literally and symbolically expresses the meaning he finds in work: to be an emblem of autonomy, work must be an act of reparation and reciprocity; when work sublimates the feelings he associates with the dunghill within, the striving for autonomy can yield sharing rather than competition.

Winstanley's first two insights, which transform bodily need and the autonomy of working into a "true religion," lead to a third insight: laborers deserve and must have title to the earth and its fruits. Initially, Winstanley had argued that the clergy's appropriation of title to the gospel deprived the poor of the freedom signified by sincere milk and "experienced speech." Now the object of his censure has changed: "They that call the earth theirs . . . hinder the mother earth from giving all her children suck" (265). Still concerned about the relationship between need and freedom, he sees that landlords deprive the poor of the freedom signified by controlling their own labor. Thus, he turns against the institutions of wage labor and property, as well as the state power that maintains them.

This insight, that freedom depends on gaining direct access to the earth, suggests that Winstanley has discovered a new meaning in the tradition of riots against enclosure. What he sees is really quite simple: "Divide England into three parts, and scarce one part is manured. So that there is enough land to maintain all her children, but many die for want or live under heavy burden of poverty all their days" (200). He contends that traditional common lands, when combined with the royal and church lands expropriated by Parliament, could ensure that labor truly feeds and frees the poor. In arguing this way, Winstanley takes seriously the traditions of the commons and mutual aid but detaches them from the ethos of traditional hierarchy and refashions them according to an egalitarian vision of individual rights, Christian fellowship, and loving labor.[2]

One is tempted to say that Winstanley has become worldly in a way he was not before. But earth, food, work, and property are for him no more external and social than spirit, milk, and speech were simply internal and individual. To be sure, he has shifted from the spirit in the body to the mortal body in which that spirit dwells, and thus from "the spirit of community" to its earthly ground. But this is not a shift from spirit, or heaven, to earth: he has not gone from "mysticism" to something "practical," or from "idealism" to something "realistic."

Winstanley calls digging a "true religion" and still situates his arguments in a millennial history that accounts for bondage, self-recognition, and worldly rebellion. "Inner and outer freedom" is still a seed that god is bringing to fruition in history—even in Winstanley's lifetime—and through the agency of the poor. But the history that he once began with Christ's crucifixion and resurrection he now begins with god's covenant

---

2. This account of Winstanley's social wilderness has focused on the inner logic of his changes and continuities. In addition, however, one could argue that since he was raised in the countryside, learned a trade in London, and then returned to the country, Winstanley was exposed to contexts and intellectual currents he was able to synthesize in unique ways. His migration between country and city might have distanced him both from the emerging market ethos of personal independence and from the ethos of peasant community. In other words, his experience could have enabled him to synthesize an urban commitment to individuality and a language of rights and a rural and traditional commitment to collective labor and mutual aid. But citing these contexts, and what he might have learned by becoming marginal to both, does not explain *why* he generated a theory that goes far beyond the ideas literally available to him. Nor do contexts explain the *meaning* of that theory, for him or for modern readers. For this reason, I have used his words to speculate about the interior of his learning process, which a purely contextual argument cannot illuminate.

with Abraham and Moses. The poor have become Israel, and England has become "the Egyptian House of Bondage, . . . the condition of the world that upholds civil interest of mine and thine and self-seeking oppressing government" (199). He now portrays himself as a Moses: "Behold, the Lord of Hosts hath sent his servant to bid you let Israel go free, that they may serve together in community of spirit and community of earthly treasure" (195).

In this way, Winstanley returns to the Puritans' own focus on the Old Testament, but he radically reformulates their version of it, and thus of the New Testament. For Winstanley recovers Christ as a Jew speaking to other Jews about a covenant with god concerning an "inheritance" to land that is to be shared. He finds in Hebrew history, as it culminates in Christ, the struggle to overcome the contradiction between the body's needs and the spirit's law and thereby to become a people entitled to land that is their inheritance. As the poor recognize themselves on the cross of this contradiction and begin to "manure unnurtured ground," they will lead an exodus that completes that history by making "the earth a common treasury."

Chapters 3 and 4 examine how Winstanley fashions his continuing commitment to the personal autonomy of "freedom within" into a theory of worldly bondage and collective action. On its face this is an extraordinary accomplishment, since it is often argued that the quest for personal autonomy precludes, is threatened by, or simply does not entail, a commitment to collective action. Orthodox psychoanalytic theory, for example, conceives of personal autonomy in a way that makes others into competitors, so that Freud follows Hobbes, as it were. Because autonomy creates not fraternity but fratricide, both theorists justify the intervention of a father and worldly authority to control instinct and enforce peace.

In historical terms, Winstanley avoids the atomism of these later theories because he precedes liberalism. But theoretically his concern with autonomy is inextricable from an ethic of sharing and a radical project of collective action. Although Winstanley's initial idea of autonomy required and sponsored his movement toward an earthly community, a psychological theory cannot sufficiently account for it. In addition, Winstanley's concern with labor, his understanding of its estrangement, and his identification with the oppression of a class of propertyless people are integral to his new project of collective action.

It is for this reason that one encounters an oft-remarked parallel between Winstanley and Marx, which is introduced in chapter 3 in the discussion of the correspondences in their accounts of estrangement. And yet there are enormous and significant differences between these two theorists, which are rooted in Winstanley's religiosity and reflected in the way he uses the Bible. Indeed, the correspondences and divergences between Winstanley and Marx are revealed best by Winstanley's recovery of the Old Testament, which no commentator has addressed. His arguments about "the Jews" become his way to synthesize his Christian psychological concerns and collective action about the earth, but they also represent a politics in which unprecedented action is based on "the spirit of inheritance." Thus, the significance of Winstanley's radicalism appears fully in chapter 4, as his scriptural language is juxtaposed with the Promethean politics that forms the bridge between Hobbes and Marx.

CHAPTER III

The Fall Revisited: Outer Bondage

Then war was not nor riches known
And no man said this or that is my own
Then first the sacred name of the king began
And things that were as common as the day
Did yield themselves and likewise did obey. . . .
Then some sage man . . .
Knowing that laws could not dwell
Unless they were observed, did first devise
The name of God, religion, heaven and hell.
            —*attributed to Sir Walter Raleigh (1603)*

By linking anxiety about nourishment to identity, and then by acknowledging a real problem with earthly nourishment in a society committed to property, Winstanley extends his theory of the Fall from an analysis of the anxious division of the personal body and the rule of the back part, to the earthly divisions of the social body and the rule of a covetous class. In his social moment, he analyzes what he believes are the constituents of a fallen society: the rule of a "branch" of mankind is enshrined in property and exploited labor, articulated politically in the "kingly power" of the state's sword and law, and defended ideologically by "the teaching power" of the clergy.

In criticizing these institutions, Winstanley focuses on the troubling and paradoxical fact that these "beasts" are "the cause of all sorrows and tears amongst mankind, for they devour abundantly and yet rise out of the sea, even from the body of deceived, covetous, dark-powered mankind in the nighttime of the world" (466). Only when people understand what in them and who among them is responsible for the "curse" they bring down on themselves can "these beasts . . . with their self-will powers . . . run into the sea again, and be swallowed up in those waters, that is into mankind, and sink like mud to the bottom" (466).

This chapter attends to Winstanley's diagnosis of what is now commonly called *estrangement,* which is at the core of his social vision. Through his argument about how fallen Adams create "works that turn against them," Winstanley extends and radicalizes the Puritans' own effort to reclaim from king and church the right to speak and act for themselves.

One ambiguity, however, is best identified at the outset. Winstanley develops a vocabulary meant to address several different audiences at once about the various ways in which they create "outer bondage." His revised account of the Fall is intended as a mythic vision of the origin of property, the state, and religion; as a diagnosis of feudal social relations, characterized by gentry landholding and peasant labor, kingship, and a state church; but also as a critique of the social basis of Puritan reformers and their Leveller critics. As a result, he uses terms such as *clergy, propriety,* and *kingly power* to serve several purposes at once and to typify conflicting kinds of property, political organization, and religion.

Like modern historians, Winstanley distinguishes among landed gentry, freeholders, and those he calls "tradesmen"; he also distinguishes between, on the one hand, the king and his gentry supporters and, on the other hand, the gentry, freeholders and artisans in opposition. He too is attentive to the different classes and forms of property and is aware of the range of political and religious differences between Calvinist Puritans and their Leveller critics. But he does not distinguish systematically among varieties of Puritanism or between the "republican" and liberal politics that derive from it. In addition, he does not address the conflicts between customary and commercial forms of property. Rather, he uses broad and virtually generic terms to suggest the commitments shared by reformers and their monarchical enemies.

To Winstanley, all the political actors of his time are bound by a commitment to some form of private property—and hence to the exploitation of labor—and by a commitment to a state that, at best, excludes the propertyless majority from participation and power. Accordingly, he contends that reformers do not reclaim for all people the political power of the king; nor do they reclaim the earth for all. By exposing the social basis and political limitations of Puritans and Levellers, Winstanley turns against them their own ideal of self-determination: reformers do not overcome the estrangement of labor, voice, and power that is "beastly" in any form of private property, state, and clerical rule.

As a result, his "social moment" provides a reading of Puritanism very different from modern accounts.[1] More important, though, his Old Testament metaphors disclose the limitations of a propertied radicalism in a way that distinguishes him from Hobbes and suggests a parallel with Marx.

PROPERTY

"Man's estate before the fall," says Winstanley, was "the last daytime of mankind," when "as the spirit was a common treasury of unity and peace within, so the earth was a common treasury of delight for the preservation of their bodies without." Consequently, "there was nothing but peace upon the face of the whole earth" (376). He still describes the Fall in terms of the "first Adam, ruling and dwelling in mankind . . . within every man and woman, which makes the whole mankind to be prisoner to him" (158). Since Winstanley now addresses social divisions, however, he adds that he must speak of Adam "in a two fold sense." The second sense is that Adam rises to rule in and as a group of people, who dominate others in order to gain exclusive control of the earth. In this second sense

> Adam is the wisdom and power of the flesh broke out and sat down in the chair of rule and dominion, in one part of mankind over another. And this is the beginner of particular interest, buying and selling the earth from one particular hand to another, saying This is Mine . . . and thereby restraining fellow creatures from seeking nourishment from their mother earth. (158)

Rather than speak simply of the Adam within each person, Winstanley now attends to classes, whose conflicts he analyses in terms of fratricide between sons. It is as if Adam, or mankind, has divided into two brothers, just as the story of Eden is followed by the story of Cain and Abel. As the "son of freedom" within the self was "trod under foot" by pride, now the poor within "the body of mankind" are oppressed by a class of covetous owners:

> Cain rose up in discontent and killed his brother Abel. The quarrel arose about the earth: for Abel's industry made the earth more fruitful than Cain, who would take away Abel's labor from him by force. These two brothers did type out or fore-run all the acting between man and man from that time

1. Winstanley does not emphasize the differences among the gentry Puritanism depicted by Perry Miller and Michael Walzer, the Puritanism of Christopher Hill's "industrious sorts," and the republicanism J. G. A. Pocock draws from Puritanism by way of the Levellers. Because he focuses on the common basis in property, he does not perceive or create differences between Puritanism as protoliberal (Hill) and protorepublican (Pocock).

to this. . . . All the great convulsions that hath been and yet is in the world is but politic, covetous, murderous Cain holding Abel, or the honest plain-dealing heart, under him, or the son of bondage persecuting the son of free-dom. (425–26)

Old Testament parables about fratricidal family dramas signify social conflict over the earth. Cain, Ishmael, and Esau represent to Winstanley the "elder brother" ruled by "the power of the flesh," who "gets the government of the kingdom (mankind) first." Abel, Isaac, and Jacob represent the oppressed "younger brother," who is nonetheless chosen "to take the birthright and blessing" from the elder brother (179). The struggle within Adam over whether to honor the soul and the Father becomes the struggle within mankind over whether to share the earth and honor the Father's "law of righteousness."

The consequences of Cain's victory is that Abel and his descendants are dispossessed:

He that sells the earth and he that buys, doth remove the landmark from the third person, because the land that was bought and sold belongs to the third man as well. . . . And the two persons that buy and sell, and leave the land that is bought for an inheritance to their children, excluding others, do mur-der the third man, because they steal away his livelihood. . . . Thou covetous person, so long as there is another man in the world besides thee, . . . the earth belongs to him as well as thee. (309)

As "the third man" is a vagabond who trespasses wherever he goes, so people become trespassers as they are "hedged out" of land once con-sidered common. Thus, the conflict of Cain and Abel refers both to the mythic origin of property and to the enclosure movement of his time.

In both cases, the act of enclosure appears to Winstanley as fratri-cide, a denial of mutuality. Mine and thine become legal; the violence of uprooting is perhaps not so visible, while the heirs of murderers and thieves call themselves Issacs, and their covenant blessed. But for Winstanley, the inheritors of land and property fall under the curse of Cain: they are marked, and property is the badge of the sin they inherit and uphold:

For the power of enclosing land and owning propriety [sic] was brought into creation by your ancestors by the sword which did first murder their fellow creatures and after plundering and stealing the land away, they left this land successively to you, their children. (269)

Indeed, the children may not personally "kill or thieve," but "pro-priety of mine and thine" is upheld by laws, prisons, and gallows, and therefore it is still "Cain killing Abel to this very day" (323). Against the Levellers and Locke, Winstanley agrees with Henry Ireton and Hobbes that property is conventional, but unlike any of them, he sees it as the denial of community truly understood. What for them is the mark of the boundaries and law that civilize, for Winstanley is the mark of Cain.[2]

"Particular propriety of mine and thine" is a social convention that turns what is common and public into a private commodity that can be bought and sold. Without direct access to land, the younger brothers must work for a wage or starve, instead of directly enjoying the fruits of their labor: "The power of the landlords lies in this: they deny common people the use and free benefit of the earth . . . unless they work for hire" (372). By working for hire, Abel and his descendants impoverish themselves and enrich owners, building the Babel that declares the pride of the victors:

> No man can be rich, but . . . by his own labors or the labors of others helping him. If a man have no help from his neighbors, he shall never gather an estate of hundreds and thousands a year. If other men help him . . . then those riches are his neighbors as well as his, for they be the fruit of other mens' labors as well as his own. (521)

But Winstanley's account of labor and property addresses more than the exploitation of peasants. Deprived of commons land and forced to work for a wage, "common people" become wage workers who must survive in a money economy on wages insufficient to buy what they need. Indeed, Winstanley complains that money is becoming "the great god," an idol invented by men. "Surely the righteous Creator . . . never did ordain that unless some of mankind do bring that mineral (silver or gold) in their hands to others of their own kind, they shall neither be fed or clothed" (270). By turning the earth and labor into money, the elder brothers supplant the Father's reason with a false god that "respects persons" (252). They also supplant the mother earth with an invention of their own making, which they believe nourishes them. Unlike the Father or the Common Mother, however, money is not available to all; unlike speech and labor that honors those parents, gaining nourishment through money leads men and women into bondage.

Once the earth is divided into parcels, and especially as money becomes the fruit of labor, actual nourishment becomes uncertain, and people therefore must "all strive to enjoy the land." The need for nour-

---

2. For a defense of Cain, see George Shulman, "Fratricide, City-Building, and Politics," *Political Theory* 14, no. 2, (May 1986): 215–38.

ishment is legitimate, but Winstanley must explain why "all of us, by the righteous law of our creation," do not gain "food and rayment freely by our righteous laboring of the earth, without working for hire or paying rent one to another" (303).

As an essential source of nourishment, the earth appears now as the primary object of "covetous" imagination and desire. People do not mistakenly imagine nourishment from this "outward object" but imagine and seek exclusive control of it and therefore compete with each other. Along with this pride that would have all to itself, the elder brother also manifests a fear and anxiety that makes him more like a bourgeois than like Hegel's aristocratic master.

The self-making men that Hobbes calls "masterless" define themselves as alone and isolated, and therefore they imagine "if they love and succor others, yet others will not love them again" (458). But they also create a world in which trust has no place. Winstanley has the elder brother say what he himself once might have declared:

> I have no riches, no certain dwelling place, no way to get a subsistence, I am crossed in all, I have no cordial friend, no succor from men; if any seem to succor me, it is for their own ends, and when they have got what they can from me, they leave me, and turn enemies. (25)

In Winstanley's interpretation, the elder brother fears he will be in want, imagines that utter independence could guarantee nourishment, and therefore tries to "draw all unto himself and leave others naked, [forcing] them to be his servants" (482). "Be not like rats and mice," Winstanley cautions the elder brother. "[Do not] draw the treasure of the earth into your hole to look upon, whilst your fellow creatures, to whom it belongs as well as you by the law of the creation, do starve for want" (448).

One might imagine that the conquering Cain, living by the sword to gain earth and honor, is too proud for mutuality, but Winstanley thinks that his heirs surely—and perhaps he as well—are too weak for mutuality. Perhaps recalling his own feelings as a tradesman, he gives voice to what he imagines the elder brother feels:

> Who will deliver me from . . . this great power of darkness in me that hinders me, so that I cannot do to others as I would have them do to me; and that enslaves me within so that I cannot quietly suffer others to enjoy their creation rights in the earth. (427)

As Winstanley tries to include both original aristocratic conqueror and "industrious sorts," his basic point emerges: that the elder brother is unwilling to share the earth is his sin; that he is incapable of sharing is his curse.[3]

By analyzing the motives of the propertied, Winstanley addresses both the landed supporters of the king and those committed to newer forms of property. And yet the poor are also part of the problem. Sometimes, Winstanley says, the younger brothers have resisted, and still resist, the elder brothers' "open and violent force," but to no avail. He also states, however, that the poor "uphold" the rich, both because it is by their own forced labor that the poor "have lifted up their landlords and others to rule in tyranny and oppression over them" (159), and because they consent to the elder brothers' claim to the earth and their labor. But the sword and gallows are always on the stage of Winstanley's social drama; the fear and punishment that perpetuate property arise from the power of the state.

KINGLY POWER

The elder brother is not only an owner but also a ruler: he creates "kingly power" to rule over the younger brother as subject as well as worker. By way of the idea of Kingly Power "ruling in one or many over others, enslaving those who in the creation are equals" (354), Winstanley tries to explain both the monarchy of Charles and the parliamentary power of elder brothers who revolt against it. Like Hobbes, Winstanley speaks of the state in the singular and plural. Unlike Hobbes, however, he uses the Puritans' arguments against a single, Kingly elder brother and then turns it against the power wielded by Puritan rebels in Parliament. The key to Winstanley's argument about kingly power is his effort to link a critique of the estranged but real power of monarchy and Parliament to a critique of their social basis in property.

Winstanley argues that the political division of the social body into "head" and "members" occurred as the elder brother abandoned "the teacher and ruler within." Tempted by the objects of creation, "he fell into blindness of mind and weakness of heart . . . and so selfish imagination, taking possession of the five senses," led him to propose himself as "a teacher and ruler" over his brothers (251–52). Since the elder

---

3. This ambiguity in Winstanley's argument reflects both his dialectical view of "weakness calling itself strength" and perhaps the difference he perceives between a commercial class and the gentry aristocracy. These parallel tensions are reflected in Hobbes's arguments about pride, which are both about "honor" and about the anxious "vainglory" of market men.

brother suppressed his own living soul and defied the god within, he became a victim of "king pride within" and the worldly agent of kingly power:

> Though this climbing power of self-love be in all, yet it rises not to its height in all, but [in] everyone that gets an authority into his hands. As many husbands, parents, masters, magistrates, that live after the flesh, do carry themselves like oppressing lords over such as are under them, not knowing that their wives, children, servants, and subjects are their fellow creatures and hath an equal privilege to share with them the blessing of liberty. (158)

To gain recognition as well as control of the earth, the elder brother claimed a "liberty to rule over the labors and persons" of those who are "fellow creatures, who are the flesh of your flesh, the bone of your bone" (335).

Winstanley's bodily language exposes the motivations and meaning of kingship in his time: the "outer ruler and teacher" creates a realm to which he claims title, making the earth and fellow creatures into his second and immortal body. By identifying his person with this realm, the king overcomes the vulnerability, need, and mortality of his personal body, which represents his real bond and equality with others. As the king pretends to represent "his" people, he appropriates to himself the right to think and act for them, becoming the head of a mute body that is flesh to his spirit. As a result, says Winstanley, the kingly elder brother becomes a law unto himself: his "prerogative" is itself declared law. From being a brother, a fellow creature of earth and spirit, the elder brother becomes a god. Therefore, he becomes "the king of the beasts," for the denial of his real limitations is manifested in the coercion of his subjects. In the name of controlling their beastliness, he releases his own:

> And the power of the sword over brethren, in armies, in arrests, in prisons, in gallows and in other inferior torments, inflicted by some upon others . . . , is Adam falling, or Cain killing Abel to this very day.[4] (323)

The younger brothers are not only Abel but also Israel suffering under Pharaoh and his taskmasters: "The condition of the world that upholds civil interest of mine and thine is Egypt, the house of bondage,

---

4. This reading of Winstanley on kingship is indebted to Norman O. Brown, *Love's Body;* Michael Rogin, "The King's Two Bodies: Lincoln, Wilson, and Nixon and Presidential Self-Sacrifice," in *Ronald Reagan, the Movie* (Berkeley and Los Angeles: University of California Press, 1987); and Peter Schwartz, from an unpublished manuscript about regicide and the English Revolution.

and truly Pharaoh's taskmasters are very many, both teachers and rulers" (199). In this way, Winstanley appropriates for his own purposes the political ideology of Parliament. The "Norman Yoke," imposed in 1066 when William conquered the land and gave it to his officers and soldiers, is "the last enslaving conquest the Enemy got over Israel" (259). "Propriety arose" from the division of the land, "which is the fruit of war from the beginning." To Winstanley, then, "Kings, lords, judges, bailiffs, and the violent bitter people called freeholders" are the descendants of William, his officers, and his common soldiers, "who are still, from that time to this, . . . imprisoning, robbing, and killing the poor enslaved English Israelites" (259). As a result of their Norman rulers and Egyptian taskmasters, "common people have no more freedom in England but only to work for elder brothers for hire." Winstanley concludes, "If this be not the burden of the Norman Yoke, let rational men judge" (288).

By its laws and sword, the state upholds the property and power of one "branch" of mankind. Indeed, "prisons and putting others to death [are] but the power of the sword, to enforce people to that government which was got by conquest and sword, and cannot stand of itself but by the same murdering sword" (271). "The law of justice," taken generally, "is but the declarative will of the conquerors, how they will have their subjects ruled." Justice is "pretended," "but the full strength of the law is to uphold the conquering sword and to preserve propriety" (387).

Therefore, if Parliament is committed to "propriety," it is not an alternative to monarchy. Indeed, that "elected body" is part of the Norman Yoke:

> And this appears clear, for when any Trustee or State Officer is to be chosen, the freeholders or landlords who are the Norman common soldiers, must be choosers. And who must be chosen? Some very rich man who is the successor of the Norman colonels or high officers. And to what end have they been chosen? But to establish that Norman Power the more forcibly over the enslaved English. (259)

Parliament professes to oppose kingly power, but any political body is "kingly" in its power as long as the poor are hedged out of land and deprived of political power. Kingly power rules "under the name of prerogative when he rules in one over others, and under the name of State Privilege of Parliament when he rules in many over others" (354). Many may rule by kingly principles because "the king's power lies in his laws, not in the name" (528).

This reasoning leads Winstanley toward a concept of sovereignty: the right and capacity to exercise power over "the persons and labors of fellow creatures" is kingly power. To be sure, Hobbes defends this sovereignty and admiringly calls it "Leviathan," whereas Winstanley laments that "this kingly power is always raised up and established by the sword, and therefore is called the Murderer, or Great Red Dragon" (354). Nonetheless, both theorists believe that parliamentary leaders are denying what actually binds them to the monarchy they attack, even as Hobbes teaches Parliament the senses in which it must be kingly, and Winstanley turns against a republican assembly for the same reasons he criticizes monarchy.

To Winstanley, a propertied republicanism, or propertied assembly, is corrupt by the very criteria that led it to condemn kingship: like a king, it makes what is private (the interest of the few) rule the public, while it uses what is public (the earth, the social body, and magistracy) for private benefit. As Winstanley warns his readers in the spring of 1649, "Covetous Kingly Power, resting in the hands of one or many men, . . . saves but part of the creation, and holds another part under bondage" (381).

Thus far in Winstanley's account the younger brothers appear solely as victims. But Winstanley knows that the issue of popular consent is crucial at a historical moment when England is deciding the fate of Charles and, thus, its political future. To speak of his own time, as government is being reconstituted, Winstanley therefore uses the Old Testament to fashion a second version of the Fall, one closer to what Hobbes calls "the transfer of right."

In this version, the elder brother rises to rule because the younger brother is a "stranger to the spirit within himself." Since the younger brother "looks upon himself as an imperfect creation," he will "seek and run abroad for a teacher and ruler" (255). Again, Winstanley links a mythic and psychological argument to Israel. To "seek to be taught and governed by fellow creatures" instead of the spirit within "is called Israel's sin in casting off the Lord and choosing Saul" (252). Rather than be governed by god, Israel wanted to be like other nations, ruled by human kings, whom Winstanley calls "stepfathers." Thus, Israel consented to the serpent within, the pride that wishes to live on its own imaginary terms (which are revealed to be a slavish imitation of how other people live). As a result, Israel consented to "objects without," in the form of "outer rulers."

Israel also asked for a king in the hope of resolving its inner conflicts over the earth: kingly power appeared outwardly because it already had appeared inwardly as the covetousness that will not and cannot share the earth (425). Moses' law, says Winstanley, had sidestepped the issue of covetousness by legally giving parcels of land to each member of every tribe so that none were "hedged out." But this policy presumed covetousness within and inevitably engendered the social divisions that led the Hebrews to create kingly power without.

By creating a visible outward ruler, the Hebrews tried to preserve themselves and represent their identity as a nation. But as Samuel warned Israel, so Winstanley instructs England: the nation becomes possessed by the king or object it creates. In this way, he teaches the English about their complicity in monarchical kingly power but also addresses several aspects of the crisis of 1649. He uses the Puritans' own comparison of themselves to Hebrews to warn them of their reluctance to remove, let alone kill, the king and to point out the issues that could lead them to create or consent to a new form of kingly power.

In addition, his account teaches that deliverance from the king, just as deliverance from Pharaoh, does not in itself bring freedom: kingly power in all its forms, as well as the need and desire for it, must be cast out. His arguments about property deny legitimacy to Parliament as constituted, but he also implies that any form of representation is a betrayal of god, who would have men and women act for themselves. It is as if Winstanley reads Exodus only up to the golden calf incident, when each member of the community was to be governed by God directly.

Israel's "fall" also addresses the widespread peasant support for the king during the Civil War. Winstanley recognizes the role of consent; he grants that the descendants of the conquered may have consented to the rule of the victor's heirs: "If you say these later kings were chosen by the people, it is possible it may be so, but surely it was when his greatness over-awed them, or else they would never have chosen him to enslave them" (310). In addition, and perhaps referring to support for a property-tied Parliament, Winstanley says that those "rich in the objects of the earth . . . are lifted up to be teachers, rulers, and lawmakers . . . by their plausible words of flattery to the plainhearted people whom they deceive, and that lie under confusion and blindness" (259).

Thus, Winstanley's two accounts of the origins and character of kingly power suggest striking analogies with Hobbes. Both tell stories of a state fashioned by covetous men engaged in fratricidal conflict over land. Indeed, Winstanley follows the logic in Hobbes's narrative: as long as men are covetous, they will feel a need to create a state that guarantees property and protects their lives. But Winstanley does not endorse Hobbes's logic because he does not accept the inevitability of its premises. The sovereignty that Hobbes defends as a saving political invention Winstanley attacks as a "false savior."

Winstanley shares the Hobbist insight that property is not natural and society not innocent: the crime of which the state is the emblem is the *social* sin of property, which is linked to the personal sin of covetousness. As a result, Winstanley also comes out as a critic of the republican or liberal government defended by the Levellers: freehold property and artisanal trade warrant political rights but "shut out" the poor from land and political power. Therefore, Winstanley insists (as Marx was to argue two centuries later) that mere political reform, even when connected to a more widespread distribution of property, does not resolve the basic problem, which is the social divisions created by property and wage labor: "He that calls any part of the creation his own particular, in this time of Israel's return from the slavery of Egyptian bondage, is [still] a destroyer of creation" (191).

This point brings us back to where Hobbes started, however, for perhaps humans are incapable of sharing the earth: property is not natural, but nonetheless it is a necessary, even salutary human convention; by making property legal, the state recognizes but regulates what makes property unavoidable. In a certain sense, Winstanley agrees with Hobbes. He sees an intimate connection between covetousness, property, and the state; he grants that a property system could arise and persist only as the creation of men with a certain character, who require a state to regulate them through laws of mine and thine. Unlike Hobbes, however, Winstanley does not consider property unavoidable because he no longer believes that acquisitive desire is natural.

Covetousness is contingent, he argues, because people have a choice about what rules them internally. Moreover, covetousness has a contingent social cause: people choose to uphold a society that in turn generates a covetous character and culture, just as "covetousness within is bred by presentment of outer objects." Accordingly, Winstanley's dialectical account of psychological and social choices discloses political possibilities that Hobbes buries.[5]

Thus, Winstanley's initial wilderness experience and his initial theory of the Fall are crucial to his social argument because only on that basis

5. It is inconceivable to Hobbes that men could share the earth peacefully. In *De Cive* he describes his thought process, asking himself

> from whence it proceeded that any man should call anything his own rather than another man's? And when I found this proceeded not from nature but from consent, [I was led to ask,] upon what impulses, when all was equally everyman's in common, did

can he make credible his demand that the earth be "restored" to a "common treasury." His social account of the Fall enables him to diagnose and criticize the social basis of monarchy and Puritan politics but presumes the profound psychological or cultural changes disclosed by his initial theory of the Fall:

> The reformation that England is now to endeavor is not to remove the Norman Yoke only and to bring us back to be governed by those laws that were before William the Conqueror, as if that were the rule or mark to aim at. No, that is not it; but the Reformation is according to the Word of God, and that is the pure Law of Righteousness before the fall.[6] (292)

Whether people truly escape Egypt or create another one depends on their commitment to "the word of God," or reason within (289). Those who are estranged from god's reason and love, which they actually embody, will relinquish their "title" to reason and the earth, alienate to "teachers and rulers" their capacity to speak and labor, and thereby create the "outward" forms of "Egyptian Bondage." Since worldly freedom depends on overcoming estrangement from the god within, the clergy now appear as a key obstacle to social change. Thus, Winstanley and Marx both focus on the social significance of religion, but Winstanley bases his argument about worldly estrangement on precisely the inner religiosity whose negation is the premise of Marx's theory.

THE CLERGY

Winstanley's view of the clergy has changed in important ways. He always rooted religion in social reality, arguing that religious ideas and

---

men think it fitting that every man should have his enclosure? And I found the reason was, that from a community of goods there must needs arise contention, whose enjoyment should be the greatest. And from that contention all kinds of calamities must invariably ensue, which by the instinct of nature every man is taught to shun.   (93)

Thus, Hobbes construes "in common" to mean up for grabs, whereas for Winstanley it means shared. Therefore, Hobbes denies that there could be "peace without subjection" and defends the state as an instrument of salvation.

6. Hobbes and Winstanley both speak of the sons' relationship to the earth (and the state) in oedipal terms. Hobbes's sons escape the maternal tyranny of the state of nature only through the creation of a paternal authority that legalizes the enclosure of the earth and enforces obedience. The desire to dominate mother earth and displace paternal authority persists, but it is enacted legally only in private life. Thus, the sovereign is an effective totem: the sons cannot politicize their oedipal desires and fantasies, and their quest for autonomy will not disrupt order. For Winstanley, the discovery of the Father within brings the maturity that renounces *exclusive* claims on the mother earth, which makes possible the reciprocity of "peace without subjection," as Hobbes puts it. In Winstanley's terms, Hobbes's sons still are seduced and overwhelmed by objects and passions and therefore require the mortal god that keeps them children; in Hobbes's terms, Winstanley's Father within is an imaginary and therefore ineffective totem.

practices, and the support of the state, provided priests a "temporal maintenance." Against Anglicans and Puritans he defended toleration and argued for the separation of church and state, partly because he believed that magistracy would then be "pure" and partly because he imagined that if the state "took back its power," Christ would rise in the people, and then all priests and ministers would lose their power.

Once he discovers social divisions, however, he realizes that those who own property and wield state power share with the clergy a deep-seated interest. Whereas before, Winstanley believed that ministers corrupted a magistracy that otherwise would be pure, he argues now that a corrupt state requires a clergy that will corrupt others. Winstanley imagines William the Conqueror promising "that if the clergy would preach him up, so that the common people might be bewitched, so as to receive him as God's anointed over them, he would give them the tenths of the land's increase yearly" (357). Thus, the clergy blind people to maintain not only their own power but also the power of owners and rulers (on which clerical power depends). In this sense, the clergy, regardless of denomination, teach people to acquiesce in property and kingly power:

> While men are gazing up to a heaven, inquiring after their happiness or fearing a hell after they are dead, their eyes are put out so that they see not what is their birthright and what is to be done by them here on earth, while they are still living. (569)

Ministers disseminate ideology, in Marxist terms, as servants of a social order that in turn maintains them.

To be sure, Winstanley knows that religion can provide the grounds for resistance, as it did in himself. He imagines a "poor enslaved man" complaining that "we that work most have the least comfort in the earth, and they that work not at all enjoy all, contrary to the scripture which says, the meek shall inherit the earth" (388). But ministers use Christ to gain submission:

> Presently the tithing priest stops his mouth with a slam and tells him that is meant to inward satisfaction of mind which the poor shall have, though they enjoy nothing at all. And so, poor creatures, it is true, they have some ease thereby, and [are] made to wait with patience while Kingly Power swims in fullness. (388–89)

In exchange for their efforts, the clergy are guaranteed tithes and protection:

> If people seem to deny tithes, then kingly power by his laws doth force the people to pay them, so there is a confederacy between the clergy and the

great red dragon. . . . The sheep of Christ shall never fare well so long as
the wolf or red dragon pays the shepard his wages. (387)

To the extent that the clergy succeed in creating consent, however, the
people will question tithes no more than property and kings, and physical coercion will be rendered unnecessary. But in the shadows, always,
stands the gallows.

In this general account of the clergy and kingly power, Winstanley
equates ministers in the state church with Presbyterian and other Puritan preachers who profess to reform it. Despite theological disagreements, they support a magistracy that enforces tithes and "fixed formal
worship" and justifies property. Yet Winstanley also retains his initial
sense that "outward bondage" appears and persists only as the creation
of "fallen Adams." Accordingly, ideas not only rationalize a given social
order but also contribute to shaping it. He says that the clergy are not
the creation of kingly power but its creators; the clergy shape those who
deny their own experience and the reason within them and therefore
seek outer teachers, rulers, and property. Indeed, Winstanley contends
that religion is "the Father that begat" all the beasts of fallen society:

> For this teaching art at first bids mankind to look abroad for a teacher and
> ruler, and to look abroad for justice and content, and when he had deceived
> them so to do, then he put mankind upon buying and selling the earth and
> her fruits, and so by that means the creation is divided. (467–68)

As this statement implies, the power to define reality, which is governed
either by the "Spirit Reason within" or by fleshly imagination, makes
religion far more than a hireling of kingly power.

The clerical beast is the social voice of the fleshly imagination that is
the source of all worldly works. Thus, Winstanley insists that "imaginary clergy-power is more terrible and dreadful" than the beasts of
property and the state (466). Although "he has come last, yet indeed he
is the Father that begat the others," for "under this power of imagination, the whole government of the world amongst the sons of men is
built" (456). Because of his analysis of the Fall, Winstanley avoids the
reductionism that makes culture into ideology and makes ideology into
a merely external rationalization of social interests.

Winstanley's sense of the power of ideas is particularly important in
his understanding of Puritanism and the Puritan clergy. As an outer savior promising to create a New Jerusalem, Winstanley declares, "Hath
not the clergy ruled over kingly power, law, and buying and selling, and
brought all under command?" Even as the arrest of Charles attests to
the ministers' power, however, Winstanley recognizes the limitations of

the Puritan form of the clerical beast. Although now these "beasts seem to persecute one another, . . . one cannot live without the other, and if one dies, all die" (466). That is because

> Kingly power depends on the law, and upon buying and selling, these three depend on the clergy to bewitch people to conform, and all of them depend on kingly power by his force to compel subjection from those that will not be bewitched. (470)

Thus, Winstanley believes that Puritan ministers are merely shifting the balance of power among the beasts. Although the ministers aspire to rule because they consider themselves spiritual men, they will learn, if in their pride they forget, that they are dependent on the sword and the propertied. Indeed, after the tumult of the 1640s ministers accept Cromwell's rule, even though he imposes religious toleration, and they even support the restoration of the monarchy they once had vowed to destroy. As Winstanley anticipates:

> If the clergy can get tithes or money they will turn as the ruling power turns, anyway, to Popery, to Protestantism, for a king, against a king, for monarchy [or] for State Government. They cry who bids the most wages; they will be on the strongest side, for an earthly maintenance. (357)

The Puritan clergy may attack specific forms of kingly power, warns Winstanley, but they never will destroy it—or always will resurrect it. That is because the clergy by definition, as it were, teach of an outward god and therefore encourage the inner alienation that is the basis of worldly estrangement. Their claim of "title" to god and the gospels, and thus of authority to speak for others, typifies the very estrangement Winstanley attacks in kingly power. By definition, too, the clergy claim title to the land and labor that typifies the estranged power of property owners. Thus, Winstanley concludes that the death of one beast would be the death of all because overcoming estrangement in one regard would undermine it in others. Conversely, none of the beasts could lead a genuine reformation because each contains the seeds of the others. Accordingly, Winstanley insists that Puritan saints may lead what they call a reformation, but their New Jerusalem never could remove the curse of Cain.

Like Winstanley, Hobbes attributes enormous power to imagination and ideas, and therefore to the clergy. Hobbes contends, however, that Puritan ministers have subverted sovereign power, which needs to be reconstructed. Accordingly, he tries to remarry Puritans to the state by appropriating their commitments to property and magistracy but insisting that only a sovereign should "personify" god's voice and will. Then the dictates of this mortal god would be voiced by clerical mouthpieces; culture would become subordinate to the state power that defines it. By reducing conscience to fancy, and then making conscience into the internalized sovereign voice, Hobbes turns a sociological insight about conventionality into a policy that harnesses the clergy to the state. Having subverted the Puritan assertion that god sanctions self-determination, Hobbes hopes to tie Puritans to the very estrangement of power they once opposed.

In this regard, the obvious difference between Winstanley and Hobbes is this: Hobbes fears anarchy because he sees Puritans trying to *reclaim* the power wielded by king and church; Winstanley sees Puritans trying to *transfer* power to themselves and therefore fears a resurrection of Egyptian bondage. Thus, Hobbes promotes a marriage between church and state that Winstanley says the Puritans never would have dissolved.

This difference, however, reflects a deeper one about god and politics. Hobbes criticizes the Puritan god and conscience as expressions of the "vain fancy" that there is a ground of judgment beyond culture, which entitles people to question the sovereign's rule. In fact, he says that the only alternative to culture is nature, in which appetite and fancy create anarchy. Winstanley also criticizes the Puritans for creating an imaginary god, but his criticism is based on an idea of god whose conventionality he denies. Believing that he himself has found a ground of judgment beyond culture, Winstanley criticizes as imaginary any idea of god that justifies human submission to worldly idols. In this way, he brings to fruition the radical potential in Puritan piety, extending it to challenge property, Parliament, and priests. As a result, however, he is twinned with his enemies, professing also to honor a standard of judgment that is not conventional, and presuming that this god speaks the same "word of power" to everyone.

CONCLUSION

By using Old Testament metaphors about fratricidal brothers, Egyptian bondage, and Israel's consent to "outer rulers," Winstanley turns from the personal body to the social body, from inner division to the estrangement of power in the world. He tries to account for "outer bondage" by linking the domination of an external power to human consent or complicity, and he therefore characterizes the poor in contradictory ways. The poor appear not only as coerced and innocent Israel, captive in Egypt and forerunner of Christ crucified by hostile power, but also as sinful Israel, choosing to betray itself into Babylonian captivity.

This is not Winstanley's incoherence, however. He is attending to contradictory, yet related, aspects of political and social reality—specifically to what is paradoxical about any form of estrangement. The insight into human imagination and consent indicates how men and women are ultimately the authors of human bondage, but it mistakenly suggests that thinking differently would suffice to destroy it. The insight into coercion depicts social institutions as objects wielding power independently of their creators and thereby indicates that freedom also depends on worldly action. But since the focus on coercion implies that people are merely victims, the former insight is necessary as a reminder of their moral agency and of complicity in their situation.

By linking "bondage within and without," Winstanley's metaphors hold these insights in tension. They are also meant to suggest that those who overcome their estrangement from the power of god within can thereby reclaim the worldly power they have relinquished to owners, teachers, and rulers. By arguing that the history of the Hebrews exemplifies this possibility, its betrayal, and its renewal, Winstanley not only subverts the logic of *Leviathan* but also presents an alternative to the understanding of radical politics we have inherited from Marx.

CHAPTER IV

Rebirth as Social Change

In that day the Lord with his sore and great and strong
sword shall punish Leviathan the piercing serpent, even
Leviathan . . . ; and He shall slay the dragon that is in
the sea.

—Isaiah 27:1

And they shall build houses, and inhabit them; and they
shall plant vineyards, and eat the fruit of them.

They shall not build, and another inhabit; they shall not
plant, and another eat.

—Isaiah 65:21—22

After his second wilderness experience, Winstanley aligns himself with
the poor in a new way. Now the poor will lead England from bondage
and social division because they will find the King of Righteousness
within, recognize their inheritance to the land that is their common
mother, and establish a covenant that makes the earth a common treasury. Following biblical usage, Winstanley calls that righteousness "the
seed of Abraham"; that inheritance, he says, is disclosed by the Old and
New testaments; and that common treasury is a Canaan that "materially fulfills" the meaning of the Hebrew covenant. Winstanley now invokes the New Testament claim that "salvation is of the Jews." History
appears to him as a narrative that runs from Abraham, through Moses
and Christ, to Christ's resurrection in and as the poor in England. But
the poor literally and directly reclaim the land in the present.

Thus, we move in Part II from the inner logic of Winstanley's turn
toward the life of the social body, to his diagnosis of estrangement and
social division, and now to his effort to embed his theory and collective
action in a history he understands differently from before. An explora-
tion of Winstanley's contention that "salvation is of the Jews" will reveal
what differentiates his understanding of radical action from Marx's.

On the one hand, Winstanley and Marx share more than a concern with the kind of estrangement defended by Hobbes. Both theorists use the Old Testament, and what they call "Jewish," to recover earthly need; joining Old Testament worldliness to the moral universalism of the New Testament, both find an earthly ground for the realization of Christ's gospel in a class of people uniquely situated to transform worldly relationships. As a result of the way each works through what Marx calls "the Jewish question," both locate their emergence as theorists, their critical perceptions on contemporary politics, and their alternative communities in a historical narrative whose purpose they believe they know and embrace wholeheartedly.

On the other hand, Winstanley's differences from Marx are signified by the fact that he literally locates the poor in *Jewish* history. That history explains and authorizes a politics of *inheritance,* and yet, like Moses and Christ, Winstanley uses the idea of inheritance to justify unprecedented action. In this way, he derives the autonomy of the poor—as he earlier had derived personal autonomy—from reverence toward what is given and not invented. Because he roots politics in the history of the Hebrews, Winstanley fashions a radicalism that links individual piety to collective action, and authority to rebellion.

In contrast, the premise of Marx's radicalism is the negation of precisely the inner religiosity and "spirit of inheritance" that are the premise of Winstanley's radicalism. Because Marx roots estrangement in the *denial* of human invention, he derives "emancipation" from the self-recognition of prideful creators and endorses the Promethean acts of creation that Winstanley identifies as the source of bondage.

As we follow Winstanley's narrative from the inside, we also witness from the outside, as it were, an example of a feudal and religious tradition metamorphosed into a systematic and radical vision of remaking history. This project, based on extant traditions, provides an alternative not only to the Puritans and to Hobbes but also to the explicitly modern radicalism of Marx.

MOVING FROM TEXTS TO HISTORY

In *The New Law of Righteousness,* after depicting how fallen Adams create a social "hell wherein one torments another," Winstanley goes on to say:

> Yet, there are three doors of hope for England. First, let everyone leave off running after others for knowledge and comfort, and wait upon the Spirit Reason . . . the true Teacher of everyone in their own inward experience. . . .

> Secondly, let everyone . . . leave off this buying and selling of land or fruits of the earth, none enclosing or hedging in any part of the earth, saying this is mine. . . . Thirdly, leave off dominion and lordship one over another, for the whole bulk of mankind is but the one living earth. . . . And let those who hitherto had no land . . . quietly enjoy land to work upon, that everyone may enjoy the benefits of his Creation. (200–201)

Those who walk through these doors leave behind clerical ideology, the market, and political domination, and therefore they are able to establish the "community of earth" and "community of spirit." "These two communities, or rather, one in two branches, is that true levelling which Christ will work . . . the greatest, first, and truest Leveller" (386). In his social moment prior to digging, Winstanley links a critique of pride to a critique of property and imagines a community that overcomes both.

Unlike the just communities depicted by other political theorists, however, Winstanley's community of earth and spirit is not self-consciously (let alone ironically) invented: it is not a fiction meant to tell the truth, but is presented as a scriptural prophecy "really and materially to be fulfilled." He has not created a "city" or found a standard in the mind, but he discloses a standard present in all and manifested in the unfolding of history.

The difference between fictional devices and irony, on the one hand, and Winstanley's spirit of prophecy and earnest embodiment, on the other, does not arise simply from his religiosity or even from its roots in Protestantism. Neither Augustine and More nor Luther and Calvin proposed a community they believed would fulfill the gospel or be established by the poor. Winstanley grounds his theory and himself in history because his recovery of the Old Testament reveals a narrative that he believes is coming to completion in his time. Writing as a witness and prophet, he promises to move from words to action.

WINSTANLEY AND THE OLD TESTAMENT

Puritans believe that god is active in history and that they testify to his truth; they authorize their struggle for religious and political self-determination by relating it to the Exodus narrative of the Old Testament. Although they call themselves Hebrews, however, they also invoke the Book of Revelation and profess to be fulfilling the prophecy of Christ's Second Coming. Thus, they reclaim for themselves Christ's promise of redemption, which they believe the Hebrews had forsaken: they cast themselves against those who deny that life's redemptive meaning can be realized in historical time. As god's grace is politicized to include the calling of the elect to transform worldly community, politics is sacralized. England becomes the stage for enacting god's will in history.

As diverse commentators have noted, Puritans do not agree about the constituents of Canaan or New Jerusalem, but they all hold to the Mosaic idea of covenant and more specifically to the Mosaic acceptance of property, priests, and the sword. At the same time, they also use the New Testament, and not only for its millennial promise: the grace symbolized by Christ becomes the criterion to distinguish those who shall be the elders entitled to wield social, political, and religious power. As J. G. A. Pocock and Christopher Hill also have argued, Levellers in the army and London begin to jettison this apocalyptic and Biblical framework. Hill's Levellers are protobourgeois defenders of a liberal, constitutional state, and Pocock's Levellers are republicans committed to a traditional freehold that is threatened by the market. But common to both accounts is the assertion that propertied politics becomes secularized as it is disconnected from a Biblical framework.

At first, Winstanley associated himself with the New Testament, and the Puritans with the Old Testament: he argued that their attachment to "Jewish, ceremonial forms of worship" betrayed the gospel. Now, however, Winstanley allies himself with the Old Testament when he attacks the religious politics of the ministers and the propertied politics of secularizing activists. Christ has not disappeared by any means, but has become the descendant of Abraham, sent by god to realize fully god's promise to the Jews of an *earthly* inheritance. Thus, those who honor god's law of righteousness are specifically described by Winstanley as "Jews," not "saints." Christ and the poor who honor him appear as the heirs of Abraham, exemplars of the good sons Isaac and Jacob and therefore entitled to the earth. In this extraordinary recasting of his argument, Jews become heroic protagonists and not only emblems of those who persecute Christ.

Accordingly, Winstanley's contention that "salvation, or restoration rather, is of the Jews" signifies his transformation from saint to social critic and digger. But what are the elements in his new view of the Old Testament? First, the history of the Hebrews discloses the idea of an earthly inheritance, which authorizes his account of righteousness; second, the history of Jewish conflicts over that inheritance provides the terms by which he criticizes Presbyterian and Leveller attempts to reform kingly power; and third, he uses that history to explain and justify the action of the poor, who will complete it because they are becoming conscious of the "seed of Abraham" or "law of righteousness" they embody. To be sure, Winstanley does not say, here is what I have discovered! But consideration of the elements in, and reasons for, his claim about the Jews will reveal his radical alternative to Puritanism and his distinctive understanding of radicalism.

When Abraham acknowledged god as his ruler, god promised that Abraham would father a great people and found a nation on land of its own:

> And I will give unto thee, and to thy seed after thee, the land wherein thou art a stranger, all the land of Canaan, for an everlasting possession; and I will be their God. . . . This is my covenant, which ye shall keep, between me and you and thy seed after thee; Every man child among you shall be circumcised . . . and it shall be a token of the covenant betwixt me and you . . . and my covenant shall be in your flesh for an everlasting covenant. (Genesis 17 : 8 – 13)

Circumcision is the outer sign, or "token," of an inner covenant whose fruit is everlasting title to the land. What is crucial here is that the blessing of the god of the Old Testament is earthly and this-worldly, a law of righteousness in the body and linked to the land, not a spirit apart from the flesh or a kingdom of heaven after death.

Thus, Winstanley identifies the poor with the Jews, as persecuted and landless "strangers," and addresses *The New Law of Righteousness* to "The Twelve Tribes of Israel that are circumcised in heart and scattered through all the nations of the earth." Winstanley's second reason for recovering the Old Testament begins to explain his use of St. Paul's phrase "circumcised in heart." God promised Abraham that he would be the seed "of many nations" but suggested that only certain of his children actually would honor god and therefore warrant god's blessing. The seed of Abraham splits into two traditions of brothers who compete for the land and god's blessing: Cain and Abel, Ishmael and Isaac, Esau and Jacob. Accordingly, Winstanley also divides "the Jews," declaring that those like Jacob are "trod under foot" by elder brothers like Esau. Winstanley goes on to clarify:

> You to whom I write are the seed of Abraham . . . but let me tell you, not the seed of Abraham after the flesh, for Ishmael and Esau are not to share in this portion, [which] they have received and spent already in unrighteousness; your portion is the Lord himself, which endures forever. And now comes the time the elder sons that are born after the flesh shall serve the younger sons, in whom the blessing lies; this is the fall of Esau and the rising of Jacob. (150)

Biblical accounts of recurring fratricidal conflicts are ambiguous, but like his contemporaries, Winstanley blatantly moralizes (and simplifies) their meaning in order to address English conflicts over the paternal estate of the king. Those Winstanley calls the elder brothers are not entitled to god's blessing of the earth because they are outwardly but not inwardly circumcised. As a result, they merely profess righteousness while acting like the king, seeking to usurp the earth for themselves, and oppressing the younger brothers.

These younger brothers are "inward Jews" because they carry a seed that Winstanley says is "the Lord himself." It is

> the law and power of righteousness which made Abraham forsake his Isaac, his dearest relations in the flesh rather than refuse the way of his Maker. . . . The Law of Righteousness, dwelling and ruling in any one is the seed of Abraham, and the several branches of men and women in whom that power rests, are children of the family of Abraham. (150)

Younger brothers can embody this seed because they are "circumcised in heart," which enables them to relinquish the covetous desire to possess the earth exclusively. As a result, they embody a "blessing" in the sense that they can deliver the whole earth from inner and outer bondage. It is for this reason that Winstanley declares:

> The nations shall know that salvation, or restoration rather, is of the Jews; that the King of Righteousness and prince of peace that removes the curse and becomes the blessing, arises up in you and from you . . . and though the seed of the flesh have cast you out for evil and you have been the despised ones of the earth . . . yet now your glory is rising. And the ancient prophecy of Zacharie shall be fulfilled: that ten men shall take hold of the skirt of him that is a Jew, saying, let us go with you, for we have heard that God is with you. (152)

By telling the poor, currently outcast and despised, that they have in them the seed of Abraham, which is their inheritance, Winstanley is teaching them, first, that the law of righteousness is within; secondly, that therefore they have title to the earth as do other people; and thirdly, that by honoring that seed they will bear a blessing for all humankind. To be a Jew inwardly is to honor the seed, insist on that inheritance, and therefore bring deliverance to all. In other words, by saying that salvation is "of the Jews," Winstanley is teaching that a people can become Israel, capable of creating a Canaan, only if they fashion a covenant that honors the seed of Abraham in each and the birthright of all to the land.

In this Canaan, Winstanley declares, "everyone that is born in the land may be fed by his mother that brought him forth, according to the Reason that rules in creation" (257):

By working together and feeding together as . . . members of one family, not lording it over another, but all looking upon each other as equals in the creation . . . thou wilt honor thy Father and Mother: Thy Father which is the spirit of community that made all and dwells in all; thy Mother which is the earth that brought us all forth and that as a true Mother loves all her children. (265)

In the name of this universal household, Winstanley says to the elder brother: "Do not hinder the Mother Earth from giving all her children suck," but instead "give thy free consent to make the earth a common treasury, without grumbling, . . . that all may enjoy the benefit of their creation" (265).

Winstanley recovers the Old Testament emphasis on the land, fratricidal conflict, and the question of legitimate title or righteousness. As a result, he situates the poor in a historical narrative that provides the grounds for rebellious action. His use of Biblical brothers, however, also signifies what is distinctive about his understanding of radicalism, for by way of them he defines politics in terms of reverence for an inheritance.

FROM ISAAC TO MOSES: THE POLITICS OF INHERITANCE

The Puritans call themselves Isaacs. Linking Christianity to a worldly calling and external worship, they create a covenant that entitles them to claim the lineage of Israel and the rightful possession of the property they accumulate. Levellers and republicans, while separating church and state, nonetheless follow the Puritans and often define themselves as Isaacs. At the same time, orthodox Puritans, as well as republicans, Hobbes, and Locke, associate Ishmael with "savages," the Irish, and white outsiders—with those deemed a threat to covenanted civilization. In these sources of the American tradition, Ishmaels have been seen as the natural and pagan antitype of Christian and, later, liberal society.

As Winstanley retains, but inverts and transforms, this idiom, he turns against the elder brothers their own Old Testament metaphors. Whereas Puritans associate Ishmael's wildness with nature, Winstanley's Ishmael, though aggrandizing and wild, is a social man who makes society a wilderness. Whereas Puritans locate the idolatry and sin of Ishmael in nature, Winstanley sees idolizing wealth and cannibalizing labor as the basis of an Ishmaelite society. He still considers Ishmael and Esau bad sons, men of the flesh, but he redefines their sin and thus includes ministers, gentry, and freeholders. Sin is the expropriation of the earth (not the poverty that results from it) and external worship (not the absence of "settled worship").

Obviously, Winstanley means these reversals to criticize his enemies, but most interesting is what they disclose about the poor and the politics he proposes for them. Puritans consider Winstanley heretical; because of his pantheism, perhaps he appears to them as a pagan Ishmael. Although dispossessed and despised as a pariah, however, he does not accept the name the Puritans give him: he neither admits the propertied to be true and chosen Isaacs, thereby seeking admission to their covenant, nor rebels self-consciously as an Ishmael, rejecting their tradition altogether. Rather, Winstanley declares that he is an Isaac or a Jacob bearing the seed of Abraham. He thereby disputes the elder brothers' exclusive claim to god's blessing and earth, giving political voice to the traditions of the poor and scriptural meaning to their entry into history.

In Winstanley's self-understanding, Isaac represents cultivators and farmers who defend the traditions of a communitarian civilization against the dispossession wrought by savage Ishmaelite landlords and freeholders. As an American Ishmael might have done, Winstanley attacks civilization and defends nature, but he uses an idea of nature to defend the bonds of community against forcible dissolution. Thus, he speaks as a good son about restoring a community and inheritance that is being "trod under foot." [1]

Indeed, by linking himself and the poor to Isaac and Jacob, Winstanley is speaking to the actual conditions of the poor, invoking allegiance to a tradition that is still alive for him and them. For as the poor resisted threats to inherited rights and folkways of community and mutual aid, so faithfulness to these traditions generated a powerful antienclosure movement and extensive rioting. That is why Hill argues that the digging colony is "merely one particularly well-documented example of a trend that was repeated in many places." [2]

1. I am indebted to Michael Rogin for my appreciation of the importance of the pairs of brothers in political thought, especially American. Much of the American discourse has been conducted in these terms, and American rebels have tended to identify themselves with people of color and with pariahs; that is to say, rebels have taken on the name Ishmael to invert the order sustained by capitalist and Christian Isaacs. In reference to this act of naming, Winstanley stands close to Thoreau, who tried to revitalize, rather than reject, the tradition of Isaacs.

2. Christopher Hill, *World Turned Upside Down*, pp. 93–101. In another work Hill says:

The artisan and peasant majority of the population . . . had behind them centuries of communal solidarity in the struggle against nature, centuries of teaching on the virtues

Reinterpreting Christ's association of salvation and "the Jews," Winstanley speaks of human action in terms of an inheritance carried as a seed. In effect, he is saying to the poor that the practices that preserve community and the principle of justice appropriate to it are apparent in their situation, both as a body of natural creatures who require the earth and as a community that has inherited certain traditions and principles. Community as such does not need to be constructed, nor does a principle of justice need to be imagined. People do not create any order and give to it any meaning they please, but act in terms of a self and world already existent, whether they admit this fact or not. Good sons and daughters accept it and therefore act self-consciously as instruments of what they do not make, toward ends they have not fixed but choose to honor. Their action is possible because it is rooted in genuine piety for what is truly not their invention.

As Winstanley now rebels against the inventions of the elder brothers, he engages in an act of loyalty within a horizon of devotion. Indeed, Winstanley's argument about inheritance and reverence enables him to speak as a Moses announcing a new exodus:

> Therefore, let Israel go free, that the poor may labor waste land and suck the breasts of their mother earth, that they starve not. . . . But I do not entreat thee, for thou art not to be entreated; but *in the name of the Lord* that hath drawn me forth to speak to thee, I say, I command thee, *To Let Israel Go Free,* and quietly to gather together into the place where I shall appoint, and hold them no longer in bondage. (265–66)

The exodus is happening; the defeat and capture of Charles is its first step or sign. The Puritans agree with Winstanley that the Civil War is part of a historical process, but Winstanley further believes it will deliver the poor from the bondage of even their reformed government. There will be an exodus within their exodus:

> The spirit now rising up by right of inheritance . . . will and shall go on to gather together the scattered of Israel, out of all Egyptian Bondage and self-seeking oppressing government, and out of all forms and customs of the

---

of Christian charity. . . . It is therefore easy to understand that in many areas there was considerable sympathy for sturdy beggars and that constables had difficulty enforcing the poor law. Few villagers, few artisans near the poverty line, would lightly believe that original sin was the sole cause of vagabondage, that men took to the road for the fun of the thing, that all beggars should be punished, that property was more important than life. The common people's hostility to the wholesome doctrine of original sin is indeed one of the most regular complaints of Perkins and his Calvinist contemporaries. (*Puritanism and Revolution* [New York: Schocken Books, 1958], pp. 232–33)

beast, to worship the Father in spirit and truth, being made to be all of one heart and one mind. And this shall more and more appear as the earth grows up to be a common treasury for all. (163)

It is "the right of inheritance" that has enabled Winstanley to unmask "the forms and customs of the beast" in its kingly, Puritan, and secular forms, and this spirit is moving the poor through and beyond these forms to establish a community of earth and spirit.

Winstanley believes that he has not invented the inheritance he reclaims or the household for the sake of which dutiful sons and daughters will act. As he later declares:

> Father, thou knowest that what I have writ and spoke concerning this light, that the earth should be restored and become a common treasury . . . was thy free revelation to me; I never read it in any book, I heard it from the mouth of no flesh, until I understood it from thy teachings within me first. I did not study or imagine the conceit of it; self-love to my own particular body does not carry me along in the managing of this business, but the power of love flowing forth to the liberty and peace of the whole creation. (329)

I have suggested that there are powerful and persuasive principles shaping this denial of invention in Winstanley's arguments about god, reverence, and, now, inheritance. I take Winstanley to be seeking both the historical sources of action by the poor and the standard they must honor if their action is to be a legitimate way to feed and free themselves. By invoking the ideas of inheritance and covenant, however, does Winstanley mean to deny the radical innovation in his interpretation of them?

Surely, god's promise of land did not include an injunction that it be shared in common, and Moses in fact gave the land to each man in each tribe rather than require them to hold the land collectively. In addition, Moses invented the priestly caste of Levites, imposed tithes to support them, and endorsed the rule of select elders. Thus, Puritan and republican elder brothers are perfectly justified in using the example of Moses to defend the institutions Winstanley attacks. Moreover, feudal traditions often gave the poor a right to the commons but embraced hierarchy and deference and enshrined the right of lords to their estates. Here again, the notion of inheritance provides support to Winstanley's enemies and little ground for his egalitarian "community of earth and spirit."

Winstanley's argument that the poor are Jews animated by a spirit of inheritance does go a long way toward explaining how piety for a living tradition can mobilize any people, including his people. But it surely does not suffice to explain or warrant the untraditional belief that the whole earth was, is, and shall be a "common treasury," a "household" without "outer teachers and rulers." Winstanley does not disguise the fact that he is calling for something unprecedented. He grants that holding land in common "is not practiced in any other nation in the world" and brazenly insists that "what other lands do, England is not to take pattern, for England (as well as other lands) hath lived under the power of the beast, Kingly Propriety" (386). The question of how to define England's reformation is "not to be answered by any text of scripture or example since the fall, but the answer is to be given in the light of itself, which is the law of righteousness or the Word of God . . . which dwells in mans heart" (289). In the context of his insistence that "salvation is of the Jews" and, thus, is defined by an inheritance, how does Winstanley justify this call for the unprecedented?

FROM MOSES TO CHRIST: TRADITION
AND THE UNPRECEDENTED

Winstanley's recovery of the Old Testament leads to the following contradiction: the Old Testament history of the Hebrews expresses Winstanley's movement toward the earth, bodily need, and a language of class conflict, but it also seems to enshrine the forms of religious and political community he once criticized as "Jewish, ceremonial, and legal." As a result, he is led into a further contradiction, for he speaks of inheritance yet calls for actions it seems to condemn or preclude.

It is precisely in these contradictions, however, that Winstanley finds the deepest reasons that "salvation is of the Jews." Most obvious, the Hebrews embody the paradox that a people imbued with "the spirit of inheritance" gave birth to two historically unprecedented developments: Moses and the first exodus, and Christ's promise that the poor shall inherit the earth. In each case, the prophet insists that the Hebrews are to "take their pattern" not from other nations but from god. To be sure, the innovations of Moses reveal the contradiction between the idea of an earthly inheritance and its particular form in property and priests. But the resolution of this historical contradiction is also manifested by the Jews, for Christ used the ideas of inheritance and birthright, covenant and righteousness.

In his radical reading of inheritance Winstanley specifically speaks as a witness to Christ against those who still adhere to Mosaic forms.

Having recovered the Old Testament and the earth, however, his witness is very different than before. He views Christ as a Jew concerned about a worldly inheritance: the animating idea of inheritance requires for its fulfillment the unprecedented historical action of overthrowing priests and property. These merely external forms of righteousness, which presume rather than transform covetousness, prevent the realization of the righteous law that is god's promise and Abraham's seed. But worldly emblems of inner covetousness can be overcome only by embodying god's spirit directly in personal and social life, which is the possibility that Winstanley believes Christ exemplified.

Thus, Winstanley's Christ speaks as a Jew to other Jews, heirs to a tradition they share with him. They may treat him as a pariah, a rebel against the traditional covenant of the fathers, but he is trying to make real its deepest meaning. Accordingly, the Old Testament split between Jacob and Esau becomes the New Testament conflict between Jesus and the Pharisees. The children of Abraham are still in conflict over the meaning of inheritance, covenant, and righteousness.

Hence, the key to Winstanley's argument lies in the distinction he makes between inward and outward Jews:

> You are the Abrahamites in whom the blessing remains, that live not now in the type, but enjoy the substance of circumcision; for he is not a Jew, that is one outward in the flesh, but he is a Jew, that is one inward, whose circumcision is of the heart. Whether he be born of the nation of the Jews extant in the world, or whether he be born of other nations in whom the blessing remains, it is Abraham's promised seed that makes a Jew; and these are they of whom it is said, salvation is of the Jews. (150)

To be a Jew "in the type" or "outward in the flesh" means to worship righteousness in a formal and external way, which is to follow the law Moses handed down after the disillusioning episode of the golden calf. In Winstanley's account, Moses created "the covenant of an outward testimony" (160) based on the Ten Commandments. As a result, "there was much equity between man and man" because "every man was limited to his own property, so that if another coveted his neighbor's wife, land, house, or servant, it was his sin and was to be punished by a general consent of the people" (490). But for Winstanley, this covenant is flawed: it only "moderates" and "curbs in" covetousness within, and thus it entails the worldly emblems of covetousness, that is, property and priests (425).

Those who are fallen can endeavor to be righteous only through "types," external and mediating forms or institutions—from a distance, as it were. By means of religious and political types the Hebrews acknowledge (their need for) god, but through external disciplines and priests rather than within themselves; they acknowledge (their need for) the earth, but indirectly, through the mediation of the "law of particular propriety"; and they acknowledge themselves as (needing) a community, but allegorically, through a "law of government" abstracted from their actual differences.

Winstanley contends that Moses was aware of the Hebrews' inability to acknowledge directly (their need for) the Father and the Common Mother. In historical terms, an "outward covenant" was the extent to which god's promises of nourishment and freedom could be realized. Thus, Winstanley's Moses says to the Hebrews:

> Though this be a law settling your peace for the moment, yet I am not he that shall restore you to your first singleness and innocency; for a Prophet shall the Lord your God raise up like me, that shall do the restoring work, and . . . he shall deliver Jacob from his sin and Israel from his transgression. (490)

"And here," adds Winstanley, "he points out Christ." Indeed, Christ appears because inner covetousness and conflict over the earth have subverted the outer covenant. Unable to honor even the types that represent righteousness, the Hebrews have become captive to hostile powers, victims of their own unrighteousness, and ripe for the acknowledgments that alone can bring deliverance.

For Winstanley, then, the Hebrews will find within themselves and their history the law and power to supersede the Mosaic inventions that circumcise outwardly. This salvation comes by way of "inward Jews," whose circumcision is "of the heart." Represented by Christ, the inward Jew rejects the worship of righteousness in types because he embodies it "in substance":

> The humane body called Christ was not the anointing, but the spirit within that body was the Christ, or the spreading power of righteousness, which was to fill the earth with himself. That body was but a house or temple for the present work, which was to draw down Moses' law and become the substance of his types. (151)

The man Jesus was Christ because in him "the righteous law dwelt bodily." Because Jesus was imbued with the spirit of righteousness, he was a Christ, or one who experienced in substance what outward Jews recognized only allegorically.

Therefore, says Winstanley, Jesus declared "that outward forms and customs and types of Moses worship . . . set forth at a distance to be our mediator, should all cease and give way to the spiritual worship of the Father" (162). By exemplifying how people can embody god's spirit directly, Jesus taught his fellow Jews how to share the earth and constitute themselves as a community without the allegorical or alienated mediation of religious and political forms.

Thus, Winstanley's use of Moses and Christ, and the distinction between outward and inward Jews, is directed to several purposes. First, he criticizes purportedly Christian ministers. Because they interpret Jesus in terms of a spirit divorced from the flesh, these would-be Christians flee the earthly life and historical and social problems that Christ actually addressed. Worshiping Jesus "at a distance," as a person and a type, ministers still are inwardly covetous and still associate righteousness with external Mosaic forms of property and religion. As before, Winstanley equates Puritans and Pharisees, teaching ministers that they are outward Jews; but now this self-recognition makes it possible to discover Jesus as an inward Jew who confronted property in order to bring freedom "while our bodies are on the earth."

Secondly, Winstanley's argument about Christ is directed at republicans or protoliberal Levellers. These reformers seem to be engaged in an endeavor comparable to Winstanley's. They subvert the worship of community through the "type" of monarchy and embody the king's spirit in their own political action. Moreover, they seem to acknowledge the earthly reality that professed Christians evade. Yet the political state of these reformers bears the same relation to earthly life in the market as the Christian spirit bears to the actual life of the flesh. By abstracting politics from earthly life, Levellers unabashedly liberate covetousness in the world while reproducing the allegory of political representation. Rather than embody righteousness directly in social life, they worship virtue through the type of an outward covenant or political community.

Winstanley's criticism of outward Jews is meant to return propertied radicals to the contradictions between law and covetous desire, between the claim of virtue and the social fact of exploitation. A reformation crucified on these contradictions cannot succeed, but facing them honestly begins to remove the cross they constitute. This acknowledgment begins the salvation that Winstanley calls "Christ rising," the disclosure of which is his third purpose in distinguishing between inward and outward Jews. For just as Christ, animated by a "spirit of inheritance," taught the Hebrews how to gain god's blessing by fulfilling promises they merely professed to honor, so the poor in England are coming to exemplify Christ's spirit, which will teach the English how to live up to the Hebrew inheritance and the gospel promise that justified their rebellion.[3]

Thus, the scriptural narrative that was current political idiom has enabled Winstanley to question the limitations of propertied radicals by honoring—but deepening and universalizing—the goal and meaning of their project. That goal is reclaiming political power and earthly title from the king. Its meaning may seem counterintuitive: unprecedented action is made possible and legitimate through the authority of an inheritance. Before proceeding further, then, let us contrast Winstanley to Marx, who seems to sever what Winstanley joins.

WINSTANLEY, MARX, AND "THE JEWISH QUESTION"

In the 1840s Marx faced a situation presenting alternatives broadly comparable to those Winstanley found in Puritanism and the Levellers. Just as Marx analyzed the "Christian" state in Germany and the explosion of liberalism in France, so he located in "the Jews" both the contradictions he sought to overcome and the means to their resolution.

In "On the Jewish Question" Marx begins by criticizing the German and Christian state that deprives Jews of political rights on the ground that they are narrowly particularistic. Against the prejudices of the Christian state, Marx argues that Jews should be emancipated because Christians are in fact as egoistic and materialistic as the Jews they stigmatize: "The Jew manifests in a distinctive way the Judaism of civil society." Indeed, the stereotype of "the Jew" exposes the truth about "the Christian," who would rise above and disguise his own narrow egotism. Accordingly, Marx declares:

> The Christian is the theorizing Jew; consequently, the Jew is the practical Christian. . . . It was only in appearance that Christianity overcame real Ju-

---

3. The fulfillment of an inheritance requires and justifies broad scope for human interpretation and agency:

> Now as Moses declared that the lamb Jesus Christ should be the great prophet to whom everyone should give ear, and delivered it in general terms, leaving the particular discoveries of his new doctrine to the lamb himself when he came . . . so, too, the new man Jesus Christ, the great prophet, declared in general terms what should be in later times, leaving it to every son and daughter to declare their particular experiences when the spirit doth rise up in them. (161)

daism. It was too refined, too spiritual, to eliminate the crudeness of practical need, except by raising it to the ethereal realm.[4] (52)

If the secret reality of the Christian is the Jew, then the Christian leads a "double life." Christian consciousness requires, and can exist only in opposition to, "vulgar" and "practical" Jewish reality. By unmasking the "religious illusion," Marx would return Christians to their real lives as Jews: "The spiritual egotism of Christianity necessarily becomes the material egotism of the Jew, celestial need is transmuted into terrestrial need, subjectivism into self-interest" (52).

Moving from Christian "heaven" to Jewish "earth," Marx emancipates Jews by enacting the liberal reduction of Christian conscience to bourgeois interest. He uses the liberal revolution in France and America to justify the emancipation of Jews in Germany, but then employs Christian stereotypes about Jews to criticize the limitations of liberalism. He condemns the liberal state on precisely the Christian ground that it does not abolish what Christians stigmatize as "Jewish," that is, narrow (bourgeois) particularity.

Thus, Marx argues that in civil society, "the private individual treats other men as means, degrades himself into the role of a mere means, and becomes the plaything of alien powers" (34). At the same time, this "bourgeois" imagines a communal and moral existence as a "citizen," but in an abstract way, as the "imaginary member of an imaginary sovereignty, divested of his real individual life and infused with an unreal universality." Therefore, political democracy or the democratic state is still Christian in its relationship to civil society: the liberal state represents an "allegorical" idea of community that presupposes a realm of real differences and exploitive social relations.

The "double life" enjoined by "political emancipation" is an advance over feudalism, but Marx rejects political reform as a form of "heavenly consciousness" that presumes, rather than transforms, the earthly reality that Winstanley calls covetous and Marx calls egoistic. Although Marx does attack Jews as "hucksters," he vindicates them in the end: he embraces a "Jewish" materialism, which begins with, and accepts, both the reality and the legitimacy of "practical need." Only this approach to need, Marx insists, can transform its "egoistic" form. For only when "the real individual man . . . in his everyday life, in his work and rela-

4. Quotations of Marx are from *Marx-Engels Reader,* ed. Robert Tucker (New York: Norton, 1978). The best account of the significance of this essay to Marx's thought can be found in Jerrold Seigel, *Marx's Fate* (Princeton: Princeton University Press, 1978).

tionships," has "absorbed into himself the abstract citizen" (46) can humans establish a community that fulfills the equally legitimate claims of the body and morality.

Against the Christian politics that stigmatizes egoism as Jewish, and against the liberal politics that emancipates it, Winstanley and Marx each seek a third alternative, an approach to need and morality that is both earthly and universal. Like Winstanley, Marx builds a transforming relationship between Jewish particularity and need and the moral universalism of Christianity. Both theorists would synthesize the universalism of the gospel (and political democracy) and the practical need of the Old Testament, giving morality an earthly ground, and giving need a "human" form.

Perhaps these similarities arise because both theorists begin their theoretical projects by criticizing religious illusions. In this regard, Marx's project does not sound very different from Winstanley's:

> The abolition of religion as the illusory happiness of men is a demand for their real happiness. The call to abandon their illusions about their condition is a call to abandon the conditions that require illusions. The criticism of religion is, therefore, the embryonic criticism of this vale of tears of which religion is the halo. Criticism has plucked the imaginary flowers from the chain not in order that man shall bear the chain without caprice or consolation, but so that he shall cast off the chain and pluck the living flower. (54)

Winstanley also criticizes the religious "halo" in order to transform this "vale of tears." Both theorists move toward "the earth" and "reason" by criticizing "heavenly" forms of religious and political consciousness. In this way, both hope to overcome alienation from the body, the earth, and others in order to reclaim the power invested in human inventions. Both turn, therefore, from criticism of religion to criticism of the state and the market. But Winstanley's difference from Marx appears in the assertion that worldly emancipation depends on embodying a spirit of righteousness men and women have not invented. Through inward piety, says Winstanley, men and women are freed from illusions about god and are empowered to confront directly their inner covetousness and worldly bondage. By orienting themselves around an inner "sun," they will be able to establish a "true religion" that realizes "freedom within and without."

To Marx, of course, *any* idea of spirit, even an embodied one, is an "illusion," a disguised human invention that alienates creators from their own power. He believes that criticism of religion is meant to disillusion man so that he will think, act, and fashion his reality as a man who has lost his illusions and regained his reason, so that he will revolve about himself as his own true sun. Religion is only the illusory sun about which man revolves so long as he does not revolve about himself. (54)

As humans realize that they always revolve about themselves and their own inventions, they can reclaim their power: "It is the task of history . . . to unmask human self-alienation in its secular form now that it has been unmasked in its sacred form" (54). Marx here conceives of a Promethean agent whose "criticism of religion ends with the doctrine that man is the supreme being for man" (60).

Winstanley believes that emancipation from illusions and bondage depends on overcoming human alienation *from* god's embodied spirit of reason, whereas Marx believes that emancipation depends on overcoming the alienation *of* human power, exemplified by the belief in god. Winstanley rebels because he has discovered how he is a created being: humans embody a spirit of righteousness they do not invent, and this realization sponsors and authorizes their rebellion. Marx rebels because he has discovered that "man is the supreme being for man": humans invent god, and this realization sponsors and authorizes their rebellion.

As this analysis suggests, Marx and Winstanley disagree not about religion as such but about truth, invention, and freedom. Winstanley calls for abolishing illusions about god so that humans can make a "true revolution" (as Marx puts it) about a sun that represents truths and values they discover but do not invent. Thus, he believes that self-creation is a prideful fantasy that must be made conscious and relinquished for the sake of freedom. He moves beyond estrangement by linking worldly freedom not to the pride of the creator but to a reverence he calls a "spirit of inheritance." Accordingly, Winstanley defines a *conditioned* human freedom: he articulates the truths, grounds, or givens that created beings must honor if their rebellion is to be *legitimate*.

In contrast, Marx believes that any truth will "fetter" human power if that authority is thought to exist independently of human invention. Thus, Winstanley's religiosity appears as the prototype of the alienation Marx would abolish in the world; the negation of piety and authority is the premise of all other worldly overcomings. Accordingly, Marx links invention and rebellion: proclaiming ultimate human authorship of all truths and any historical circumstances, he associates salvation with Promethean invention made conscious and explicit. As a result, his radicalism exposes the self-denial in Winstanley's idea of reverence but elides the question of legitimacy. That question is central to Winstanley and leads him to insist on the bond between authority and action, or piety and rebellion. His theory thereby exposes Marx's failure to define explicitly the legitimate exercise of human power but elides the question of his own human authorship. Winstanley and Marx are led toward an earthly radicalism by their critiques of Christian and liberal politics, and each discovers a historical protagonist that synthesizes moral universalism and practical need. But their contrasting views of authority and rebellion lead to contrasting views of that protagonist and the historical possibilities it embodies.

Marx grants that "the resurrection of the dead" can empower historical action, as it did in the English and French revolutions, but he insists that the use of past (Biblical and Roman) models also expresses a need for self-deception. Thus, he argues that the Puritans' redemptive vision of history did enable them to act, but specifically by disguising both the novelty and the social limitations of their politics. In his language, political "poetry" is at odds with the "sober prose" necessary for a self-consciously radical politics. Accordingly, he declares that the proletariat will make a revolution not in the name of "dead generations" but by "letting the dead bury their dead."

Winstanley's poetry of reverence recovers the inheritance of dead generations. Indeed, he believes that the poor will be the literal resurrection of Christ's spirit in the social body. They become historical actors to the extent that they recognize themselves as bearers of Abraham's seed and witnesses to Christ's embodiment of it. Through his argument about a Jewish salvation, Winstanley links a millennial vision of history to a self-consciously radical politics, derives from inheritance unprecedented action, finds in piety the grounds for revolt, and speaks a poetry of redemption to justify the prosaic work of digging. Thus, he exemplifies a radicalism that synthesizes precisely what Marx says radicalism must sever. This interpretation of Winstanley's belief that salvation is of the Jews, and a contrast with Marx, can be extended by turning first to Winstanley's account of Christ's resurrection in and as the poor, and then to his vision of what digging will be and mean.

CHRIST RISING IN THE POOR

Jesus established the forerunner of the community of earth and spirit more by his death than by his life: "When that humane body was laid into the earth, the spirit which indeed is Christ came again a second time upon the apostles and brethren" (204). The death of his mortal body created a mystic body, as sons and daughters bore witness to the spirit that was in Christ. The blood of the lamb, washing white the sins of the apostles, united them into a regenerate spiritual community. Now, Winstanley argues, the spirit of the lamb is rising to knit together those who honor it:

> For as the man Christ Jesus swallowed up Moses and so the spirit dwelt bodily in that lamb . . . even so . . . that same spirit that filled every member of that one body should in these last days be sent into whole mankind, and every branch shall be a joint or member of the mystical body. (160–61)

Believing that Christ's spirit "is coming a second time in the personal appearance of sons and daughters" (152), Winstanley announces an agent unprecedented in human history:

> The Father is now raising up a people to Himself out of the dust, that is, out of the lowest and most despised sort of people, that are counted the dust of the earth, mankind, that are trod under foot. In these and from these shall the law of Righteousness break forth first. (186)

Just as god led the Hebrews out of Egypt, so too

> when this universal power of righteousness is spread upon the earth, it shall destroy Babylon, the great City of fleshly confusion . . . ; that is, he will pull down the government and kingdom of the world out of the hands of tyrannical, unreasonable acting flesh [and] into the hands of spiritual Israel, that so there may be no complainings, no burden, nor poor in Canaan . . . that it may be a land flowing with milk and honey. (181)

This new deliverance will do away with types altogether, Winstanley believes, including the worship of Christ "as a single man":

> For everyone shall know the Law, and everyone shall obey the Law, for it shall be writ in everyone's heart; and everyone that is subject to Reasons law shall enjoy the benefit of sonship. And that is, in respect to outward community, to work together, and eat bread together, and by so doing to lift up the creation from the bondage of self-interest or particular propriety of mine and thine. (198)

Accordingly, "though Israel's separation out of Egypt amazed the world," Winstanley insists that "this ministration of the spirit, now rising up by right of inheritance, will take peace from the world much more" (163).

What is the meaning of this mystical language? Winstanley believes that the spirit of Christ is "trod under foot" in the poor because they do not know, or cannot honor, their nature (that the law of righteousness is in each), are prevented from addressing their needs (for earth as well as sincere milk), and therefore cannot gain their freedom (by the right exercise of their capacities for labor as well as speech). Winstanley says that the spirit of Christ is rising in the poor because he believes that they are discovering the needs, capacities, and truths to which Christ testified, and which Winstanley makes explicit as the new law of righteousness. As they become conscious of what in themselves has been trod under foot, they act in new ways. But what makes this consciousness possible?

To say that the Father "leads" men and women to consciousness of this law, as he led Winstanley, means that adults are being led to new insights as they reason about the experience of dispossession and hunger, the tradition of mutual aid and common labor, and the memory of inheritance and title. They are not led by the Father's reason to just any insights: that *Christ* is rising means that the poor are beginning to act in accordance with a pattern or standard that truly could feed and free everyone, not only themselves.

Christ rises *first* in the poor because Winstanley believes that they alone are in a position to articulate a standard of righteousness that represents a universal salvation. To include themselves in the community and gain recognition for their needs and capacities, they must articulate the idea that a genuine human redemption cannot deny the full humanity of any class of people. Winstanley believes the poor are "chosen" specifically because the character of their particular experience will enable them to find and formulate truths that are common to all. Thus, their "experimental knowledge" will bear fruit as a law that is also "the Word of God." As Christ rises in the poor, Winstanley says, Christ can rise *as* the poor, in the body of society.

Let us return to the recurrent question: how does the language of Christ's Second Coming relate to Winstanley's belief that salvation is of the Jews? Winstanley's Christ was a prophet who reminded his people that their freedom depended not on burying the dead but on resurrecting insights that had been trod under foot. Hence Winstanley's language of resurrection emphasizes the role of memory, the recovery of what has been lost to consciousness and action, which yields the unprecedented. Specifically, he believes that the appearance of the poor in history and their legitimacy as actors are inextricably bound, just as Christ reminded Hebrews captive to Rome that Israel's initial appearance as a free people depended on being "a holy nation." Salvation is of the Jews because their historical experience linked freedom and righteousness and culminated in Christ's witness to their capacity to resurrect this insight.

Thus, Winstanley's vision of Christ rising is not a mystical flight from politics but a powerful account of the experiences from which social revolution arises and of the standards that make it legitimate. That Winstanley's poetry is not an alternative to the prose of politics, however, is only clear once the final reason that he believes salvation to be of the Jews has been considered. As the connection between freedom and righteousness takes the specific form of faithfulness to a covenant, so Winstanley's vision of digging is best understood as an effort to conceptualize the kind of covenant, or true religion, that will guide practical action and establish Canaan.

DIGGING

Winstanley's vision of digging reveals his rosy expectations for what appears as an agrarian theorist's unrealistic dream. But that vision has a sober political core—the idea of a covenant that will establish "the beginning of public freedom to the whole land" (439). Like Moses and Christ, Winstanley asks: what must humans choose to do if they are to become and be free? And like his models (and his Puritan enemies), he answers: establish the right relation to god. But what does this answer mean politically? The Hebrews could reach Canaan only because together they made a covenant to honor their god, which can be understood as consenting to live by the authority of certain truths, values, and commitments. The Bible teaches that the choice to live by this god, or this authority, turns slaves into a people of the covenant, and therefore free.

But why free? On the one hand, the premise here is that only a free being can choose to make and keep a covenant; thus, Winstanley's project, to paraphrase Nietzsche, is to breed a creature with the right to make promises. On the other hand, freedom also depends on the content of the promise, on what it is to which people bind themselves. The premise here, again based on the Bible, is that only by covenanting to specific values and commitments, to *their* god, can a people develop both the inner freedom of creatures capable of making and keeping promises and the outer freedom of creatures whose promises eliminate worldly bondage.

Following Christ, Winstanley would have the poor become capable of a covenant that "inwardly circumcises" so that they can live as "equal members of one household." By teaching them to embody righteousness directly, their covenant will enable them to meet their needs in a way that engenders their inner and worldly freedom. Having used the Bible to disclose the contradictions of his age, the earthly radicalism that diagnoses them, and the agent that resolves them, he now uses the Biblical idea of covenant to define the promises that resolution requires. At the same time, the diggers' covenant is intended to be a practical alternative to the market.

But what are the elements of this covenant, which will turn an enslaved people into diggers, and England into Canaan? Winstanley starts with necessity, poverty, and hunger: diggers promise to work together and eat together rather than work for another and try to live on wages. That is what god demanded in Winstanley's trance, but the logic behind this promise is rather obvious. All people require food, and therefore have a right to nourishment, but only by "freely laboring one with another" can all of them satisfy the need and enjoy the right. The covenant to work and eat together, however, takes the particular form of a promise to "manure the earth." Since idle land and the obstruction of landlords cause *unnecessary* starvation, diggers promise to cultivate "unnurtured" commons, church, and royal lands. By raising crops to keep cattle alive in the winter, and by using cattle to fertilize the land, the manuring of the earth not only feeds and empowers the poor but increases land utilization and yield.

Winstanley believes that by promising to manure the earth, diggers will bring other benefits to England. By improving its land, England "will be enriched with all commodities within itself" (349). Moreover, by increasing production and "pulling down the price of corn," digging will raise the real income of workers and prevent famine (414). In addition, because there will be food and work for all, rather than the hunger and dispossession fostered by enclosures, "within a short time, there will be no beggar and idle person in England" (414). As a result, all people will be secure from violent, masterless men, and these men no longer will be punished for a poverty that is not their fault. Indeed, "the whole land will be united in love and strength," and England will fulfill the Biblical promise of Canaan (414).[5]

Winstanley's intentions, however, are not merely ameliorative. By promising not "to give or take hire," the poor will challenge the emerg-

5. The alternatives to digging, says Winstanley, are unpalatable. Charity must be raised out of men's estates, "which is a hardship for many," and "the mass of money" so raised could "never supply the wants" of the poor. Further, many in poverty are "ashamed to take collection money and therefore they are desperate and will rather rob and steal and disturb the land." Those ashamed to beg, but unwilling to steal, "would do any work for hire" at any wages and consign themselves to Egyptian servitude (349).

ing market in labor and land, for there will be no one to work enclosed land or buy commodities with wages. "Some will say, This is My
Land. . . . Then said the Lord, Let such a one labor that parcel of land
by his own hands, none helping him" (195). As more people promise
to withhold their labor from landlords, "all the commons and waste
ground in England and in the whole world shall be taken in by the
people" (260). The diggers' promise to work and eat together will not
violate the title of landlords but will meet immediate needs, subvert the
market, preserve rural communities, and provide an alternative way to
modernize England. From the outset, then, the issue of hunger has
an ethical and political component for Winstanley (as it did for the
Hebrews).

But what will enable the poor to make and keep the promise to work
the earth as a common treasury? Does Winstanley presume the "inner
freedom" that enables people to share the earth? Winstanley is well
aware that many of the poor, despite traditions of mutual aid, are monarchical and deferential, desperate and isolated, impulsive and greedy.
In part, therefore, he believes that he must "wait on the rising of Christ
in the poor," as if to say that the diggers' covenant is a visible sign of a
grace already experienced. But he also believes that digging can be an
instrument in the process of Christ rising: by calling digging a true religion, he must mean that it is a conversion experience that works a profound transformation.

Winstanley's enthusiasm for digging is based, perhaps, on the Exodus story itself. Like the Hebrews, the poor at first might consent only
in an external sense to the principles of the digger community; but
Winstanley hopes that involvement in its practices will teach the self-
respect that he discovered introspectively and thereby generate collective power. As outward Jews become inwardly circumcised, they will remain committed to each other and the law of righteousness even if they
go hungry because of a bad crop or the harassment of local landlords.

Involvement in the community will inwardly circumcise, however,
only if people live without the forms and types of outward community.
In affirmative terms, diggers must promise to

> leave every man to stand and fall to his own master: if the power of covet-
> ousness be his master or king that rules in his heart, let him stand and fall to
> him; and if the power of love and righteousness . . . rule in his heart, let him
> stand and fall to him. (283)

By engaging in practices that treat everyone as "equals in creation, every
man being a perfect creation of himself" (159), poor people will over-

come their "slavish fear," which will make it less likely that outer teachers and rulers can emerge from their midst (269). Similarly, Winstanley believes that common work will teach the reality and value of sharing, even as discovering god's inward authority will make people more capable of sharing. Living with people who really do try to preserve each other, he hopes, will heal the wounds of mistrust and teach the truth of interdependence.[6]

Therefore, the diggers' covenant also creates freedom by requiring people to promise *not* to do certain things. Winstanley imagines that diggers will covenant with each other to reject outer teachers and rulers, and the sword and property they live by. But this means that diggers also must resist their own covetous impulses to idleness, violence, envy and theft. He is concerned that diggers will "lose the benefits of sonship" if they fall into covetousness and discord, and he is emphatic that diggers promise not to take already enclosed land, which would make them slaves of their resentment. If they become like Cain, they will have succumbed to the curse they should cast out. With this in mind, Winstanley says to the elder brothers:

> We shall meddle with none of your properties (but what is called common), til the spirit in you makes you cast up your lands and goods, which were got and still are kept in your hands by murder and theft. And then we shall take it from the spirit that hath conquered you, and not from our swords. (272)

Since the diggers must promise to abjure the sword, which signifies the pride of playing god, how does Winstanley address the problem of broken promises and the issue of punishment? Winstanley imagines

---

6. For reasons already discussed, Winstanley believes that manuring the earth is essential to these lessons and inner changes. Such labor acknowledges a person's connectedness to the earth and others and thereby counteracts the fantasies of unreal independence that lead the elder brothers to mastery and possession. A properly covenanted community, however, will be "the Lord of creation":

> The earth is the Lord's, that is, man's, who is the Lord of creation in every branch of mankind; for as diverse members of our human bodies make one body perfect, so every particular man is but a member or branch of mankind; and mankind living in the light of obedience to reason, the King of Righteousness, is thereby made a fit and complete Lord of the creation. And the whole earth is this Lord's, man, subject to spirit. (261)

Title to the mother earth is only legitimate if universal and shared; but also, just as the Father's power over the soul is legitimate because the Father truly feeds and frees it, so mankind's power over the earth is legitimate only if that power feeds and frees the earth (which in turn feeds and frees the bodies of men and women). Recognizing the earth as in some sense a subject in its own right, with its own needs and rights, is essential to establishing a legitimate relationship to it. With respect to nature as mother, the autonomy of the human species is premised on reciprocity with a source of nourishment that is a subject.

someone asking him, What if some of the diggers steal? If "everyone
shall have meat, drink, and clothes," he responds, "what need have they
to steal?" (198). Nonetheless, he suggests a form of punishment that
does not harm the body, jeopardize human equality, or violate the
promise to let each person "stand and fall to his own master."

"All punishments which are to be inflicted among creatures called
men," says Winstanley, "are only such as to make the offender know his
maker and live in the community of the righteous law of love, one with
another" (193). If a person engages in any act that violates their covenant, even the most serious, "whereby he begins to bring the curse again
upon creation, he shall not be imprisoned, hanged, or killed." Rather,

> he shall be made to work the earth . . . and none shall help him; he shall have
> a mark set upon him all the time so that everyone's eye may be upon him. He
> shall be a servant until such time as the spirit in him makes him know himself
> to be equal to others in creation. (197)

He shall be made a servant, since he is already a slave to covetousness; "none shall have communion with him" because he already
has broken the bond of mutual preservation. The punishment of solitary
labor perhaps is meant to make explicit the fact that the offender has
repudiated life with others by treating himself as an exception, acting
like Cain, as if he were alone in the world. Internal exile, however, also
is intended to teach that no one is "a lord over any, for all men looked at
in the bulk are but the creation, the living earth." Punishment, like
prophecy, is an effort to call people back to themselves, or to the Father
within them, by revealing to them the "reason" in the covenant they
violated. By enforcing solitary labor, other diggers act as responsible
peers—equals—who do not claim for themselves a power no human is
authorized to wield.

Whereas "utopian" political theorists create fictional communities in
order to work a perspective shift on their readers, Winstanley imagines
such a shift occurring in fact, on the commons, through new practices.
His vision surely suggests an agrarian theorist's pastoral dream, but
when put in the context of poverty and oppression, it also reflects a
powerful and sober effort to think through what it would require to
strengthen the poor. To fight poverty, the poor must fear it less as individuals; to fight "cursed propriety" and domination means having to
face hardship, austerity, and intimidation. To reach Canaan, the poor
must overcome deference, withstand the bribes and punishment of the
strong, and resist the temptation of private and resentful acts, like theft,
which leave the general condition of poverty unchanged. There are

easier ways to perish, and there are ways to survive that leave everything unchanged. Winstanley hopes that by covenanting to live together as diggers, the poor will strengthen themselves to face what they must, learning to wield "Christ's sword of love" while "filling our bellies with good actions of freedom" (471).

CONCLUSION

In *The New Law of Righteousness* Winstanley roots in history the political action by which the poor shall reclaim their earthly inheritance. He thereby provides an illuminating example of a feudal and religious tradition fostering a radical politics. In contrast to Michael Walzer's argument in *Revolution of the Saints,* Winstanley reveals that neither an abrupt rupture with the past nor an ascetic and fanatic ideology is essential to radicalism. Of course, one might follow Marx and associate Winstanley's language of "restoration" with the sentimental socialism of a William Morris, with the nostalgic and resentful wish to will backward. But it is clear that Winstanley is defending traditions still alive in his present, although under attack. More important, he obviously transforms the principles of traditional community into a forward-looking alternative that restores what is threatened, but in a changed form. Thus, he avoids both the sentimentality of later agrarian or pastoral radicals, who idealize the life they would restore, and the fanaticism of ascetic priests of revolution, who demonize the life they would destroy.

In affirmative terms, Winstanley visualizes an alternative to feudalism and emerging liberalism. Although his understanding of community, nature, and god owes a great deal to the experience and discourse of feudal culture, he subjects these givens to a more modern—that is, middle-class—sensibility. He defends the commons, but through a language of rights; he defends mutual aid, but through a language of equality. His project is to build a community that still sees itself as a household and nature as the common mother, and as a result, he preserves a sense of rightful and natural dependence. Yet he rejects aristocratic and peasant attachments to inequality, idleness, and deference. By synthesizing commitments to shared community and individual reason, he fashions an alternative to both the inequality of feudalism and what comes to be the "possessive individualism" of liberalism. Through shared labor, a commitment to reason, and an ethic based on love, his Canaan would weave together autonomous and equal individuals.

Winstanley creates a vision of radicalism that is systematic in its analysis of bondage and freedom, rooted in living traditions, democratic in its premises and practices, and libidinous in its understanding of work and community. In terms of his understanding that "salvation is of the Jews," his radicalism is the fruit of his reverence and the commitments it engenders. In modern terms, his reverence betokens a unique vision of modernization that empowers the poor by both honoring and transforming their traditions.

Now let us turn to what happens when Winstanley actually digs the earth, encounters brutal harassment, and takes a truer measure of the poor. As he moves from saint and digger to citizen, we can, along with him, grapple with the contradictions in his vision.

PART THREE

The Political Moment

In man creature and creator are united; in man there is
material, fragment, excess, dirt, nonsense, chaos; in man
there is also creator, form-giver, hammer hardness, spectator
divinity, and seventh day. . . . And your pity is for the
"creature in man," for what must be formed, broken, forged,
torn, burnt, made incandescent, and purified—that which
necessarily must and should suffer. And our pity—do you not
comprehend whom our converse pity is for when it resists
your pity as the worst of all pamperings and weaknesses?
                                                    —*Nietzsche*

Between October 1648 and January 1649, when Winstanley turned
toward the earth and social radicalism, the New Model Army had
captured the king and, in Pride's Purge, removed from Parliament those
monarchical and Presbyterian members unwilling to act decisively
against Charles. He was executed on January 26, four days after *The
New Law of Righteousness* appeared. In the next months the course of
the English Revolution was decided. Although the monarchy and the
House of Lords were abolished by Parliament in February, and a modi-
fied "Agreement of the People" was being discussed, Leveller and army
radicals nonetheless began to suspect that they had been deceived and
used by Cromwell and his supporters. As it became clear that parliamentary promises to consider land and electoral reform would not ma-
terialize, Levellers called for the appointment of agitators and the recall
of the General Council of the army, a demand that had led to the famed
Putney debates in the fall of 1647.

A Leveller pamphlet written early in the spring of 1649, *England's
New Chains,* expressed the view that a "new state tyranny" was in the
offing. In late March, Leveller leaders John Lilburne, Richard Overton,
and William Walwyn were imprisoned in the Tower. In early April, as
Winstanley began to dig, mutinies broke out when soldiers who refused
to be shipped to Ireland were demobilized without payment of arrears.

In support of them and the activists in the Tower, there was a major demonstration in London in late April. Early in May one mutineer was executed in a show of force and resolve, but even more serious mutinies occurred. The mutinous regiments were defeated decisively at Burford on May 14, and the army was professionalized into precisely the mercenary body that agitators at Putney had defined as the basis of tyranny. England was officially declared a republic on May 19, but silenced Leveller radicals knew it fell far short of the reformed liberal society they had hoped to achieve.

As Michael Walzer writes in *Exodus and Revolution,* "In the early years of the Puritan Revolution [people] thought that the moment of fulfillment had arrived."[1] But after the king had been executed and the mutinies suppressed, says Walzer, the English had come of age politically. In his reading, a revolution that began with New Testament promises of democracy, unanimity, and perfection was forced toward "tough-minded realism." Political actors accepted what Walzer calls the prosaic realities and carnal needs that must be addressed by any "this-worldly" or "exodus politics," which Walzer associates with the Old Testament.

Cromwell, like the chastened Moses after the incident of the golden calf, taught the English to accept the necessity of outer rulers and teachers (and thus of property and priests), the legitimacy of violence to enforce a covenant, and the inevitability of "better and worse" being the criteria by which to judge success and justice. Walzer uses Marx's contrast of heavenly and earthly to stand him on his head: Walzer condemns as Christian and otherworldly any effort to criticize or overcome the Jewish realities represented by Moses. Cromwell, like Moses, represents for Walzer the value of a radicalism that accepts earthly limitation.[2]

1. Michael Walzer, *Exodus Revolution* (New York: Basic Books, 1985), p. 112.
2. In *The Revolution of the Saints* (New York: Atheneum, 1968) Walzer links the millennial vision of the New Testament to the political vocation of Puritan saints, whose apocalyptic framework enabled them to remake themselves and the world. New Testament apocalypse fueled an Old Testament exodus, the practical achievement and exercise of power. Walzer links the Old and New testaments in order to cast the Puritans—and Leninists—as ascetic priests of revolution. In doing so, he appears to use the Puritans to defend Lenin against Rosa Luxemburg, and the Old Left against the New Left: ideological rigidity and political violence, he says, were and are unavoidable and essential for making the transition to modernity. In fact, however, Walzer demonizes radicalism by insisting that it must be fanatically ideological and violent. He is not defending Lenin but burying radicalism by conflating it with Leninism.
In *Exodus and Revolution* Walzer splits the Old and New testaments, divorcing radical visions from "the hard labor" of an earthly political vocation. Now those visions allow men to flee from the "carnal realities" attested to by "exodus" politics. Now he uses the

In the terms used by Christopher Hill, however, the rise of Cromwell is not the beginning of wisdom but the end of revolution. For Hill, the coalition against the Norman Yoke broke apart once the king was killed: the class nature of the revolution was exposed as "the better sort" regrouped around Cromwell to defend property and political rule by the propertied. Walzer, looking from above, counts as maturity what Hill, looking from below, depicts as repression and betrayal.

It is by way of Marx's account of the Revolution of 1848 in France that Hill almost directly draws his analysis, and it is against Marx that Walzer directs his argument. In Marx's analysis, the February revolt against Louis Philippe was a "beautiful revolution" because political "poetry" about liberty and equality disguised the reality of class contradictions and thereby mobilized artisans and workers to support the bourgeoisie. Since workers believed the "beautiful phrases," they ousted the king but also agitated for a "social republic." Their effort to fulfill the poetry of February, however, generated what Marx called the "ugly revolution," when the propertied turned against, and massacred, the workers.[3]

Puritans to defend Karl Kautsky against Lenin as well as Luxemburg and to defend the Democratic party in the United States against ideologues of the New Left and Old Left (and presumably of the Right as well). Still convinced of the association between radicalism and fanaticism, Walzer defends social democratic politics explicitly. That politics is now associated with the Old Testament, and demonized radicalism with the New Testament.

Walzer's argument in favor of social democracy and against radicalism as he caricatures it, or in favor of social democracy as the only "realistic" form political radicalism can take, is of interest not only to those tracking the course of "Jewish intellectuals" away from their political roots. For Walzer casts his argument in specifically "Jewish" terms in order to challenge Marx and his heirs. He contends that the millennial dreams associated with Marx are in fact "Christian" or New Testament dreams of an otherworldly heaven that devalues and perverts practical politics. Thus, Marx appears as a millennial Christian thinker: concocting apocalyptic historical dreams to evade troubling earthly realities, Marx is really an assimilated Jew, taken in by gentile Hegelianisms, an apostate following Revelation rather than the "better or worse" morality of Exodus. In his own version of "On the Jewish Question" Walzer unmasks as Christian Marx's radical dream of transforming bourgeois egoism, to which Walzer would reconcile the reader. As a result, Walzer's exodus politics amounts to a social democratic alternative to bourgeois Jewishness.

3. In "The Class Struggles in France" Marx says:

The February Revolution was the beautiful revolution, the revolution of universal sympathy, because the antagonisms which had flared up in it against the monarchy slumbered peacefully side by side, still undeveloped because the social struggle which formed its background had won only a joyous existence of phrases, words. The June Revolution is the ugly revolution, the repulsive revolution, because things have taken the place of phrases, because the republic uncovered the head of the monster itself, by striking off the crown that shielded and concealed it.

The monster was the social question, the class struggle. See Karl Marx, *Surveys from Exile: Political Writings*, ed. David Fernbach (New York: Vintage, 1974), vol. 2, p. 60.

For the leaders of the political revolution, the ugliness was the specter of social revolution; for the poor, the ugliness was the reality of class rule and repression, once disguised by beautiful political phrases. In the terms of "On the Jewish Question," Marx expected that the workers' defeat would discredit the poetry of a merely "political emancipation" and thereby generate a directly social revolution. Then, he declared, the real exodus will have begun: "The present generation is like the Jews, whom Moses led through the wilderness. They not only have a new world to conquer; they must perish in order to make room for the men who are equal to a new world." [4]

Thus, whereas Walzer argues that Cromwell's political maturity was shown when he gave up the dream of a holy nation and accepted earthly limitations, Hill follows Marx and argues that Cromwell had achieved political sobriety about the social limitations of his class. Walzer finds in the priests of Moses the birth of realism about political education, and in the sword and purges of Moses the birth of honesty about violence; Hill, again following Marx, takes the priests and purges as signs of the emergence of overt class rule.

Accordingly, differing views of what constitutes realism and maturity (and thus disillusionment and betrayal), elicited by the issue of what a true exodus entails, are at stake in how one reads the course of the English Revolution. These concerns became the center of Winstanley's attention as he began to dig and to face repression. His struggle with the elder brothers' sense of realism, and with his own, constituted a "political moment" that yielded significant innovations in his thought.

Like Walzer and Hill, Winstanley developed arguments about political realism and maturity, using the concept of a genuine exodus to criticize the elder brothers and defend digging. Like Walzer, he professed to recover an Old Testament politics, but for him this did not mean reducing revolution to reform. Rather, his synthesis of the Old and New testaments generated an earthly radicalism committed to the real interests of the poor. Like Hill and Marx, then, Winstanley exposed and criticized the limitations of the propertied class leading a merely political reformation, but he did so *because* he was serious about Biblical language and the meaning of exodus. He did not reduce political speech to a merely poetic illusion. As a result, Winstanley developed a rare kind of *political* radicalism, which politicized both the poetry of redemption and the earthly interests of the poor. But the specific context for his political moment was the digging experiment itself.

4. Ibid., p. 112.

Winstanley and four others began to dig on St. George's Hill on April 1, 1649, before the repression of the Levellers and the mutinous regiments. In this context, his millennial hopes perhaps appear understandable. Unlike Marx, he believed the promises of liberty and righteousness made by those leading the reformation: he knew their interests currently diverged from his, but he believed that Christ rising would lead everyone to be "of one heart and mind" (124). Thus, he urged his readers:

> Seriously in love and humility consider this business of public community which I am carried forth . . . to advance as much as I can. And I can do no other, the law of love in my heart does so constrain me. . . . I hate none, I love all, I delight to see everyone live comfortably. . . . Therefore, if you find any selfishness in this work or discover anything that is destructive to the whole creation . . . , open your hearts as freely to me in declaring my weakness to me, as I have been open hearted in declaring that which I find and feel much life and strength in. (291)

Winstanley wrote these words, and the pamphlets of the next year, while living in a hut on "waste land," suffering hunger and "manuring the earth," convinced that he was contributing to a significant historical change:

> And the truth is, experience shows us, that in this work of Community in the earth and in the fruits of the earth, is seen plainly a pitched battle between the Lamb and Dragon, between the Spirit of love . . . which is the lamb appearing in the flesh, and the power of envy, pride, and unrighteousness which is the dragon appearing in the flesh. And these two powers strive in the heart of every single man, and make single men strive in opposition one against another. (281)

As he would say much later, "this difference between lords of manors and the poor about the common land is the greatest controversy that hath rise up this last 600 years" (420).

Although Winstanley could not use terms like capitalism and socialism, or borrow from the social sciences the ostensibly neutral language of "modernization," he was aware that whether the poor retain or regain access to common lands was the crucial issue on which hinged England's exodus or path of development. Contrary to Walzer again, the contrast is not between the heaven of dreams and the earthly politics represented by Cromwell but between the earthly realities represented by the poor and those represented by Cromwell, and between the contrasting political languages by which those realities were articulated.

Winstanley's own sense of significance, however, was not shared by observers, who appeared not to take diggers seriously. Toward the end of April, when the number of diggers had increased to fifty, one commentator remarked:

> The new-fangled people that begin to dig on St. George's Hill in Surrey say they are like Adam, they expect a general restoration of the earth to its first condition, that they themselves were called to seek and begin this great work which will shortly go on throughout the whole earth. . . . They profess a great deal of mildness and would have the world believe they have dreamed dreams, seen visions, heard voices, and have dictates beyond man's knowing. They profess they will not fight, knowing that not to be good for them.

But there was an underside of fear in the barely veiled cynicism:

> What this fanatical insurrection may grow into cannot be conceived, for Mahomet had as small and despicable a beginning, whose damnable infections have spread themselves many hundreds of years since over the face of half the Universe.[5]

Correspondingly, local property owners were scornful but scared. They called on the Council of State to intervene militarily. The officer sent to investigate by General Fairfax reported that the landlords were being unduly alarmist, but Winstanley and another digger named Everard nevertheless were brought before Fairfax for an interview on April 20. On that same day, a week before the demonstration in London, Winstanley's *The True Levellers Standard* appeared. In this, his first pamphlet since digging began, he claimed that "the old world . . . is running up like parchment in the fire" (252) but he also objected that "you who are the powers of England" only "pretend to throw down that Norman Yoke," while in fact "[you] lift up . . . slavish tyranny" and "hold the people as much in bondage as the Bastard Conqueror himself" (259).

Fairfax refused to intervene in what he considered a local affair without significance, but local property owners forced or bribed their tenants to raid the diggers repeatedly, each time destroying crops and huts and beating people (including a pregnant woman who miscarried as a result). Because the colony continued to grow, in late July landlords went to court, bringing an action for trespassing against the diggers. When diggers refused to plead through a lawyer, they were condemned unheard. Since they had no assets to pay the fines imposed by the court, several were jailed, and bailiffs attempted to confiscate the cows Win-

5. David Petergorsky, *Left-Wing Democracy*, pp. 165–66.

stanley was tending for someone else. A Keystone Cops episode of cow chasing ensued; but though comical to read about, the cows were beaten, and they became for Winstanley a symbol of the elder brother's treatment of the earth, the poor, and himself.

In September the colony moved from St. George's Hill to nearby Cobham Heath, presumably in the hope of being left alone. But Francis Drake (lord of the manor at St. George's Hill and a member of Parliament purged by Colonel Pride) joined forces with Parson Platt (lord of the manor at Cobham and a local minister) to continue the harassment and begin as well a local boycott. In December 1649 Fairfax finally was pressured by Drake and Platt to call in his troops, and although by and large they did not intervene physically, their presence emboldened the locals, who destroyed houses, corn, and tools and beat cows and diggers. Since other digger colonies appeared that winter, however, Winstanley found reasons for hope. Unbelievably, by April 1650 the colony at Cobham could boast of eleven acres planted, six or seven houses built, and the beginnings of a national digger network. But in late April the colony was destroyed, finally and irrevocably.

The next three chapters explore how these circumstances politicized but also tested Winstanley's reverence. That reverence had now caused Winstanley to adopt the perspective and activities of the citizen. His synthesis of the Old and New testaments enabled him to address human needs and unmask ideology while speaking of rights, justice, and freedom. As he focused on a specifically national context in which people disagree about political institutions, political concepts, and how to get to Canaan, he came to grant the legitimacy of conflicting interpretations and interests. Thus, he developed a politics of dialogue that included a legitimate role for representative government and the exercise of state power. Having developed a psychological alternative to covetous individualism, and a social alternative to the market, he now created a political alternative to the covenant and reformation of Puritans and Levellers.

In part, however, Winstanley's reverence undermined the politicization it sponsored because it kept him bound to the purity of inward religiosity declared by Jeremiah:

> Behold, the days come, saith the Lord, that I will make a new covenant with the house of Israel. . . . Not according to the covenant I made with their fa-

thers in the day that I took them by the hand to bring them out of the land of
Egypt, which my covenant they brake. . . . [But] I will put my law in their
inward parts, and write it in their hearts. . . . And . . . they shall all know
me, from the least of them unto the greatest of them. (Jeremiah 31:31–34)

Marx's criticism of Luther therefore applies to Winstanley: "He liberated man from external religiosity by making religiosity the innermost
essence of man. He liberated the body from its chains because he fet-
tered the heart with chains" (60). Since the god who becomes the essence of man (presumably as the conscience) still robs man of his power
of invention and alienates him from something in himself (like anger),
Marx takes his version of "the Jewish Question" to its final conclusion,
which "is a matter of confession, no more. To have its sins forgiven,
mankind has only to declare them to be what they really are" (15).

In contrast, Winstanley still attached a stigma to human imagination,
anger, and power. His denial of man as creator, however routine for a
religious thinker, was the basis of a republican politics in which created
beings become citizens acting within horizons beyond human invention.
But he therefore entered the agon of politics in the belief that sons and
daughters would not be tainted by the prideful transgressions it required. Unwilling to grant the pride in his own politics, "to confess his
sins to be what they are," he felt increasingly implicated in "the curse of
pride" he meant to heal. In the context of his persecution by the elder
brothers, his guilt drew him toward a cross that was partly of his own
making. The narrative of Christ rising embodied a dream of purity that
contradicted the citizen politics it fostered but also cast the shadow
of crucifixion over the dream and the politics. Even as Winstanley
was pressed toward self-sacrifice, however, he began, as Marx put it,
"to struggle against his own internal priest, against his own priestly nature" (60).

CHAPTER V

Speaking Truth to Power

When great Men disagree
About Supremacy,
Then do they warn poor men
To aid and assist them
In setting up their self-will power,
And thus they do the poor devour.
            —*from the diggers' Christmas Carol*

"But 'glory' doesn't mean 'a nice knock-down argument,'"
Alice objected. "When I use a word," Humpty Dumpty said,
in a rather scornful tone, "it means just what I choose it to
mean—neither more nor less." "The question is," said Alice,
"whether you *can* make words mean so many different
things." "The question is," said Humpty Dumpty, "which is
to be master—that's all."
                        —*Lewis Carroll*

This chapter analyzes how the reversals of the spring and summer of
1649 lead Winstanley to a new understanding of political language and
of the state as a potentially legitimate institution. Learning to act as a
citizen, and not only as a saint who is a spokesman for the poor, he
comes to describe England's reformation as a political process of creating a "public community" and "public freedom." In *True Levellers
Standard, A Watchword to the City of London and the Army,* and *A
New Years Gift* Winstanley uses already formulated arguments about
class and inner covetousness to explain why elder brothers turn against
the poor, but for the first time he analyzes the meaning of the political
principles by which the Revolution was justified. By clarifying key concepts, he criticizes the betrayal of revolutionary promises, justifies digging, and proposes the actions that would make Parliament legitimate.
Winstanley's arguments reflect his newfound sense that the social body
requires the political form of a representative assembly. He does not em-

brace, but begins to work toward, the idea of a public community that takes account of conflicting social interests through public-spirited debate about principles.

WHAT IS HAPPENING TO THE REFORMATION?

Winstanley says that in the early 1640s elder brothers "complained of oppression . . . because their lands, inclosures, copyholds were intangled, and because their trades were destroyed by monopolizing patents. Thereupon, you that were the gentry when you assembled in Parliament called upon the common people to come and help you cast out oppression" (357). The common people knew the gentry "were summoned by the king's writ and chosen by the freeholders that were the successors of William the Conqueror's soldiers" (304). Nonetheless, "we looked upon you to be our chief counsel" because we too "groaned under the burden of the bad government . . . of the late King Charles" and because "you promised, in the name of the Almighty, to make us a free people" (304). Therefore, "we of the commonality" answered your call "to deliver this distressed, bleeding, dying nation out of bondage." A war began "between the king that represented William the Conqueror, and the body of the people that were enslaved" (303).

From his vantage point in the spring of 1649, however, Winstanley believes "you that complained were helped and freed" because "the top bow is lopped off the tree of tyranny, and kingly power in that particular is cast out" (357). But the poor are no better off: "Alas, oppression is a great tree still, and keeps the sun of freedom from the poor commons still." We remain in the shadow of "the horrible cheating that is in buying and selling," the "power of tithing priests over the tenths of our labor," "the power of lords of manors holding the free use of the commons and waste lands from the poor," and "the intolerable oppression either of bad laws or of bad judges corrupting good laws" (357). Unless these "branches" also are "lopped off," and the "great roots" of covetousness "grubbed up," the poor will not enjoy freedom; indeed, "the great spread tree of kingly power" will "grow again and recover fresh strength."

The problem is not simply a matter of omission, of not carrying reformation far enough. By the summer Winstanley openly declares that the elder brothers never intended to uproot the tree of tyranny: the problem is not only their ignorance of what needs to be done but also their conscious intentions. Charles is gone, "yet his Colonels" (the lords of manors), "his counsellors and divines" (the lawyers and priests), and "his inferior officers and soldiers" (the freeholders and landlords) "are all striving to get into a body again that they may set up a new Norman Slavery over us" (330). Thus, the Civil War appears as a conflict among Norman descendants who never intended to lift the Norman Yoke: in the spring and summer of 1649 they regroup to consolidate and protect the power their fratricidal conflict had shaken temporarily.

Although the metaphor of the tree evokes root and branch social change, Winstanley relies on more direct bodily metaphors to describe the reimposition of the Norman Yoke. For the elder brothers form themselves into a new "body," located in Parliament and imposed on the "body" of the people (304, 330). Indeed, Winstanley invokes the classic monarchical metaphor of the people as a horse ridden by the king: the elder brothers "get the foot fast in the stirrup . . . to lift themselves up again into the Norman saddle." Winstanley fears that "you had killed him that rode on you that you may get up into his saddle to ride on others" (335). New tyrants with particular interests and oppressive intent use republican terms like liberty to disguise their designs. "Thou blindfolded, drowsy England," Winstanley warns, "the Enemy is upon thy back . . . and wilt thou not look out?" (335).

WHY THIS IS HAPPENING: INTENTIONS, MOTIVES, AND MEANINGS

Winstanley senses that there is a terrible disparity between what the elder brothers say and what they do (and fail to do). Initially, he argues that the Revolution's leaders are deceived both about the meaning of their words and about what they are doing. They genuinely, but mistakenly, believe that their actions fulfill the promise of freedom. They genuinely believe "it a righteous thing that some men are clothed with the objects of the earth, and so-called rich men . . . should be magistrates to rule over the poor, and that the poor should be servants, nay slaves, to the rich" (179).

A selfishness that denies the Golden Rule is only part of the problem, and it bothers Winstanley less than the fact that the elder brother is self-righteous and cannot conceive that there is a difference between what he calls god or justice and what is truly of the spirit and for the public good. True righteousness, however, requires making judgments about the difference between what one desires and what one calls good, and thus requires humility in the face of our capacity for selfishness and rationalization, for confusion and delusion. But the elder brother "cherishes himself within: he thinks whatever he doth is good and whatever crosses that power in his heart doth cross the Lord" (227). He calls his selfish rule righteous and means it.

Yet Winstanley knows that the elder brothers are not wholly deluded, and thus he holds them responsible for what they say and do. He sees, for example, that what elder brothers "call sin in the common people," such as the appropriation of the earth, "is counted no sin in the action of them that maintain the kingdom" (324). He and they agree that theft is bad, that righteousness involves giving each his due, and that freedom requires access to the earth. They have linked the criterion of giving each his due to ideas of political and economic self-determination, but they do not see that their own control of the earth, which deprives the poor of land, is unrighteous according to their own criteria.

Accordingly, Winstanley tries to teach the elder brothers about the words they use seriously but mistakenly. He turns the criteria they profess against their interpretations of their own concepts and actions. Given their self-righteousness, however, he also tries to reveal the covetousness unconsciously ruling them. While arguing with them "like men, that can speak and act rationally" (282), he also must expose them as "devils" who "would be angels of light" (171). Using himself as an example, Winstanley says:

> If I delight in any way of flesh, as to seek peace in creatures abroad . . . [and] I do hear the words of experience from some others, declaring such actions to be the powers of the flesh, . . . Presently, those words take peace . . . from proud flesh and fill the whole soul with anger . . . and torment. And this is another operation which *pure language* produces, which is a lancing of the dead flesh that the disease may be cured. For this wounding . . . is medicine to heal him. (234)

If they could admit their real motivations—and face their shame—they would relinquish the fig leaves of ideological speech, understand the true meaning of their words, and act differently.

Winstanley also comes to believe that elder brothers consciously engage in "Machiavellian cheats":

> Every man is ready to say they fight for the country, and what they do, they do for the good of the country. . . . But if, when they have the power to settle freedom, they takest [*sic*] possession of the earth into their own particular hands and makest their brothers work for them . . . they have fought and acted for themselves, not for their country. Here their hypocrisy is discov-

ered. . . . Common Freedom, which is the rule I would have practiced and not talked on, was the pretense, but particular freedom to themselves was their intent. (516)

According to this interpretation, the elder brothers *intend* to oppress the poor and know this is not righteous, but they also know they can succeed in their design only by promising freedom. They are not blind and self-righteous blowhards but cynics. Winstanley therefore holds them responsible in a more direct way and considers their sin less excusable.

Even here, however, Winstanley asks why the Revolution's leaders feel compelled to violate norms they understand. They believe that gaining earthly nourishment requires the oppression of others, even though they know that is not just. In a world ruled by covetousness they come to believe that there is only domination or submission, so they strive to be masters rather than slaves. Thus, they knowingly use language to mobilize support for the selfish aims they disguise. They understand that title to the earth is essential to the freedom of anyone, but are "afraid and ashamed to own" this insight "because it comes clothed in a clownish garment" (316). Ashamed that others would call them foolish idealists, and fearful that such a freedom for all would leave them vulnerable to domination, they choose to engage in "cheats."

In this interpretation, covetousness blinds the elder brothers, not to the meaning of words, but to the possibility of enacting them in a way that gains what they deserve without sacrificing others. The pedagogical problem for Winstanley, then, is to persuade them to understand their interest and identity differently so that they no longer scorn the idea of mutuality. That task requires unmasking their cynicism to expose the fear "that if they love and succor others, yet others will not love them." Only then will they admit their need and learn to address their fear.

Winstanley's two accounts suggest both that rulers are deceived about the actions their claims really entail and that rulers understand concepts but feel compelled to violate them. Winstanley speaks not to two audiences, however, but rather to one audience he understands in two different ways. He is not being incoherent but responding precisely to real tensions in Puritan politics.

In *The Machiavellian Moment* J. G. A. Pocock argues that Puritans manifest the tensions among vocabularies of custom, grace, and republican liberty, each of which addresses earthly interests in a principled and open way. He insists that within each vocabulary there is no tension between claims to freedom and arguments about property, a claim that precludes the assertion that the Puritans were deceptive, or deceived,

about the relationship between their words and their interests. By recovering the real intentions of actors and the meaning they ascribed to
their words, Pocock opposes those theorists, like Hobbes and Marx,
who reduce complexities of speech and action to the ideological reflection of either individual appetite and self-interest or simple bourgeois
class interest. Pocock thereby subverts, indeed, buries, the idea that political language is *ideological,* in the sense of mystifying or hiding underlying social interests, as if the alternative to reductionism is taking the
elder brothers literally at their word.

Winstanley uses the vocabularies of grace, custom, and liberty, but he
attends to the tension between the universalist language of saint and
citizen and limited social interests. He is sensitive to a disparity between
claims and acts that Pocock seems to deny and attests to a contradiction
between social interests and political language that Pocock obscures. As
a result, Winstanley explains what Pocock ignores—a contemporary
skepticism about the intentions and "hypocrisy" of Puritans so widespread as to include monarchists, Levellers, and, perhaps most fa-
mously, Hobbes. In contrast to Hobbes and Marx, however, Winstanley
does not use such disparities to reject the political discourse of his time
but criticizes ideology without devaluing speech. Yet he is vulnerable to
Hobbes's argument about the conventionality of language and to Marx's
argument about unresolvable class conflict. Contrasting Winstanley
first with Hobbes and then with Marx will reveal what is fruitful in
Winstanley's politics of dialogue as well as the tensions at the heart of
political engagement itself.

TAKING SPEECH SERIOUSLY: WINSTANLEY
AND HOBBES

Like Pocock and Winstanley, Hobbes roots the English Civil War in
interpretative conflict about political concepts derived from religion,
political tradition, and republicanism. Hobbes argues that these vocabularies undermine political authority and preclude its reconstitution.
Indeed, he believes that making *judgments* (about words like justice and
freedom) is the emblem of rebellion and invariably causes an anarchy of
proliferating interpretations, a state of war, for which political language
itself provides no resolution.

It is not surprising, then, that Hobbes uses the Garden of Eden story
to depict the reformers as Adam, to equate sin with the political judgment
of authority, to associate politically explosive concepts with the fatal

apple, and sovereign power with god. God's reproof to Adam and Eve, he says, "clearly though allegorically signifieth that the commands of them that have the right to command are not by his subjects to be censured or disputed" (L/157). Since it is a short and virtually foreordained step from judgment of rulers to regicide, Hobbes's god asks Adam, "Who told thee that he was a tyrant? Hast thou eaten of the tree . . . ? For why dost thou call him a tyrant . . . except that thou, being a private man, usurpest to thyself the knowledge of good and evil?" (DC/245).

Hobbes therefore discredits the available languages of political judgment as well as the motives of political actors; but he also constructs a mortal god that rules a garden in which words no longer are apples tempting Adam to rebel. By redefining justice and covenant, freedom and magistracy, he creates a vocabulary designed to defend authority. Once justice is redefined narrowly as the keeping of covenants, covenanted authority cannot be called unjust, and it is the rebel who becomes unjust by definition. Once freedom is redefined to mean what the law permits, no one can assert that authority deprives people of their liberty. If magistracy is redefined as any power that provides protection, no one can complain of tyranny as long as they are likely to continue living.[1]

Winstanley agrees with Hobbes that the English are in a wilderness condition because of what Winstanley calls "the particular and confining ways" in which they define political interests and concepts. Hobbes says this is the bitter political fruit of the natural temptation to judge rulers by necessarily self-serving opinion. In contrast, Winstanley maintains that the English have failed to exercise properly the "justice and judgment" by which they must endeavor righteousness. Attacking as a Norman Yoke the emerging state power that Hobbes tries to strengthen and legitimize, Winstanley finds in political language itself the grounds for *shared* judgments, the criteria for a public or political response to England's situation.

To Winstanley, for example, the concept *magistracy* involves criteria by which to judge whether speech and action violate or honor its mean-

---

1. To Hobbes, judgment about human art is analogous to Adam and Eve's judgment about god's art because judgment is "the most ancient and diabolical of temptations" (DC/245). To judge is to "pry into" what is given by god or the mortal god and "transgress the bounds god hath set us and gaze upon him irreverently" (L/344). Hobbes worries that gazing irreverently on human art will strip us down to god's art, our nakedness, which he fears. Winstanley reveres the nakedness that is god's art in a way that Hobbes cannot and does not, and therefore he wants to strip away the veils of culture. Notice, however, that both attack "irreverence."

ing. "Magistracy," he says, "is a good name, and the mystery of iniquity hath not only got this but other excellent names . . . that under the cover of a good name, he may go undiscovered; and he puts bad names on things that are good" (472). If rulers divide the earth and mankind, acting in "particular and confining ways," then they are tyrants who do not warrant the name of magistracy, which involves criteria of trusteeship and universality of benefit. If rulers call themselves magistrates, then they either are deceived or are using the word as a "cover" to disguise their true intent and real interests.

Accordingly, Winstanley engages in a process of shaming: "The babes and sucklings will draw off his veil and show all his nakedness and shame him" (473). By assimilating language to innocent nature, or childhood, and opposing it to the veils of a corrupt culture, he suggests the authenticity of the child's speech. His commonsense or naively literal approach to the meaning of words exposes the nakedness of those who use words deceptively. Thus, their shame is an admission that they have violated standards they themselves embrace, and not only invoke. Those standards indicate how they could be clothed in righteousness: one need not abandon political speech or human judgment in order to find a common ground for peace; political speech provides the standards for justifiable criticism and for a new order.

Winstanley's image of the child shaming—and teaching—authority, however, also suggests precisely the indignant self-righteousness or innocent certainty that Hobbes fears. By associating his words with "babes and sucklings," Winstanley dissimulates his own adult act of interpretation, suggesting that the meaning of words is natural or god-given, fixed or virtually innate, rather than conventional, ambiguous, and learned. How, then, does Winstanley justify his claim that he has the right understanding of words and the actions they entail?

Winstanley repeatedly reminds his readers of key parliamentary declarations. The first was the Solemn League and Covenant, adopted in September 1643, which promised to endeavor a "real reformation" for the sake of liberty. The second was the proclamation of February 1649, which asserted "that it had been found by experience . . . that the Office of King in this Nation . . . is unnecessary, burdensome, and dangerous to the liberty, safety, and public interest of the people of this nation and ought to be abolished." The third was the act of May 1649, which declared England a "Free Commonwealth" to be governed by "representatives of the people in Parliament . . . without any King or House of Lords." From these declarations Winstanley draws his key concepts: the *covenant* (sworn by each person with every other person and with god) to *endeavor a reformation* that brings *freedom* to all by making England a *commonwealth.*

Winstanley asks two sets of questions. First, what is the meaning of these words? (Do people use the concepts correctly?) Secondly, what actions do the words require? (Do people act according to the meaning of their words?) By grappling with these questions, Winstanley justifies his contention that there is a profound disparity between what the elder brothers say and what they do. He thereby can show how the meanings of their own words justify digging and require them to act differently.

According to Winstanley, the liberty that the English have covenanted to seek "lies where a man receives nourishment," and thus he says that freedom "lies herein principally, to have the land of their nativity for their livelihood" (287). How does he justify this assertion? First, "natural experience," especially in the Civil War, reveals that "all men seek the earth" because "they see their freedom lies in plenty and their bondage in poverty" (520). Secondly, he looks at their use of the word *free.* For example, the elder brothers taught him that a servant or hireling is not free (and therefore not entitled to political rights) because being free requires that one not work for wages, not depend on another for a livelihood, and not be subjected to another's will (428).

On precisely these grounds the rebels had maintained that the king violated the public good and enslaved the people: he controlled their livelihood and deprived them of the right to speak and act politically. For the rebels, freedom links nourishment and self-determination and is constituted politically in terms of rights. By their own criteria, then, the elder brothers are justified in associating property with freedom, but Winstanley also is justified in calling the ownership of property a "half freedom" (519) since it gives some their birthright to the earth at the cost of others' being made "unfree."[2]

2. Christopher Hill argues that in the common usage of the time, all wage laborers were by definition unfree:

> Even the Levellers, the most radical of all seventeenth-century political groupings, would have excluded paupers and servants (i.e., wage laborers) from the franchise, because they were unfree. The leveller franchise would have been restricted to "freeborn Englishmen." Wage-laborers and paupers had lost their birthright because they had become economically dependent on others; they had lost their property in their own persons and labor. . . . There is plenty of confirmatory evidence for Professor Macpherson's argument that in the sixteenth and seventeenth century those in receipt of wages were regarded as unfree. ("Pottage for Freeborn Englishmen: Attitudes to Wage Labor," in *Change and Continuity in 17th Century England* [Cambridge: Harvard University Press, 1975], pp. 223–24)

As this analysis suggests, the third way Winstanley justifies his argument about freedom is through the idea of righteousness, which he associates with the Golden Rule and with the principle of giving and receiving our due (according to our nature and necessity as creatures). Winstanley says the elder brothers should ask, would I want to be hedged out of the earth and forced to be a hireling? They also should ask, what are the benefits of creation, and what is required for all people to enjoy them? These two perspectives comprise the "True Leveller's Standard," which excludes or excepts no one, brings real benefits to all, and honors the lessons of usage and experience. According to this standard, Winstanley says, "if the reformation be according to the Word of God," the poor must have a right to consent actively to their government, as some of the Levellers maintained; but also the English must grant that "the poorest he hath as true a title and just a right to the land as the richest man" (321).

Because the concept of freedom is deeply implicated with needs and power and with ideas of membership and entitlement, it is the flip side of Winstanley's idea of justice. For him, justice or righteousness is a regulative idea of equity that distributes access to, and control of, nourishment, whereas freedom is gaining that nourishment in the right sort of way. Thus, in Winstanley's understanding, Parliament's promise to "make England a free people" and the declaration that England is a "commonwealth" are logically related. Winstanley follows the strongest and most literal sense of the word *commonwealth:* "to warrant the name of commonwealth," he says, Parliament must make the land a "common treasury to all her children" (323). But he also invokes a more flexible and strategic sense of the word: "Unless we that are poor commoners have some part of the land to live upon freely, as well as the gentry, [then] it cannot be a commonwealth" (348).

Because he has built on, but also transformed, the elder brothers' understanding of freedom, Winstanley speaks of learning:

> Is our 8 years war come round about to lay us down again in the kennel of injustice as much or more than before? Are we no further learned yet? O ye rulers of England . . . Will you always hold us in one Lesson? Surely you will make dunces of us; then all the boys in other lands will laugh at us: Come, I pray let us . . . go forward in our learning. (361)

There are, however, two senses of learning he has in mind. In the first, one learns about freedom by reasoning about one's own uses of a word and its regulating criteria, by attending honestly to one's experience,

and by examining that to which England has covenanted. This sense of
learning suggests the conventionality of Winstanley's interpretations
and points to the inductive process by which he arrived at them. Indeed,
he comes increasingly to rely on people's ability to "speak like men, rationally," about the "reason and equity" of their standards and practices (287).

In a second sense, however, learning originates with god. By declaring that god is initially the author of his ideas, he does not mean to deny
that he is working within the ordinary usage of words, for he insists on
taking that seriously. Partly, he is accounting for the transforming perspective that *preceded* his reevaluation of concepts and practices. As he
rhymes, a year after digging:

> Freedom is the mark at which all men should aim
> But what true freedom is, few men doth know by name.
> But now a light is rise and nere shall fall
> How every man by name shall freedom call. (ESU/9)

Only through the light within, he believes, is he able to criticize the particular interpretations and practices others accept as natural. In this
way, he escapes the trap of either believing in the elder brothers' justice
or believing that there is no such thing as justice, in the same way as he
once escaped the trap of either believing in their god or believing there is
no god.

However, Winstanley also invokes god in order to assert that his interpretation of freedom is the only right one. Apparently, to have shown
how his interpretation is better is not sufficient, especially since his
understanding of *better* breaks with received wisdom. It is as if his continuing sense that his legitimacy depends on reverence for god, for an
authority he has not invented, is extended to include reverence for language as an authority we also do not invent: god's truth is the meaning
that inheres to words, which he has distinguished from the meanings we
imagine.

Winstanley's reverence for the spoken word and its meaning, once
expressed as the idea of bearing witness, now appears in the liberty of a
citizen, who speaks to clarify the covenant and acts to affirm it. In Biblical terms, covenanting gives rise to the vocation of prophecy: the
prophet is a citizen who testifies to the meaning of promises and, thus,
to the disparity between what people have promised and their practices.
In this way, Winstanley links his scriptural project to the republican
project of citizenship, which distinguishes between what is public,

shared, and virtuous and what is private, exclusive, and corrupt. In contrast to Hobbes, then, Winstanley draws on a history of concepts and commitments, usage and criteria, in an effort to suggest the shared (and god-given) meanings that could provide a just peace.

Addressing the elder brothers in this way, however, does not answer Hobbes's most troubling insight. Hobbes turns to the state and relies on the technical device of redefining concepts, in part because he believes that history, common discourse, and political dialogue do not provide a common ground that could end the Civil War. Indeed, it appears that the Civil War and the dispossession of the poor testify to fundamental, perhaps irreconcilable, conflicts about precisely the norms that Winstanley's dialogic politics must presume are shared.

It seems that Winstanley's belief in a truth beyond human invention, his seriousness about speech, and his desire for political engagement require him to believe that the elder brothers could and will listen to him—and even change—though he himself has analyzed the covetousness and interests that make this outcome unlikely. To explore this contradiction further, however, one must contrast Winstanley with Marx.

TAKING SPEECH SERIOUSLY: WINSTANLEY AND MARX

In Pocock's terms, Hobbes replaces the language of conscience, political tradition, and republican virtue with the liberal language of appetite, interest, and rationality. Treating the latter as a scientific solution to the problems created by the former, Hobbes moves beyond Puritanism. Marx uses a theory of history, class struggle, and ideology to discuss the contradiction between political "poetry" of the saintly citizen and his prosaic interests as a member of an emerging bourgeois class. In this way, Marx moves not only beyond the poetry of Puritanism but also beyond the prose of Hobbes and liberalism.

In his famous introduction to *The Eighteenth Brumaire of Louis Bonaparte* Marx grants that middle-class revolutionaries believed their words (for a time) but insists that words function only as tools of self-deception, disguise, and mobilization. In "the stern classical tradition of the Roman republic," or in "the language, passions, and illusions of the Old Testament," revolutionaries in France and England found "the ideals, art forms, and self-deceptions they needed in order to hide from themselves the limited bourgeois content of their struggles and to maintain their enthusiasm at the high level appropriate to great historical tragedy." In describing how bourgeois revolutionaries "resurrect the dead," Marx uses a rarely noted metaphor:

> In the same way, the beginner who has learned a new language always re-translates it into his mother tongue: he can only be said to have appropriated the spirit of the new language and to be able to express himself in it freely, when he can manipulate it without reference to the old, and when he forgets his original language while using the new one.

He goes on to say that "bourgeois society in its sober reality created its own true interpreters," who followed the prescient Hobbes, in effect separating from the past and speaking a prose appropriate to the new world they had created.[3]

Accordingly, Marx himself does not take the "mother tongue" to be meaningful, and just as he expects the bourgeoisie to speak the sober prose of class interest, so too he expects the proletariat to speak a prose appropriate to its own class interests. Diverging forms of prose will yield no common political ground or culture, which appears only through mystified poetry. The point here is not to make the argument that Winstanley was a revolutionary who "timidly conjures up the spir-its of the past to help" him make a new world. Rather, Marx's theory implies that Winstanley could not establish the right perspective on the elder brothers' language, and therefore his own, because he lacked a theory of history and class struggle. Moreover, as long as there is a propertied class, one infers from Marx, no kind of dialogue can lead rulers to interpret political phrases in a way that genuinely includes all people.

Even though Marx is manifestly animated by a sense of injustice, and thus by a sense of the meaning of the word *justice,* he only considers such concepts as poetry to be read in terms of ideological function. The way he exposes the social content *behind* words leads him to deny, in effect, that there could be a meaning or content *in* words. At most, he imagines a class whose universal interest guarantees that each will re-ceive his or her due. That is, his rage at injustice appears as the claim that there is no real justice but only succeeding (and increasingly univer-sal) forms of class rule.

While Marx wraps his argument about ideology in the mantle of a historical science of class struggle, Winstanley wears a sense of betrayal on his sleeve. As the "younger brother," Winstanley continues to take

---

3. *Surveys from Exile: Marx's Political Writings,* ed. David Fernbach (New York: Random House, 1973), 2:147–49.

seriously the concepts the elder brothers taught but now violate. Indeed, Winstanley's discovery of his own critical voice has depended not on rejecting the mother tongue but on making it his own, transforming it in a way he can own. Moreover, the poetry of saint and citizen provides him, as that poetry in fact provides Marx, with the criteria by which to criticize a revolution with limited "social content." Because Winstanley does not deny his debt to the mother tongue, however, he exposes ideology in the name of disclosing the meaningfulness of speech. Therefore, he is concerned not just with the poor, for he believes the elder brothers betray what is best in themselves when they betray their words and others.

Behind the difference between Marx and Winstanley lies a deeper tension pervasive in the tradition of political theory at least since Plato's struggle with the Sophists: the relationship between might and right in language. Consider the encounter between Socrates and Thrasymachus in Book I of Plato's *Republic*. Thrasymachus perhaps can be seen as the first social scientist. He announces that justice is the rule of the strong: what people call justice is really what the strong have defined it to be, and what they define it to be is a function of their interests. As an angry unmasker of ideology, Thrasymachus not only exposes the content behind phrases but also denies that the word *justice* has a meaning by which one could judge interests or acts as unjust. Socrates grants that what people call justice surely may reflect the interests of the strong, but he insists that when we say justice, we do not *mean* the rule of the strong. We mean something like fairness or each person receiving, having, and doing what is due.

Whereas Thrasymachus looks at what we call justice in sociological terms, Socrates explores the meaning of the concept and the actions it entails. Readers who dismiss the Socratic case as an example of foolish "idealism" compared to Thrasymachus's "realism" ignore the Socratic rejoinder: if Thrasymachus were wholly right, why is he such an angry man? He is angry because he knows that what people call justice is often unjust. But how does he know that? What people call justice violates the word's meaning, which he knows but which he refuses to "own." [4]

Like Thrasymachus's argument, Marx's disillusioning science of class ultimately arises from a sense of justice that it discounts and cannot ex-

4. The argument in this chapter about the relationship between a class analysis and a Socratic commitment to the meaning of words is deeply indebted to Hanna Fenichel Pitkin, *Wittgenstein and Justice* (Berkeley and Los Angeles: University of California Press, 1972), chapter 5 in particular.

plain (since, after all, if justice really is the rule of the strong, then how can Marx account for his indignation?). Like Marx, Winstanley has the Thrasymachian insight, but unlike Marx, he also follows Socrates and uses the meaning of the word *justice* to criticize practices people call just. Therefore, Winstanley *addresses* the elder brothers, whereas Marx analyzes them, addressing only the proletariat. Nonetheless, Marx and Thrasymachus might well question Winstanley's belief that the elder brothers could choose to act differently.

Winstanley does not lack a theory of the social interests that create a rule of the strong, nor does he lack a theory of history in which those interests develop, for he argues that conflict between elder and younger brothers is precisely the key fact in a history that culminates in "universal community." But this historical scheme is based on the idea of universal grace, as god "leads" *all* people to know and honor righteousness. Thus, Winstanley engages in the dialogue Marx precludes because of faith in a historical process different from Marx's. He is not naive about social interests, but his theory of history teaches that people are free beings and rational because they are children not of modes of production but of god. All can be "redeemed" because each is endowed with a capacity for "justice and judgment" that is not, he believes, ultimately determined by social position (or covetousness).

Winstanley *must* believe in the accessibility of the elder brothers because otherwise he would violate his animating faith, which also, despite all the evidence he himself offers to the contrary, makes possible his politics of speech and engagement. More broadly, perhaps a politics of dialogue must be premised on a faith in the capacity for "justice and judgment," even if not theologically derived. Accordingly, Winstanley may be trapped in a contradictory position, but not because of a failure of insight into power relations: if commitments to membership, mutuality, and choice are essential to, or the premise of, political dialogue, then they always will be contradicted by actual social divisions and will not mesh with a class analysis and its compelling insights about "the rule of the strong."

Thus, Winstanley, without the advantage of hindsight and bound to a millennial faith and a politics of dialogue, asserts the historical possibility of persuading the elder brothers to be faithful to a covenant they profess to uphold but whose meanings they interpret in a way that excludes the poor. Writing as a prophet who teaches the rights and obligations that could create freedom for all, Winstanley makes two kinds of arguments, which now can be explored. First, he argues that digging is rightful, and neither illegal nor dangerous to public liberty. What warrants digging also discloses the obligations of those in power, so secondly, he outlines what Parliament must do if it is to be legitimate and deserve to be called a magistracy.

HOW THE COVENANT DEFINES RIGHT ACTION

To Winstanley, getting one's words right does not suffice: words must be lived and acted. As a digger, he says he bears witness to "the substantial truth, brought forth into action, which the ministers have preached of and all religious men have made profession of" (408). Owning speech in action is essential because "certainly, God . . . is not a God of words only, but of deeds; for it is a badge of hypocrisy for a man to say and not to do" (407). Since the elder brothers harass the diggers, however, Winstanley must clarify how digging is a way of "owning" the "covenant and oath to endeavor reformation and to bring in liberty." One passage in the *True Levellers Standard* contains the key elements in Winstanley's argument. The diggers are harassed, he says:

> because they stand to maintain a universal liberty and freedom which is not only our birthright, which our Maker gives us, but which thou hast promised to restore unto us . . . and which likewise we have bought with our money, in taxes, freequartering, and bloodshed. (256)

First, they have a right to dig because the earth is their birthright: "The earth was not made for some but for all to live comfortably upon the fruits of it because all require it" (199). Secondly, human need and god's promised inheritance yield an argument about the promises between people. Winstanley says to Parliament: "You promised that if we would adventure person and purse to restore England from under that Norman oppression, you would make us a free people" (343). Given the meaning of freedom and Parliament's promise, digging is legitimate.

But thirdly, Winstanley shifts from *what* is promised to the fact that a promise is a bargain or contract:

> For Parliament promised, if we would pay taxes, give freequarter and adventure our lives against Charles and his party, they would make us a free people. These three being done by us, as well as by themselves, we claim this our bargain by law of contract with them, to be a free people with them. (276)

They acted as they did on the presumption that their promise entails reciprocity and real benefits, especially since the parties promised to make mutual and real sacrifices. If they do not gain land and freedom, "what benefit shall the common people have (that suffered most in the wars) by the victory that is got over the king? It had been better for the common people that there had been no such conquest, for they are impoverished in their estates by freequarter and taxes" (287).

Of course, the elder brothers deny that the national covenant entitles the poor to the earth, and instead insist that digging is illegal, a form of trespass or theft. Therefore, Winstanley develops a fourth argument, educating them about title to the earth. Where does title come from, such that some men can label others trespassers or thieves? "The king held title as he was conqueror," and the lords hold title to the commons "by no stronger hold than the king's will"; and since "the kings head is cut off," Winstanley argues, the lords "have lost their royalty to the common land," at the very least (288).

The question of title is now not legal but political. Just as William conquered England and "took the land for his own and called that his freedom," so, too, "seeing all sorts of people have given assistance to recovering England from under the Norman Yoke, surely all sorts, both gentry in their enclosures and commonality in their commons, ought to have freedom, not compelling one to work for wages for another" (287). On the grounds of their contribution to the conquest, "we plead our propriety in the common land as truly our own by virtue of this victory over the king," and not only because elder brothers promised freedom (343).

By asking how title originates, however, Winstanley suggests that might makes right, which means he loses any basis for objecting to the elder brothers' effort to forcibly reimpose the Norman Yoke on the poor. He therefore asks, What made, or makes, the conquest of Charles legitimate? The elder brothers had justified an admittedly illegal revolt (and mobilized the poor) by invoking a higher principle of legitimacy, "*Salus Populi*, the safety, peace and preservation of the whole body of the people, excepting none." This "ancient fundamental" law "gave life and strength to the Parliament and Army to take up arms against the king; for they had not the least letter of any written law for their warrant at that time, all the laws being for the King and none against him" (430).

Only an appeal to *salus populi* made conquest politically possible and justifiable, and only honoring that principle makes conquest legitimate. Otherwise, it will be said that "the gentry of England assembled in Parliament, killed the king for his power and government as a thief kills a true man for his money" (308). In the light of *salus populi*, elder brothers appear as a robber band, whereas diggers appear as the "life and marrow of the Parliament's cause" (366). Contrary to what elder brothers maintain, the action of diggers honors the only law that justified revolt and that now governs what is determined to be legal or illegal. That Winstanley argues this way reveals two fundamental shifts in his understanding of politics: he has begun to define the actions that would make Parliament legitimate, and (as will be explored in the next chapter) he has accepted that violence can be legitimate.[5]

LEGITIMATE STATE POWER

In *The New Law of Righteousness* Winstanley seemed unambiguously opposed to the state. Its origins in violence and its character as an instrument of class rule made it tainted, dangerous, and unjust. As he begins to dig, he again invokes Israel's mistake in choosing Saul, declaring: "We told you . . . we were not against any that would have Magistrate and laws to govern, as the Nations of the world are governed, but . . . we shall need neither the one nor the other" (282). By August 1649, however, he has formulated a political argument about what the Parliament and Army must do to be legitimate: "While we are in pursuit of the covenant, [we] expect that Parliament that made the covenant . . . to assist us herein, against all who oppose us in this righteous work of making the earth a common treasury" (326). Now he insists:

> You blame us who are Common People as though we would have no government; truly Gentlemen, we desire a righteous government with all our hearts, but the government we have gives freedom and livelihood to the gentry . . . and the poor that works to get it can hardly live and if they cannot work like slaves then they must starve. (361)

5. When Winstanley says that conquest confers rights (to the spoils), he sounds like Hobbes, who argues that conquerors win the right to rule, and it is the recognition of that right that creates peace. But here the difference with Winstanley emerges, for Winstanley says:

> If this freedom [to the earth] be denied the common people . . . then Parliament, Army, and Judges will deny equity and reason, whereupon the laws of a well-governed commonwealth ought to be built. If this equity be denied, then there can be no law but club law among the people; and if the sword must reign, then every party will be striving to bear the sword; and then, farewell peace. (373)

Both theorists fear "club law," but Winstanley derives it from illegitimate rule, whereas Hobbes derives it precisely from arguments about legitimacy. Therefore, Winstanley seeks peace by locating the principle that warrants the exercise of power and rights, whereas it is this very effort that Hobbes would prevent, for it jeopardizes the sovereignty of any state power.

In December Winstanley finds a Biblical metaphor for legitimate outer rulers:

> We hope that there will not be any kingly power over us to rule at will and we to be slaves, as the power has been, but that you will rule in love as Moses and Joshua did the children of Israel before any kingly power came in, and the Parliament will be as the elders of Israel, chosen freely by the people to advise . . . and assist . . . us. (348)

To honor the covenant and be a good authority, like Moses and Joshua, what must Parliament do? "If the fault lies in the laws, and much does, burn your old law books . . . and set up a government upon your own foundation: do not put new wine into old bottles, but as your government must be new, so let the laws be new" (358). This means, as Moses instructed the Hebrews, "look not upon other lands to be your pattern," but make laws that honor the "True Levellers Standard."

But what acts show reverence for that standard? If freedom "lies herein principally, to have the land of their nativity for their livelihood," then the main thing Parliament should "look upon is the land, which calls upon her children to be freed from the entanglements of Norman taskmasters" (304). That is because "our freedom must not lie within the clasps of a book, in words that may be read; nor in the bare title of victory; but it must be a freedom really enjoyed or else it will do us no good" (429). At the very least, then, the poor must be allowed to dig the commons. To truly establish freedom, however, Parliament must approach social bondage systematically and institutionally. As Winstanley says, "The king's blood was not our burden, it was those oppressing Norman laws whereby he enslaved us" (308). "Mistake me not, I do not say cast out the persons of men: No, I do not desire their fingers to ache; but I say cast out their power, whereby they hold the people in bondage, as the king held them in bondage" (372). Therefore, "all the several limbs and members must be cast out before kingly power can be pulled up root and branch." Since Parliament has abolished the monarchy and the House of Lords, Winstanley advises, "take away the power of Lords of Manors, and of Tithing Priests, and the intolerable oppression of judges" (372). Only these actions, and not mere regicide, constitute "the beginning of public freedom to the whole land" (439).

Winstanley knows, however, that "the nation's representative" has been chosen from the Norman taskmasters who oppress the poor. In theory, Parliament could be chosen by the few and still represent the many, but even this arrangement would not fulfill the requirements of freedom, for as Winstanley says of Joshua, rulers must be freely chosen by all the people. And strategically, Winstanley knows that the composition of Parliament must change if it is to encourage social change. Accordingly, in the winter of 1650 he argues that if Parliament is to fulfill its promise of freedom, it must create a government of representatives chosen by all the people.

Parliament's acts to cast out the king and establish England as a free commonwealth justify such political reform. Only if the people "enjoy successive Parliaments . . . shall we be freed from the corruption of particular men" acting as "perpetual governors" (ESU/9). After all, that was Parliament's objection to monarchy:

> If any should assume a power to abide constantly in that Parliamentary seat, and so to rule as if they were conquerors over the people . . . then they do thereby endeavor to bring in Kingly power, and themselves . . . corrupt commonwealth government. (ESU/10–11)

When Winstanley reminds his readers that "Parliament declared what they did . . . not for themselves but for the public freedom," he takes that to mean "everyone shall have his full liberty in the land for his livelihood and likewise in the choice of the representing power" (ESU/12).

Once again, Winstanley appears naive about the elder brothers even as he analyzes the "yoke" they impose. Politically or rhetorically, however, his problem is formulating a policy that attends to their sense of interest while honoring the meaning of their words and the interests of others. "If you establish the old Norman laws," he warns, "then you pull down the guilt of King Charles' blood on your own heads," and, he adds, "give just occasion to the common people never to trust the fair words of a Parliament any more, as you were always slow in trusting the king" (307). And as the king learned, when "the people fall off from you, you shall fall of a sudden like a great tree that is undermined at the root" (390). But the rulers can secure their particular interest in a way that also benefits the poor: "Let the gentry have their enclosures and the poor their commons" (305). This minimum demand acknowledges the rulers' own right to land while granting the poor their right as well. If elder brothers granted the rights and needs of others, Winstanley maintains, they also would feel more secure in the enjoyment of their own.[6]

---

6. The immediate danger is not a revolt of the poor but a counterrevolution by supporters of monarchy. In a delicate maneuver, Winstanley is trying to reinforce the republican political loyalties of the men who killed the king, by reminding them that without the support of the poor, their own liberties and rights (especially to property) will be subject once again to arbitrary power. In other words, he is trying to persuade them that the royalists are greater enemies than the poor (307).

But Winstanley also asks, as if wondering aloud, "Surely, if these lords and freeholders have their enclosures established to them in peace, is not that freedom enough? Must they needs have the Commons Lands likewise?" (307). He knows they do not really need the common lands, but since he knows their anxiety, he fears they will be "as Ahab, that was restless til he had Naboth's Vineyard, and so in the midst of abundance yet they will eat the bread out of the poors mouths" (307). By picturing them as Ahab, for whom nothing was enough, Winstanley means to warn them of self-destruction, but his image also suggests his own doubts about their ability to act differently.

WINSTANLEY AS CITIZEN: THEORY AND ACTION

What is striking about Winstanley's defense of digging and his argument about legitimate government is his ability to relate issues of need and interest to a political understanding of freedom and justice. He works out a political understanding of the tension in the existence of creatures shaped both by their needs and by their capacity for choice. He now gives a political response to his abiding question: how can humans meet their needs in a way that makes and keeps them free? In terms of rights and the meaning of a political covenant, diggers demand control over their livelihood and the right to exercise their agency as free men and women seeking to establish "public community" (291).

By turning the questions of what people need into the question of what they are entitled to, Winstanley gives necessity and social interests a political form and makes digging a political act. By politicizing bodily necessities and household concerns in terms of justice and for the sake of freedom, he puts earthly realities into political terms. By insisting that a legitimate government must address earthly need, and by insisting that freedom is to be felt and enjoyed in daily life, he also gives politics an earthly ground. Winstanley's politics attends to daily realities (how people feed themselves) while his understanding of daily life incorporates the intentionality and choice implicit in political speech.

In this way, Winstanley joins what most political theorists separate: need, or what is most basic (and necessary to existence); and freedom, or what is most noble and meaningful (and necessary to the good life). Whereas many theorists split need and freedom because they lack a mediating or synthesizing idea of justice, Winstanley's concern for justice discloses a political way to grant legitimacy to both. Citizenship becomes the activity of meeting needs in political terms and through specifically political forms.[7]

The politicization implied in this theory of citizenship and public community is confirmed by another and related development. Before he began digging, Winstanley imagined a unitary community in which particularity was effaced, "swallowed in love," as people achieved unanimity about words and deeds. He could not grant the possibility of legitimate differences because that would have implied the conventionality—and above all, the particularity—of his interpretation, which would have brought into doubt his claim to be god's instrument and undermined his own sense of legitimacy. In this regard he was like the elder brothers, but he felt enormous pressure to succeed where they had failed.[8]

During Winstanley's year as a digger, however, he is forced to confront the problem of plurality, of reconciling diverse and conflicting interests and interpretations. He still insists that his motives are pure: "Self-love to my own particular body does not carry me along in the managing of this business" (329). He still believes that abolishing property is the best way to guarantee everyone's freedom. But he grants that the gentry's enclosures do represent freedom, although "only for them" and at the expense of the poor. He therefore accepts their right to enclosures if the poor (by equity) have a right to land as well. As a result, he grants that a legitimate commonwealth could be based on enclosures and commons.

Thus, his argument about commonwealth moves from the idea of a unitary household to something like the idea of the Hebrew nation composed of tribes that are different and sometimes in conflict. A "commonwealth's government" exists to reconcile such differences; people become citizens when they learn that they must take into account their differences and their similarities. Winstanley starts to accept a certain plurality of differences within the boundary of assuring that all people can enjoy the earth, which everyone defines as crucial to freedom (305, 308, 326, 413).

7. These arguments are indebted to Hanna Fenichel Pitkin, "Justice: On Relating Public and Private," *Political Theory* 9, no. 3 (August 1981): 327–52.
8. Winstanley's idea of truth and Marx's idea of science are attempts to claim that they do not disguise limited social interests and that they, as authors, are not subject to the corruption of limited interest or particularistic imagination. Their words do not conceal. For both theorists, the experience of revolution and the disparity between words and actions appear to have generated an intense desire to find a language that releases humans from ideological discourse.

In his year as a digger, then, Winstanley becomes a citizen by struggling to reconcile his sense of a unitary and god-given community
grounded in a fixed standard of righteousness and his awareness that he
lives in a world of diversity and conflict. This struggle is salutary: he
avoids both the relativism that disavows judgment and the fixity that
denies plurality; he learns how community is a political creation and
neither automatic nor manifestly god-given. God-given truths no longer
preclude politics but rather mark the perimeters of legitimate political
action. As a result, he no longer enters the agon of politics to abolish it
but instead accepts it in order to make society and its members more
just and free.

The practical import of these developments is that after a year of digging, in the spring of 1650, Winstanley urges the poor to "take the Engagement," the oath of loyalty to the republic, in spite of Parliament's
obvious deficiencies and its failure thus far to fulfill its promises. How is
this change to be interpreted?

There is no doubt that Winstanley still operates within the millennial
framework of Exodus: he still hopes to uproot kingly power and establish instead a true commonwealth. But he has developed a more strategic view of social change. He now conceives an outward and political
form of the Father's internal magistracy and the poor's agency; "True
Magistracy" has become the political expression of what was once
simply an internal and social process. That he brings politics and magistracy to the foreground in this way, however, does not require that he
take the Engagement. Surely, he knows that the formal declaration of a
republic represents only "the bare title of a victory" and thus only a
"freedom to be read" rather than enjoyed. Therefore, his changing sense
of what the poor require must have led him to pledge his loyalty in spite
of his reservations.

In the most practical political terms, Winstanley must know that the
diggers' survival requires state protection from local gentry and freeholders. If the poor take the Engagement, he can demand that protection in return. The desperation one might read in this act is mitigated by
the fact that the purged Parliament was considering electoral reform,
which gave hope to those seeking land reform. This too would justify
taking the Engagement.

In the long run, and granting his uncertainty about Parliament's final
position, Winstanley seems to believe that establishing republican *principles* is still the precondition for making the English a free people. He
pledges not so much to the government as to principles by which it de-

clares itself legitimate. Those principles justify further social change, for they entitle the poor to demand an independent ground in the earth, "successive Parliaments," and "their freedom in choosing their representatives" (ESU/10).

In hindsight, of course, we know that Winstanley is mistaken about what is possible. But he also takes the Engagement for reasons far deeper than strategic gambles. Winstanley has covenanted not only to obey god but also to see to it that god is obeyed; he cannot abandon the revolution and pretend that he, at least, has fulfilled his obligations. In this sense, his reverence has brought him more deeply into the morally problematic political world. Indeed, for the sake of the freedom of the poor he had endorsed bloodshed; by justifying digging in terms of the king's conquest, he has made himself complicit in moral transgression and the nation's blood guilt. Therefore, his innocence now hinges on redeeming such sacrifices by actually establishing freedom. He cannot refuse to pledge, but at all costs he must succeed in reforming the regime, to whose destiny he is deeply bound by the piety that requires him to justify and atone for his transgressions.

CHAPTER VI

The Curse of Cain

Freedom is not won,
Neither by sword nor gun,
Though we have eight years stay'd,
And have our moneys pay'd:
Then clubs and diamonds cast away,
For harts and spades must win the day.
　　　　　　　　　　　　—a digger song

For although martial severity, self-discipline and danger have
been the conspicuous characteristics of my strange life . . . if I
lived *like* a soldier, it would have been a silly
misapprehension to believe that I should therefore live *as* a
soldier; yes, if it is permissible to describe and define
intellectually an emotional treasure as noble as freedom, then
it may be said that to live like a soldier but not as a soldier,
figuratively but not literally, to be allowed in short to live
symbolically, spells true freedom.
　　　　　　　　—Thomas Mann, Felix Krull

In the year of digging, Winstanley modifies his basic views about leadership and violence so that certain fissures and pressures appear in his
thought and action. He maintains his initial belief that the politics of
"the Dragon" reenacts Cain's crime, and he defends dialogue and nonviolence as the politics of "the Lamb"; but he also argues that the diggers are conquerors entitled to a share of the "spoils" won in the armed
victory over Charles.

Winstanley's analysis of political violence is not fixed and static, nor
is it an abstract account by one whose hands feel clean. As his effort to
distinguish absolutely between the politics of the Dragon and of the
Lamb becomes an effort to justify when each is appropriate and legitimate, he himself takes on the transgression of violence and the hopeless
task of redeeming it. As this man of love becomes a citizen, he confronts

a dilemma: can Abel, the younger brother, regain his inheritance without becoming like Cain?

WINSTANLEY'S INITIAL POSITION

In March 1649 a triumphant army had just deposed the king and forced his execution. Levellers tried to take advantage of this situation, to gain acceptance for an "Agreement of the People" that would extend the franchise and reform Parliament. But in the debate about their proposal, Cromwell and even more radical intellectuals like Milton agreed that there was no social basis even for Leveller democracy. Christopher Hill concurs: "The mass of the population was unsophisticated politically and still under the influence of landlords and pastors: to give such men the vote . . . would be to strengthen rather than weaken the power of the conservatives."[1] Therefore, until the poor were prepared for self-rule, leaders must not be subject to popular control. On these grounds, however, army and Parliamentary leaders suppressed the Levellers and mutinous regiments. They purported to follow Moses' example: reaching Canaan required violence against rebellious Hebrews and war against external enemies.

As a result, by 1651 many ex-rebels agreed with Hobbes that England could escape the wilderness of the interregnum only by acknowledging the centrality of sovereignty and the sword to any stable, let alone just, order. In Hobbes's drama of the state of nature, the murdered father returns in the scientific dress of Leviathan: insisting that "covenants without the sword are but words," and denying that the state requires a justification beyond the protection of social existence itself, Hobbes appropriates the Mosaic model and turns it to secular purposes. He defends what is now called a monopoly of legitimate violence, which would become the premise for the private pursuit of all other goods.[2]

Before the mutinies and purges in the spring of 1649, Winstanley had

---

1. Christopher Hill, *God's Englishman: Oliver Cromwell and the English Revolution* (New York: Dial Press, 1970), pp. 206–8.

2. A Thrasymachian therefore might say that conquest, or might, is the basis of right and argue that there is no justice (L/219). Such men are correct about might, Hobbes says, but incorrect about justice: sovereign law is just by definition; there is no standard of justice behind, beneath, or higher than the law, except the natural law that says justice is keeping covenants, that is, obeying constituted law. The alternative to this understanding, he says, is an endless cycle of rebellion:

> They will all of them justify the war by which their power was first gotten and whereon they think their right dependeth and not on the possession. As if, for example, the

developed his own arguments about "what is to be done." Unlike the Puritans and Hobbes, Winstanley in *The New Law of Righteousness* unequivocally denounced violence as "the power of the flesh" and rejected a reformation led by "outer saviors" or controlled by "the hands of the few" (181–82). The premise of his argument was that violence is the most extreme denial of an equality between creatures that derives from the fact that all embody a spirit that is greater than each. Thus, says Winstanley:

> If any man can say, he can give life, then he hath the power to take away life; but if the power of life and death be only in the hands of the Lord, then surely he is a murderer of the creation that takes away the life of his fellow creature, man, by any law whatsoever. (197)

Like violence, therefore, the claim to be an "outer savior" also dishonors the god within and violates the limits that define humanness. In each case, the effort to "be as a god" makes people "fight and devour like beasts" rather than be "moderate and speak and carry themselves like men, rationally" (282).

Like other modern critics of political violence, Winstanley articulated the limits that should define human action and argued that means are ends in the making: we betray our ends if we do not honor them in our present action; if we profess to be lifting the curse of pride, then we must renounce whatever constitutes it. Accordingly, Winstanley argued, Puritan radicals present neither a real alternative to kingly power nor a living example of what he called "a power contrary" (382). Indeed, he appeared to believe that no politics, let alone violence, can "settle" the reformation, that is, "build up" a true alternative to kingly power:

> The whole earth is corrupt and it cannot be purged by the hand of creatures, for all creatures lie under the curse and groan to be delivered, and the more they strive the more they entangle themselves in the mud. . . . Surely no flesh can settle this work for all flesh is corrupt; this work shall be done by the power of the Lord, killing covetousness and making mankind generally to be of one heart and one mind. (186–87)

The "work" of "killing covetousness," Winstanley maintained, will be accomplished "without either sword or weapons" and without "self-

---

right of the Kings of England did depend on the goodness of the cause of William the Conqueror . . . wherein whilst they needlessly think to justify themselves, they justify all the successful rebellions that ambition shall at any time raise against them. . . . There is scarce a commonwealth in the world whose beginnings can in conscience be justified. (L/506) ish counsellors and selfish governors," but rather "by the universal spirit of the divine power, which is Christ in mankind, making them all to act in one spirit and in and after one law of reason and equity" (181–82). The only power that can lift the curse of pride and violence is "a power contrary, . . . love and patience acted with a cheerful life" (456). Since "Christ came not to destroy but to save," one who honors him does not abjure all action but honors his method, which works "on the flesh but not by the flesh," by wielding "the sword of love, patience, and truth" (181, 471).

Before examining what Winstanley meant by the sword of Christ and how he then wields it as a digger, let us consider first the political implications of his initial argument by contrasting it to an explicit defense of the legitimacy of leadership and violence. J. G. A. Pocock, for instance, views the New Model Army before the mutinies of 1649 as an armed prophet: violence is not only an ineluctable fact of political life but also an essential and unavoidable means to found and preserve a republic. Following Machiavelli, Pocock writes that "Prophets, whether true or false, require the sword because they are innovators":

> The prophet's inspiration and mission do not deliver him from the political context created by innovation, and he must continue to use secular arms for reasons inherent in that context. . . . [Innovation] makes enemies who are fervent because they know what they have lost, and friends who are lukewarm because they do not yet know what they have gained, not having yet had enough experience of it: precisely the problem of the fleshpots of Egypt.[3]

Such a political argument has its own moral underpinning: just as moral virtue arises specifically from acknowledging and taking responsibility for violence, so republican virtue arises only when citizens take collective responsibility for it. For moral and political reasons, then, Machiavelli condemns those who foist responsibility for violence onto god or mercenaries. People become citizens only when they are willing to jeopardize their souls and risk their bodies—literally to fight for their freedom. And that sort of citizenship is engendered by the emulation of great leaders.

From this point of view, Winstanley is selfish and irresponsible. He is too concerned with his personal goodness to do good. As Bertolt Brecht warns, "Take care when you leave the world / You were not only good /

3. J. G. A. Pocock, *The Machiavellian Moment* (Princeton: Princeton University Press, 1975), pp. 171–72.

But leave a good world." Moreover, Winstanley dooms his cause to defeat because, again in Brecht's words, "Only force helps where force
rules; only men help where men are." As Lenin argues, if the gift of freedom requires the sword of iron, then those like Winstanley, whom
Lenin calls "slaves of love," will never be free.[4]

Winstanley, however, was making an argument about political effec-
tiveness as well as moral goodness, which he believed are related. The
armed prophet

> that seems to prevail over another says, God gave him his victory, though his
> conquest be tyranny over his brothers, making the King of Righteousness the
> author of sorrows. . . . Victories that are got by the sword are but victories
> of the Murderer, and the joy of those victories is but the joy of Cain, when he
> had killed his brother Abel. (297)

What are the consequences of such victories? "Freedom gotten by the
sword is an established bondage to some part of creation. . . . Victory
gotten by the sword is a victory that slaves get one over another"
(378–79). The losers become the slaves of the new tyrants, who themselves are slaves to covetousness within. In time the conquered rise up
and kill their masters, and the process is repeated. "For if I kill you" in
the name of god, justice, or freedom, "I am a murderer. If a third man
comes and kills me for murdering you, he is a murderer of me; and so by
the government of first Adam, murder hath been called justice when it is
but the curse" (193).

Winstanley's point is that a state built on conquest is built on division, and division and inequality generate potentially violent resentment
and discontent. Then the victors will feel compelled to reenact their
fratricidal crime:

> Oh, saith imaginary, covetous, proud, self-seeking flesh, If I take not the
> sword to restrain the unruliness of mankind, we shall not live one by an-
> other. But his interest is not in love to peace, but that he may rule over all
> himself and beat down others under him. (488)

What outer saviors call a righteous necessity is the result of a victory
that creates slaves. Winstanley tells the victors that the crimes with
which the polity begins will be its bad conscience; the divisions which
its foundation initiates are crimes whose effects will haunt the rulers.

4. Bertolt Brecht, *Poems 1913–1956* (New York: Methuen, 1976); V. I. Lenin, *What
Is to Be Done?* (New York: International Publishers, 1969).

The community will be weak at its roots, in the hearts of its members, because change cannot be forced. An order can be legitimate and stable only if it is made by all, equally and consensually.

But what is the point of making this argument against violence *after* a victorious war? In *The New Law of Righteousness* it sounds as if Winstanley had stood aside from violence for moral and political reasons, convinced it could not give birth to freedom. Yet he grants that it is by "wars, councils, and the hands of men" that "the government of Esau shall be beaten down and the enemy shall destroy one another" (205). Thus, the fight of the Dragons appears to prepare the way for the spirit of the Lamb, which generates nonviolent social change. "England, know this," he declares at the outset of digging, "thy striving now is not only Dragon against Dragon . . . but now thou beginst to fight against the Lamb, the Dove, the meek spirit, the power of love" (297). Once the parliamentary Dragon has destroyed the monarchical Dragon, the "hand of the Lord . . . will be the healer, restorer, and giver of the New Law of Righteousness, by spreading himself everywhere and so drawing all things into himself" (205).

One has the uneasy feeling that Winstanley's noninvolvement has entitled him to play the agent of Christ: the innocent younger brother is entitled to a freedom that is partly the result of Parliament's sinful victory over Charles, from which he is meant to stand apart so that he can embody "a power contrary." To be sure, Winstanley believes that noninvolvement is intended as a gift to the elder brothers: because the poor are innocent, they will be able to wash white others' sins by bearing witness to the spirit of the Lamb. But he also wishes to stay pure: he can redeem the crimes of others, and bring in freedom, without himself transgressing or suffering the guilt that requires expiation. This dream, that one can become a citizen while remaining a saint, is transformed and jeopardized by his experience as a digger.[5]

5. There is considerable ambiguity in Winstanley's account of the redemptive narrative because he seems uncertain about the role of the dragon and the sword. In part, he says that any victory gotten by the sword is the victory of Cain. But he also insists that war is necessary because it alone can destroy kingly power, in part by discrediting violence:

> When you see Army against Army, it is but Kingly Power dividing, tearing, and devouring itself; for as he riseth by his own sword so he shall fall by his sword . . . til the creation be cleansed of these plagues; and that curse which hath destroyed the earth shall now in a period of time destroy itself. (467)

As violence destroys kingly power, but also discredits itself, a power contrary can be demonstrated by those whose hands are clean.

HARASSMENT

Beginning in June 1649 diggers were physically beaten, their huts and crops destroyed, and several of them arrested and tried for trespassing. Winstanley's August pamphlet, *A Watchword to the City of London and the Army,* is particularly crucial because it explains their physical and legal harassment through a theory of the new Norman Yoke and justifies nonviolent digging as the way to wield "the sword of Christ." His narrative in this pamphlet, however, is repeatedly broken by anguished references to the plight of the cows he tended, which bailiffs physically abused and tried to confiscate in an effort to gain payment in kind for the damages assessed by the court. Winstanley intentionally uses the cows to symbolize what is at stake in his differences with the elder brothers. Unlike his other literary devices and metaphors, however, Winstanley's references to the cows actually fracture his narrative form and political argument and create an extremely disjointed, even rambling, text. Winstanley cannot master his own metaphor, but it discloses the feelings and contradictions that shape—and misshape—Winstanley's arguments about violence and nonviolence.

How the elder brothers use, sell, and beat the cows provides a metaphor for how they treat the poor and the earth. Most obviously, the Normans rob the people of their livelihood and nourishment: "And this Norman camp are got into so numerous a body already that they have appointed sutlers to drive away the cows which were my livelihood" (331). As Winstanley says of himself, "If I could not get meat to eat, I would feed on bread, milk and cheese, and if they take the cows . . . then I'll feed on bread and beer" (328). Meanwhile, the cows "were to be killed to victual the camp, that is, to feed . . . freeholders and others, the snapsack boys and ammunition drabs that helped drive away the cows, that they might be encouraged by a belly full of stolen goods to stick the closer to the business another time" (331).

Thus, the cows represent both the poor and an "unnurtured" source of nourishment. Indeed, the transformation of nourishment and fellow creatures into commodities for others is literally an act of violence: as the Normans take away the cows, "they beat them with their clubs, that the cows heads and sides did swell, which grieved tender hearts to see" (329). Accordingly, the Normans' attitude toward the cows represents the exact opposite of digging: they deny reciprocity with the earth and with "fellow creatures." This alone explains why the fury of this Norman camp against the diggers is so great that they would not only drive away all the cows upon the ground, but spoil the corn too, and when they had done all this mischief, the bailiffs and other Norman snapsack boys went howling and shouting as if they were dancing at a whitson ale, so glad they are to do mischief to the diggers. (335)

Winstanley is especially concerned about the cows because they do not belong to him: he is a trustee tending this source of nourishment, a fellow creature. He says he told the bailiffs, "Here is my body, take me that I may come to speak to those Normans that have stolen our land from us, and let the cows go, for they are not mine" (328). By taking the cows, elder brothers hypocritically disregard rightful ownership, but the whole episode also exposes the hypocrisy of their profession to uphold law and virtue, to be trustees for the people and the land.

"This power of covetousness is he that does countenance murder and theft in them that maintain the kingdom by the sword of iron and punishes it in others" (324). The law itself is merely a tool of this covetousness, believes Winstanley, who points out that the jury that decided in the freeholders' favor "was made of rich freeholders and such as stand strongly for the Norman power; and though our digging upon that barren common land hath done the common much good, yet this jury brings in damages of ten pounds a man" (327). "Under the color of justice," the elder brothers rob the poor of their livelihood, confiscate and abuse the nourishment they hold in trust, engage in "theft and tumult," deprive people of the right to speak, and themselves refuse to speak "like men" (336). It must be "that the god from whom they claim title to the land as proper to them, shutting out others, is covetousness the murderer, the swordly power, the great red dragon, who is called the god of this world" (385).

At the same time, the cows symbolize what Winstanley takes to be the truth about diggers and himself, which is the innocent suffering endured by those who try to nourish the earth and others. Just as the "reason in creation" is upheld by the cows providing milk and manure, so too the diggers only meant to feed the poor and "nurture unnurtured ground." Like the innocent cows, the diggers

> have plowed and dig'd upon Georges Hill in Surrey, to sow corn for the succor of man, offering no offence to any, but carrying ourselves in love and peace towards all, having no intent to meddle with any mans enclosures or propriety, til it be freely given us by themselves, but [intending] only to improve the commons and waste lands . . . for the relief of ourselves and others. (301)

Like the cows, diggers are punished for an act of love that is blameless
and even praiseworthy.

Obviously, diggers are not cows; but Winstanley maintains that like
cows they are the innocent victims of persecution by evil people. When
he laments the plight of the cows, he draws an important distinction:
"And yet these cows were never upon George Hill, and never digged
upon that ground, and yet the poor beasts must suffer because they give
milk to feed me" (329). Unlike the cows, the diggers *choose* to be on
George Hill; nonetheless, Winstanley insists that diggers are as innocent
as the cows. Eager to prove that diggers are neither trespassers nor
transgressors of any moral law, he declares:

> We find . . . love in our hearts toward all, to enemies as well as friends; we
> would have none live in beggary, poverty, or sorrow, but [hope] that every-
> one might enjoy the benefit of his creation: we have peace in our hearts and
> quiet rejoicing in our work, filled with sweet content, though we have but a
> dish of roots and bread for our food. (262)

In part, Winstanley is trying to assuage the fears of the elder brothers
in order to survive: they project their own impulses and motives onto
diggers, and thus misunderstand them: "Enemies filled with fury falsely
report of us that we have intent to fortify ourselves and afterwards to
fight against others and take away their goods from them, which is a
thing we abhor" (281). Theft and violence characterize the elder brothers, however, not the diggers: "Community will force nothing from anyone, but only take what is given in love" (383). He encourages his
enemies: "Cherish the diggers, for they love you and would not have
your finger ache if they could help it; and why be so bitter against
them?" (333).

Of course, Winstanley knows the elder brothers are "so furious
against us" because "we endeavor to dig up their tithes, lawyers, fees,
prisons, and all that art and trade of darkness whereby they get money
under color of law" (335). When he says, "All we desire is to live quietly
in the land of our nativity by our righteous labor, upon common land
that is our own," he knows full well that he hopes thereby to uproot
their government and property. The rulers are right to see the diggers as
making more than an innocent claim to a small piece of land: "Freedom
is the man that will turn the world upside down, therefore no wonder he
hath enemies" (316). But Winstanley insists that he is committing no
transgression, intending no harm, and even engaging in an "act of love."
How does he feel justified in this assertion?

THE POLITICS OF LOVE

Winstanley can maintain that digging is an act of love in the paternal sense of seeking what is best:

> Alas, you poor blind earth moles, you strive to take away my livelihood and the liberty of this poor weak frame, my body of flesh, which is my house I dwell in for a time; but I strive to cast down your kingdom of Darkness, and to open Hell gates and to break asunder the Devils bands wherewith you are tied, that you, my enemies, may live in peace. And that is all the harm I would have you to have. (333)

Until the elder brothers undergo the shift in perspective he calls "Christ rising," however, the diggers will be seen as, and in fact be, a threat to those who gain nourishment through the labor of others.

Despite disagreements about what is best, however, elder brothers can see the truth of his loving intentions by *how* he acts. Thus, his refusal to take their property by force demonstrates that he intends not to jeopardize their rightful interest in nourishment. By letting each person "stand and fall to his own master" (283), and by insisting on rational speech and rejecting coercion, Winstanley accords respect or love to each person as a peer. Thus, he keeps appealing to the rulers, "Let our cause have a public trial," in which the merits of his proposals can be debated, subject to "the judgement of all rational and righteous men" (407).

Speaking to Mr. Drake, "a Parliament man" and "therefore a man counted able to speak rationally," Winstanley argues: "We know if your laws be built on reason and equity, you ought both to have heard us speak and read our answer, for that is no righteous law whereby to keep a commonwealth in peace, when one sort shall be suffered to speak but not another" (321). Speech and deliberation are essentially human; the question of what is best ought to be settled by rational debate between people treated as equals:

> Let your ministers plead with us the Scriptures, and let your lawyers plead with us in the equity and reason of your own law. And if you prove us transgressors, then we shall lay down our work and acknowledge that we have trespassed against you, and then punish us. But if we prove by Scripture and Reason that undeniably the land belongs to one as well as another, then you shall own our work, justify our cause, and declare that you have done wrong to Christ. (338)

That he is willing to honor the conclusions of rational discourse demonstrates to the elder brothers how "to carry yourselves like man to man," that is, to honor the Christian message they profess. Thus, he asserts:

You will see in time . . . that our actions and conversation is the very life of scripture and holds forth the true power of God and Christ. For is not the end of all preaching, praying, and profession wrapped up in this action, namely, Love your Enemies and do to all men as you would they should do to you? (365)

The Golden Rule, which entails loving one's enemies, is "the substantial truth brought forth into action" by the diggers. Winstanley loves his enemies not only because of the truth to which he bears witness but also because of the way he testifies to it. In affirmative terms, diggers must "speak like men" because that is how they deserve to be treated; in negative terms, diggers cannot resort to violence if the elder brothers refuse to talk or listen. Accordingly, he says that when elder brothers physically abuse them, "we must not fight but suffer" (275) in order to maintain the integrity of their position and honor the Golden Rule:

Our spirit waits in quiet and peace upon our Father for deliverance; and if he give our blood into thy hand for thee to spill, know this, that He is our Almighty Captain. . . . Our blood and life shall not be unwilling to be delivered up in meekness to maintain universal liberty, that so the curse on our part may be taken off creation. (256)

Such is the logic of his reverence, whose consequences he has reckoned carefully: "We shall not be startled, neither at prison nor Death, while we are about this work [because] we have been made to sit down and count what it may cost us in undertaking such a work, and we know the full sum, and are resolved to give all that we have to buy this pearl which we see in the field" (263). Winstanley's nonviolence is not blind adherence to principle but a conscious choice about the best way to undertake reform.

What, then, does Winstanley mean by saying that diggers use "the sword of Christ," a "sword of love, patience and truth" (471)? In part, the image suggests how the diggers should surmount in themselves the covetousness they would overcome in others. As he says, those who wield the sword of Christ live by a love found within. If violence is a weakness, then love is a power that strengthens a person internally, enabling him or her to overcome resentment and vengefulness. By bearing witness to the power of this love, one is reminded of its presence in others. The sword of Christ is also the patience to accept that the struggle against the flesh is a painful process, a fight in which the enemy is one's own weakness and pride. By extension, Christ's sword is the patience to accept the pace of love's struggle with this enemy in others. Finally, Christ's sword is the truth that humans are responsible for what rules, and rules in, them. This truth binds diggers to acknowledge the same individual responsibility in others.

In these ways, Christ's sword "kills covetousness" in the diggers by teaching them the mutuality they must exemplify to others. Diggers must overcome their own impulses toward self-righteousness and "rash anger," their own inclination to deny the humanity of their enemies, and their own desire to strike back violently. Only then will the diggers' action toward (the flesh in) others embody the love that heals, the patience that succors, and the truths that empower and bind. By wielding the sword of Christ, diggers will transform themselves and thereby affirm the elder brothers' power and responsibility to struggle against evil.

As this analysis suggests, Winstanley believes his love can help engender love in others; he believes that nonviolent action will transform those who witness it as well as those who engage in it. He notes the change in those who once were enemies:

> Many of the country people that were offended at first now begin to be moderate and see righteousness in our work, and to own it, excepting one or two covetous freeholders that would have all the commons to themselves. . . . And we expect that these angry neighbors, whom we never wronged, will in time see their furious rashness to be their folly, and become moderate and speak and carry themselves like men, rationally, and leave off pushing with their horns like beasts. (282)

But on what grounds can Winstanley "hope in time that love and patience will conquer our furious enemies"? (335). In his account of covetousness, people avoid knowledge of the flesh that rules them by attributing their own violent impulses to their enemies. To Winstanley, however, the Dragon and the Lamb not only "make single men strive in opposition one against another," but also "these two powers strive in the heart of every single man," in the form of the "spirit of love" and the "power of envy, pride, and unrighteousness" (281). Accordingly, diggers "put our bodies in thy hand" in order to force the elder brothers to confront the inner conflict they externalize.

As yielding, beaten bodies, diggers will strip freeholders' violence of its ideological cover, exposing the rage that keeps them from acknowledging their Christian professions: "If you say [that God] bids you to love your enemies, then I demand of you, why do you . . . stir up the people to beat, to imprison, to put to death?" (291). Then, elder brothers can face the truth of Winstanley's declaration about them: "You lie under the power of death and bondage and know not, or at least doth not actually hold forth that you know that spirit which in words you seem to profess. You speak and preach the life of love, but you have not the power of it" (445).

Facing their own rage inwardly, on the appropriate battlefield, elder brothers can make the "experimental discovery" of "the Dragon appearing in the flesh." Thus, digger nonviolence, like their speech, is intended to "lance" the self-righteous armor of the flesh, "leaving you naked and bare, and making you ashamed." But the "wound" diggers inflict is meant to cure: diggers demonstrate a "power contrary," "that powerful spirit of love," which elder brothers also will discover striving within them.

As the metaphor of the sword suggests, Winstanley tries to fight evil and affirm a power contrary by living as a soldier, not literally, but figuratively. Only by fighting symbolically, he believes, can one exemplify the self-respect and equality in the name of which one acts and thereby change one's adversaries without betraying one's principles. Thus, Winstanley develops a practice of nonviolence for reasons not unlike those of religious activists in the early civil rights movement in the United States. Like Winstanley, Martin Luther King believed that nonviolent resistance confronted the nation not only with its evil and the reality of the poor, but also with the right way to own its democratic and Christian professions. Accordingly, each believed that shaming adversaries is an act of love that helps restore them to the love within and to their brethren in the body of mankind. As Winstanley puts it, "I look upon you as part of the creation that must be restored" (391). Indeed, "covetous, hardhearted, self-seeking children . . . openly seekest [love's] destruction," but those testifying to Christ "bear all things patiently" because "love secretly seekest thy preservation" (297).

The nonviolent protests of god's beloved sons and daughters arises from a violation of dignity and mutuality, which must be honored by rebels if they are to maintain their integrity and demonstrate a power contrary. It is because of a common commitment to such a politics of limits that one also can compare Winstanley to Camus: both articulate a kind of action that does not involve self-betrayal, and both define such action in terms of the capacity to "speak and carry ourselves like men, rationally," as Winstanley puts it. For both theorists, the rebel demonstrates truth without imposing it—a truth that acknowledges the love and reason in each person and requires genuine consent. Accordingly, Winstanley and Camus reject monologue (tyranny), babble (ideology), and silence (violence) as inappropriate to the estate of humans.

To be sure, the parallel with Camus can go only so far. Camus points up what is problematic in the nonviolence devised by religious thinkers. In the absence of god, Camus argues, moral limits can be discovered only by way of the transgression and guilt that reveal them. Moreover, in the absence of moral certainty, a rebel always risks transgression. Finally, violence is unjustifiable, but it may be unavoidable. Since evil is the inescapable shadow of morality, the rebel must renounce the idea of purity and recognize the impossibility of salvation. Thus, Camus's rebel does not radically dissociate Cain and Abel or moralize politics in terms of innocence and salvation.

In contrast, Winstanley begins with reverence for god-given limits and therefore becomes a rebel who believes he can avoid transgression altogether. Because of his faith in a god whose purposes he embodies, he believes that limits can be learned without crime, which jeopardizes innocence. Indeed, his faith in god precludes the tragic recognition that is the basis of Camus's argument about rebellion: Winstanley radically dissociates Abel's reverence for god-given limits and Cain's transgression. Elder brothers may learn about the god within and mutual recognition by confronting their own transgression, but diggers insist that innocence is the basis of their own rebellion. Correspondingly, Winstanley sees that digging has made his enemies angry but does not admit that he himself is justifiably angry and because of that anger turns the world upside down. It is the claim of innocence, and the disclaimer of anger, whose causes and political consequences need to be examined.[6]

6. Camus must find a principle of limits without relying on a theological perspective; but like Winstanley, he insists that people must renounce the desire to play god, which he interprets as a prideful denial of the limits of the human estate. For both, those who rebel against injustice are justified only if they act in terms of what is common to all humans. As Camus says, "The freedom the rebel claims, he claims for all; the freedom he refuses, he refuses to all. He is not only slave against master, but man against the world of master and slave" (*The Rebel* [New York: Random House 1956], p. 284). Thus, Camus's rebel speaks in the name of a natural community: "It is for the sake of everyone in the world that the slave asserts himself when he comes to the conclusion that a command has infringed on something in him which does not belong to him alone, but which is common ground where all men—even the man who insults and oppresses him—have a natural community" (16). In a similar way, Winstanley uses the reason and love within each (but not belonging to anyone) and the natural community grounded in the earth (which belongs to all and includes even the oppressor) to define legitimate action and criticize prideful politics.

Both theorists want to avoid the human effort to father themselves and deny limitation. But Camus, without a god, insists that men must give up ideology and revolution, for he fears that these lead rebels to play god and commit murder in the name of bringing salvation in historical time. In contrast, Winstanley's theodicy, which reveals the possibility of salvation but also the legitimate way to seek it, frees him to engage in a far more systematic radicalism. But Winstanley is far less profound in his understanding of the moral dilemma in politics. He does not suffer on the cross Camus erects between transgression and moral limits; therefore, he is *immoral* in Camus's terms, since he insists on his *innocence*.

VIOLENCE, ANGER, AND TRANSGRESSION

Let us grant that Winstanley has principled moral and political reasons to criticize the armed prophet and reject violence; that he is prudent in his refusal to "harm" a vastly superior and armed force, and that he is trying to change his adversaries by exemplifying a power contrary; even that he is motivated by love to the extent that he does act with a respect his enemies merely profess. But his identification with the cows and his claim to be the loving and innocent victim of others' violent transgressions do not simply exemplify a power contrary. For although the diggers themselves renounce violence, they also endorse the conquest—even violent conquest—of the king. And although Winstanley declares himself to be purely loving, he also demonstrates the right use of the anger he disclaims.

In *The New Law of Righteousness* Winstanley insisted that the poor should remain wholly innocent of involvement in the victories of succeeding Cains. In June 1649, however, Winstanley argues that the army and Parliament are accountable to the poor because they were chosen as "servants" of the "whole body of the English people" for "an appointed time" and "a particular work" (276). If a dragon has become the servant of the poor, they are in turn responsible for the action of what is now their agent. So the poor are to inherit the earth by virtue of their involvement, not withdrawal. No longer beneficiaries of the conflict between dragons because they are innocent bystanders, the poor now are beneficiaries because they authorize a victorious dragon they contend is their servant. The poor have become conquerors, entitled to a share in the "spoils of victory." Yet Winstanley still defines these spoils as the fruit of sin. By making the Dragon their agent, haven't the poor become Cains? Or is violence no longer sinful if it makes freedom possible?

To gain title to the earth, Winstanley here claims responsibility for the victory over Charles. But conquest involves the sacrifice of innocents (including the king, "whose blood was not our burden") and reflects the prideful presumption that one is entitled to take another's life. By claiming the fruits of conquest, he has become complicit in the blood crimes he continues to condemn. He still insists on the purity of his motives and ultimate intentions, but he has violated or contradicted both his claim to love and the nonviolence required by the Golden Rule. Thus, his argument about conquest is likely to *feel* like the justification of a crime, a deed about which he must have ambivalent feelings. How, then, does he reconcile his claim to conquest and title and his feelings and arguments about pride and violence?

Winstanley does not explicitly address this contradiction in himself and the poor, but his own guilt appears indirectly in his reiterated desire to make the conquest legitimate, which would atone, one surmises, for his own sense of transgression. His feelings are reflected through his argument to and about the elder brothers: *they* can justify the transgression of violence by creating a community that excludes none and recognizes all. Implicitly, then, his own atonement depends on their action. If Parliament does not restore the earth to the "whole body of the people," Winstanley is left feeling responsible for blood crimes it prevents him from redeeming. Thus, he admits his own problem with transgression implicitly, but not explicitly, in the urgency of his efforts to ensure that Parliament truly acts as the servant of the poor.

In each pamphlet as a digger he argues that Parliament will not be a Cain if it honors the "fundamental law" that justified taking up arms: it should share the land with all who participated in the conquest, and it should renounce violence within the nation. Now that the king is cast out, Winstanley believes that he must teach Parliament and the army how to be servants of the Lamb (and faithful to the word of god, which is love) as well as servants of the poor (and faithful to the covenant of men, which is liberty).

While still insisting that violence is never justified because it violates any righteous end, Winstanley now argues that it can be justified, but only if it leads to that end. He still insists that people have no right to kill because they lack the power to create life; that is, a death cannot be redeemed by any other compensating act. But he also implies that humans do have the power of redemption—or at least a legitimate way to atone. Winstanley still maintains that crimes of slavery and violence can be cleansed only by a Lamb whose spirit is pure. But now he also says that transgressions committed to uproot slavery can be expiated if those who are complicit begin to honor the spirit of the Lamb. The poor still represent that spirit, but now they are conquerors who must purify their own sins.

One might expect that Winstanley's idea of personal legitimacy would have changed, as well, so that he no longer feels bound to notions of purity and innocence and no longer defines righteousness in terms of meekness. But he continues to make such assertions, along with pious and unequivocal rejections of violence. Thus, one sees him splitting, his claims as a conqueror and his assertions of meekness alternating within a single paragraph even as the contradiction goes unacknowledged. He could reconcile the contradiction explicitly, through the idea of a reborn commonwealth that would provide both the limit and warrant of violence and the means to atone for it. But he never addresses directly his contradictory statements about violence and love, nor does he analyze his own complicity in the relationship between transgression and atonement; therefore, he does not work through his conflicting notions of what constitutes legitimate action.

It is in his argument that the diggers are wholly loving, however, that one finds his other attempt to resolve the dilemma of violence and guilt. As building a reborn commonwealth is one way to expiate violent crimes, so digger nonviolence is another. The transgression entailed by asserting that the poor are conquerors is both denied and admitted in Winstanley's portrayal of diggers as wholly loving. Although he argues explicitly that their innocence and love are proved by their nonviolence, it implicitly atones for their complicity in violence. Principles aside, Winstanley's nonviolence works out the anger and guilt he denies.

As a result, however, a further splitting and another form of self-denial emerge: in his effort to atone, Winstanley portrays diggers as wholly loving, identifies them with the innocent and beaten cows, and thereby dissimulates the very anger that makes digging—and nonviolence—possible. Diggers, in fact, are soldiers of Christ only because they use their indignation and rage rightly. Indeed, the point of digging is to turn fearful and ashamed "dogs," as he calls tenants who obediently follow the landlords' orders, into a certain kind of fighter (367–68). Rather than turn against themselves in obsequious self-hatred or ascetic self-punishment, diggers give their anger a principled form and thus become masters of themselves.

How they master their anger can be seen in the following passage, in which Winstanley may well be speaking of himself:

> Reason is that living power of light that is in all things. . . . It lies in the bottom of love, of justice, of wisdom; for if the Spirit Reason did not uphold and moderate these, they would be madness, nay, they could not be called by their names; for Reason guides them in order and leads them to their right end, which is not to preserve a part, but the whole creation. [Reason] makes justice to be justice, or love to be love: for without this moderator and ruler, they would be madness, the self-willedness of the flesh, and not that which we call them. (104–5)

The desire for love and justice, which entails anger at their denial, is guided by reason to preserve the whole rather than released as murderous "self-willedness of the flesh." But it is this anger, which enables diggers to "fight like men, not beasts," that Winstanley feels compelled to deny.

Erik Erikson's reflections about Gandhi apply to Winstanley: "I seemed to sense the presence of a kind of untruth in the very protestation of truth; of something unclean when all the words spelled out an unreal purity; above all, of violence where non-violence was the professed issue." Erikson's point is that those who work for peace, for a politics that does not uphold the curse of violence, must be aware of their ambivalence, of the potential love in hate and the presence of hate in love. Winstanley displays what he sees in others: a pretension of love masking rage—although he does not act murderously. Erikson goes on to say of himself: "My job is not to pierce the pretense, but to ask why it is necessary at all."[7]

Following Nietzsche, one could say that Winstanley is a Christian who embraces nonviolence because he is incapable of acting otherwise: he turns his impotence into a moral virtue while fantasizing the punishment of the powerful. I cannot disprove this interpretation, but my feeling is that Winstanley is not rationalizing impotence. If he were really weak, he could not fight servitude, overcome his fear of social ostracism, and put his body on the line by taking over the commons land. If there is a weakness in Winstanley, it is his unwillingness or inability to face his own anger, which he nonetheless puts to good use. It is his self-denial that has a bad smell—the smell of the dunghill, because according to his own analysis, the will to purity is a sure sign of anger directed against something in the self that is considered unclean.

The culture of the elder brothers defines godliness as being "moderate" and "reasonable." In the Putney debates all the disputants agreed that moderate behavior was a sign of godliness, of one's willingness to consider another's point of view and thus to seek the public good. But this norm of civility can be oppressive because those who are dispossessed are likely to be unhappy, angry, and immoderate. If their anger is expressed outright, it is taken as a symptom of wildness, irrationality, or selfishness and is used to justify their continued oppression. In the effort to appear moderate, therefore, the powerless may dissimulate, or turn against themselves the anger it is not legitimate to express openly. Some of this may be going on in Winstanley, whose desire to be legitimate takes the form of claiming to be the real Isaac, who fulfills the elder brothers' professed values. By this angry inversion, he tries to sat-

7. Erik Erikson, *Gandhi's Truth* (New York: Norton, 1969), pp. 231, 239.

isfy norms that, given his circumstances and interests, create a difficult contradiction between how he actually feels and how he feels obliged to behave.

In Winstanley this contradiction takes a particularly intense form because of his diagnosis of the angry and immoderate behavior of the elder brothers. They believe that the "zealous" service of God and country is a legitimate way to use their anger. Winstanley argues, however, that their conscious anger derives from the unconscious rage that he, like them, associates with the back part and with pride. Thus, he believes that their acknowledged anger at their enemies disguises a deeper and unacknowledged anger in themselves. Ruled by this shameful anger, they are "the devils within" who lack "the inward power" to live up to their professions to saintliness (378).

Because the elder brothers feel entitled by their god to be angry, Winstanley calls their god covetousness. He insists that god alone has the right to be angry, whereas the good son is obliged to relinquish the pride of "judgment and vengeance." By submitting to god's will, he would radically distinguish himself from Cain and justify his own assertion that no unconscious pride rules him. Thus, he "commits our cause to thee, O King of Righteousness, to judge between us and them that strive against us" (396) because this decision is not in his personal power as a body nor in his authority as a creature. Since final judgments are not for him, or any mortal, to make, he feels free to focus on his own limited "work," which is to testify to the spirit of love.

But it also can be said that Winstanley feels loving because he has surrendered vengeance to a god he believes will vindicate him:

> This power of love is the King of Righteousness . . . the restoring power that is now rising up to change all things into his own nature. . . . He will be your judge, for vengeance is his. And for any wrong you have done me, as I can tell you of many, yet I have given all matters of judgment and vengeance into his hand, and I am sure he will do right and discover him that is the true trespasser that takes away my rights from me. (332)

Because Winstanley believes that god will do the dirty work of purging and restoring covetous creatures, he is not ruled by his desire to punish; by surrendering it to a god whose righteousness and power he can trust, he does overcome vengefulness in his own action.

Yet the very fact that Winstanley "gives" vengeance to god suggests that he is not totally like the harmless cows, nor totally unlike those angry others who persecute them. Moreover, by splitting off his anger, he preserves his sense of innocence and legitimacy; but he cannot make an argument that anger is legitimate, or that it can be given a legitimate form. As a result, Winstanley is driven into an emotional corner by his angry feelings about harassment, the failure of the revolution, and the sacrifices he is prevented from redeeming.

VENGEANCE AND SELF-SACRIFICE

Since Winstanley and his colony are subject to harassment, while the blood crimes of the conquest go unredeemed, he begins a dialogue with god:

> Ever since I did obey thy voice, to speak and act this truth [that the earth should become a common treasury], I am hated, reproached, and oppressed on every side. And so I see, Father, that England yet does choose to fight with the sword of iron and covetousness, rather than by the sword of the spirit, which is love. And what thy purpose is with this land, or with my body, I know not; but establish thy power in me, and then do what pleases thee. (328–29)

He asks god, Is it thy will that the diggers and cows be punished? This question raises another: which of thy purposes do I really embody? Winstanley must reconsider whether in fact he is honoring god's will. His introspection leads him in two contrasting directions, each of which works out the anger he cannot own directly.

If it is god's will that he should be hated, he must stay humble to reaffirm that he is the reverent son who above all else loves his father: "I'll stand and see what he will do with me, for as yet I know not. . . . And so I said, Father do what thou wilt, this cause is thine, and thou knowest that the love to righteousness makes me do what I do" (328). Humbling himself to what appears to be god's will, he renews his faith that god loves him:

> These and such like sweet thoughts dwelt upon my heart as I went along, and I felt myself like a man in a storm, standing under shelter upon a hill in peace, waiting til the storm be over to see the end of it, and of many other things that my eye is fixed upon. (329)

Imagining himself sheltered by god's love for him, however, he also can dream of god's vengeance on those who harass him:

> And you all must and shall be torn to pieces and scattered and shamed for your excessive pride, covetousness, hardness of heart, self-love, and hypocrisy. And your verbal professions shall be loathed by all and be cast out, as

stinking imaginary dung of false-hearted ones, who profess love in words and in actions deny love. (447)

If Winstanley admitted he were angry at god as well as at other creatures, he would not feel legitimate. Since the only legitimate anger is god's, who has the right to judge and punish, Winstanley's own anger appears in fantasies of divine retribution, while he continues to declare that he loves purely.

For instance, as Moses, the mouthpiece of god, Winstanley feels entitled to announce god's wrath:

> In the name of the Lord that hath drawn me forth to speak to thee . . . I command thee, to let Israel go free. . . . If thou wilt not . . . then know that whereas I brought ten plagues upon [Pharaoh], I will multiply my plagues upon thee, til I make thee wary and miserably ashamed. (265)

As if struck by the violence of his words, however, he adds, "This conquest over thee shall be got, not by sword or weapon, but by my spirit, saith the Lord of Hosts" (265). The anger he surrenders to god often overwhelms even the idiom of Christ:

> O ye rulers of the earth, kiss the son . . . least his anger fall upon you. . . . He shook heaven and earth when Moses law was cast out, but he will shake heaven and earth even now much more, and nothing shall stand but what is lovely; be wise, scorn not the counsel of the poor, least you be whipped by your own rod. (390)

Especially after the episode with the cows, Winstanley's declarations of his own meekness are colored by his anger:

> Though you should kill my body or starve me in prison, yet know, the more you strive, the more troubles your hearts shall be filled with, and do the worst you can to hinder public freedom, you shall come off losers in the end. (332)

But he immediately adds: "I mean, you shall lose your kingdom of darkness, though I lose my livelihood, the poor cows" (333).

Thus, his growing rage increasingly effaces the boundary between angry god and loving son: if the elder brothers do not "put into sincere action" their "promises, oaths, and engagements," says Winstanley, "the lamb will show himself to be a lion and tear you to pieces for your most abominable dissembling hypocrisy, and give your land to a people who better deserve it" (386).[8]

8. There is evidence for a Nietzschean argument about the resentment of the weak in Winstanley's repeated references to the *pity* he feels for the elder brothers, specifically for

As he collapses the distinction that assures his legitimacy, Winstanley reveals the anger about which he is ambivalent. That ambivalence is indicated in his other response to the suffering of the diggers, cows, and himself: his indignation and his fantasies of vengeance are paralleled by a growing guilt. It is noteworthy that in his description the cows suffer because *he* is on the commons; they are sacrificed because they gave *him* milk or nurtured *his* action. It is likely that the treatment of the cows also symbolizes his sense that the diggers, too, are punished for the visions he had; the cows' suffering symbolizes the price others pay for his actions, which he desperately insists are not transgressions dictated by his pride but acts of love enjoined by god's will.

In part, his words suggest that whereas the cows are really innocent, he is not, and therefore it is he, not they, who deserves to suffer. It is as if Isaac, having witnessed the truly innocent suffering of the ram sacrificed in his stead, had insisted that he too must suffer to atone for that sacrifice. In part, however, Winstanley maintains that it is love for god that led him to the commons and caused others' suffering; god is the author of his actions. But he cannot angrily blame god, and instead he feels responsible as the willing instrument of god, even if it was god's will that he carried out.

Accordingly, whereas Job indignantly contends with god and proclaims his unwillingness to suffer, Winstanley insists on his "worthiness" to suffer (393). Job truly feels innocent and righteous, but Winstanley feels called to suffer, as if he does not feel innocent or feels obliged to prove his innocence (which otherwise is in jeopardy). His unexpiated guilt and his unacceptable anger drive him into the paradoxical position of embracing the suffering about which he is indignant. Indeed, perhaps

---

the suffering that god will inflict on them or that their own covetousness will cause them. He pities not only their defeated "striving as it were for life" but also the torment they *will* suffer:

> There is a time appointed of the righteous judge, that all flesh shall see itself in its own colors, and when the flesh doth see itself in its own beastly shape, he will appear so deformed, so piteous a confused chaos of misery and shame, that the sight thereof shall be a great torment to himself. (223)

Their impending suffering enables him to say, "I pity you for the torment your spirit must go through" (391). He pities the elder brothers for the suffering he *anticipates* they will undergo, and indeed, wills on them. Psychologically, Winstanley's belief that god will punish (and restore) allows him to indulge feelings of pity while displacing his angry feelings onto god, who does the punishing. Thus, his analysis of the elder brothers suggests Nietzsche's arguments about resentment and weakness, but so do his own declarations of pity.

he feels "worthy" to suffer because he does hate the elder brothers as well as the god whose will apparently requires suffering.

He had hoped that his love could redeem the transgression of others; then he had hoped that his love could redeem his own transgressions; but now his attempt at redemption generates more anger and entails more suffering. The example of the crucified Christ, which he had hoped to avoid, returns as an answer to his need for atonement. Enraged at the persecution of Christ in and as the poor, Winstanley feels obliged to identify with the crucified Christ and offers himself for sacrifice.[9]

Winstanley resists the notion that dirty human hands have a right to shape the world. As the instrument of god, he would "turn the world upside down" without committing transgression. As his year as a digger unfolds, he struggles with that desire for purity, especially as he discovers that his idea of goodness causes others to suffer and fails to build a better world. Though he is pulled toward an overt acknowledgment of legitimate violence, he never openly accepts his anger or complicity in transgression. At the same time, however, he offers a powerful example of what it means to sublimate anger, to give it a principled and political form, and therefore to shape the world in a more loving way. His politics arise, then, from the admirable desire not to make the world worse in the struggle to make it just, but also from the questionable need to remain pure.

9. In a very insightful essay about psychology and politics, Susan Griffin argues:

There are two kinds of anger. The first is accurate and appropriate; it is *known*. But the second is not accurately placed. It is displaced and therefore *unknown*. The first anger . . . liberates one, both in mind and body. But the second anger . . . imprisons. It becomes obsessive; it turns into bitterness; it leads to self-defeat; it turns us against ourselves. Because this second anger hides another and deeper anger, the true anger, of which one is ashamed. Therefore . . . [one] who does not explore her own emotions is in danger of turning against herself.

What Griffin says about the "deeper" anger applies to Winstanley, for it seems likely that he lives, as she suggests, "with the constant and inarticulate feeling that one's inner self is evil, wrong, or even repulsive. And moreover, since one is hiding, one is actually lying, and this lie compounds one's feelings of wrongness. It is thus inevitable that displaced anger will lead to self-hatred and even to a desire for self-punishment" (Susan Griffin, "The Way of All Ideology," *Signs* 7, no. 3 [Spring 1982]: 641–60).

CHAPTER VII

Sexual Politics and the Beast Within

Those moralists who command man first of all and above all
to gain control of himself thus afflict him with a peculiar
disease. . . . Whatever may henceforth push, pull, attract, or
impel . . . from inside or outside, it will always seem to him
as if his self-control were endangered. . . . He stands . . . the
eternal guardian of his castle, since he has turned himself into
a castle. Of course, he can achieve *greatness* this way. But he
has certainly become insufferable for others, difficult for
himself, and impoverished and cut off from the most
beautiful fortuities of his soul. Also from all further
instruction. For one must be able to lose oneself occasionally
if one wants to learn something from things different from
oneself.

—Nietzsche

In December 1649 Parson Platt finally succeeded in persuading General
Fairfax to intervene, and for the first time since June the army stood by
while tenant farmers destroyed the diggers' shacks. Winstanley knows
that Christ was not crucified only by Pilate: he was betrayed by Judas,
one of the apostles. In the winter of 1649–50 Winstanley begins to account for the complicity of the poor in the failure of the revolution and
in the harassment of the diggers; he begins to speak directly to the poor,
who have been doing Platt's dirty work.

To some degree Winstanley portrays the poor as innocent victims of
false promises: "If common freedom were not pretended, the commoners of the land would never dance after the pipe of self-seeking
wits" (534). The poor clearly understand freedom but have been betrayed and coerced. Accordingly, he says that "the poor tenants pulled
down our houses" because they feared "they should be turned out

of service or their livings." Nonetheless, Winstanley does not excuse the poor:

> If any fearful and covetous tenant[s] . . . do beat the poor men off from planting the Commons, then they have broke the Engagement and Law of the land, and both Lords and tenants are conspiring to uphold or bring in the Kingly and Lordly Power again . . . and are traitors to the Commonwealth of England. (412)

The poor are not simply "poor enforced slaves"; they choose to be victims when instead they could dig.

Accordingly, Winstanley addresses their fear in order to engender different choices. To his "brethren" he says, "let not slavish fear possess the hearts of the poor" because, he insists, "the army hath purchased your freedom, . . . the Parliament hath declared for your freedom, and all the laws of the commonwealth are your protection" (413). He also reminds the poor that digging could bring real benefits to those with desperate needs: "Will you live in straits and die in poverty when you may live comfortably?" (408). The prevention of famine, the indignity of begging, the danger of theft, are mentioned as "encouragements, out of many, to move you to stand up for your freedom in the land by acting with plow and spade upon the commons." Indeed, he says, "nothing is wanting on your part but courage and faithfulness" (413).

Although increasingly ambivalent about the younger brothers, Winstanley's initial view of them lacks the demonic element found in his attitude toward the elder brothers. In the spring of 1650, however, Winstanley announces his discovery of a "beast" in the poor. He writes a "Vindication of the Diggers, who are slandered with the Ranting action. And my end is only to advance the kingdom of peace in and among mankind, which is and will be torn to pieces by the ranting power, if reason do not kill this five headed or sensitive Beast" (403).

Ranters play Judas to his Christ because they profess love and community and reject the Puritan ethic and property, but embrace sexual promiscuity and idleness, foment quarrels, seduce or rape digger women, father bastard offspring, and tempt young adults with their libertine ways. "Beware of this ranting practice: for it is that golden, pleasing, and deceitful bait whereby foolish young men are taken, ensnared, and wrapped up in many bondages. It is a nursery of idleness, hardness of heart, and hypocrisy, making men to speak one thing and do another, that they may enjoy their destroying delights" (ESU/14). While Winstanley criticizes the ranters, however, the elder brothers use the "ranter

practice" to slander and discredit the diggers, as if the diggers were ranters or made ranters possible.

As Winstanley's antinomian revolt of the spirit is ensnared in a revolt of the flesh, he is caught between the ranter Beast and the kingly
Dragon. His cultural alternative to ranters and the Protestant ethic
clarifies Winstanley's complicated relationship to his own Puritan antecedents and leads into the heart of the tensions that animate his thought
and politics.

THE RANTERS

Who were the ranters? They included demobilized troops and defeated Levellers, unemployed vagabonds and rebellious young people,
religious "seekers" and former political activists. These people had been
led to an individualist, relativist hedonism, which reflected outrage
at political oppression, ridicule of Puritan hypocrisy, cynicism about
moral standards, and despair about worldly commitments of any sort.
In defiance of Puritan injunctions about work, love, and political obedience, and in despair about political resistance, they cynically, angrily,
and joyously embraced the bodily present.

Conservative Puritans, perceiving what they considered a revolt of
the flesh, charged that ranters would have

> no Christ within; no scripture to be a rule; no ordinances, no law, but their
> lusts; no heaven or glory but here; no sin but what men fancied to be so; no
> condemnation of sin but in the consciences of ignorant ones.[1]

According to Christopher Hill, however, there was a positive and liber-
ating truth in what the elder brothers condemned as blasphemy:

> [The ranters'] materialistic pantheism is a denial of the dualism which sepa-
> rates God in heaven from sinful man on earth. . . . God is not a Great Task-
> master: he is member of the community of my one flesh, one matter. The
> world is not a vale of tears. . . . Ranters insisted that matter is good because
> we live here and now.[2]

That all matter is good because the spirit is embodied in the flesh meant
to ranters that judgment and sin were eliminated along with law and the
Puritan covenant of works.

---

1. Quoted in Christopher Hill, *The World Turned Upside Down* (New York: Viking, 1972), p. 190.
2. Ibid., p. 165.

When a conservative like Richard Baxter warned that they merely intended to sanction "hideous blasphemy and continuous whoredom," however, he was not without grounds. Ranter Laurence Clarkson, for example, confirmed Baxter's fears:

> There is no such act as drunkenness, adultery, and theft in God. . . . Sin hath its conception only in the imagination. . . . What act soever is done by thee in light and love is light and lovely, though it be that act called adultery. . . . No matter what Scripture, saints, or churches say, if that within thee do not condemn thee, thou shalt not be condemned.[3]

But ranters quite consciously used the idea of Christian liberty to expose the conventionality, and thus the social purpose, of Puritan ideas of sin. Sin was a way to sanctify property, the patriarchal family, and the state: it is not by chance that Clarkson specified theft and adultery, which presume that the earth and women are property. Ranters also tried to release people from the personal torment and inner division engendered by ideas of sin, which stigmatized sexuality and repressed each person's sense of inner justification.

Freedom from Puritan moral restraints was expressed by ranters in several ways. They declared their freedom by swearing: Abiezzer Coppe said he had suppressed himself for twenty-seven years and then simply *let go*. Hill remarks about Coppe:

> Great tensions must lie behind attitudes to swearing, whether in his indulgence after 1646 or in his earlier repression. . . . Swearing was an act of defiance, both of God and of middle class standards. . . . Bibliolatry led to a [Puritan] phobia about swearing; rejection of the Bible made it possible again, and with it, a release of the repression which gave the Puritan middle class their moral energy.[4]

For ranters, release from repression also meant the freedom to embrace sexuality without shame or guilt. And letting go of guilt meant that ranters did not feel compelled to justify themselves through diligent labor in a calling. In fact, they reveled in idleness, the Puritan nightmare. In the name of love and spirit, ranters attacked the Puritan ethic of chastity and repression, compulsive labor and anxious self-control. Hill says:

> The Ranter emphasis on love is perhaps mainly a negative reaction to nascent capitalism, a cry for human brotherhood, freedom, and unity against

3. Ibid., p. 172.
4. Ibid., p. 160.

the divisive forces of a harsh ethic enforced by the harsh discipline of the market. . . . Much of Ranterism was less a new ethic than an extension downward of the attitudes of the traditional leisure classes—dislike of labor, sexual promiscuity, swearing, an emphasis on works rather than faith. All these linked the upper and lower classes in opposition to the intermediate proponents of the Protestant Ethic.[5]

Overthrowing the internal tyranny of the Puritan superego meant that anger, no longer directed against the self, was directed at external enemies: swearing, promiscuity, and idleness were loaded with angry defiance and self-consciously political intent. Coppe declared that "honor, nobility, gentility, property, superfluity" had been the "father of hellish, horrid pride, . . . yea, the cause of all the blood that hath ever been shed, from the blood of the righteous Abel to the blood of the last Levellers that were shot to death." Their blood cried out for vengeance: "Now the necks of horrid pride" must be "chopped off at one blow" so that "parity, equality, community" might establish "universal love, universal peace, and perfect freedom."[6]

But ranters disavowed discipline and therefore the vocation of conscientious political labor. Although politically aware, they were disillusioned about the possibility of organized political activity and hostile to the strictures it entailed. Ranters were not soldiers, even of Christ, but Dionysians. They undermined family, property, and the state not through organized politics but by subverting their basis in personal repression. The ranters acted as cultural guerrillas, stirring up what the Puritan fathers repressed.

In Hill's wonderful and sympathetic account, surely shaped by the "counterculture" of the 1960s, ranters carried political revolt onto the terrain of culture. Hill emphasizes the similarities between ranters and Winstanley, for each located spirit in the body and the body in nature, trying to overcome possessiveness and social division. Each developed an analysis of Puritan superego and law, linking psychological repression to the rule of a class and its moral standards. Each made an antinomian attack on judgments and laws as fleshly inventions and defended instead a new community knit together by the power of love.

Ranters, however, intentionally disrupted the digger colony and apparently considered Winstanley a prig, a charlatan, and a hypocrite. In turn, Winstanley condemned them as a "beast" that "tempted" and

5. Ibid., p. 274.
6. Ibid., pp. 168–69.

then "devoured" the poor. He was sensitive to what Hill minimizes in the ranters: not only did they displace politics into cultural revolt, but their effort to subvert Puritan values and institutions also seemed to undermine the possibility of enduring commitments to work and worldly accomplishment, conjugal love, and an organized moral life. They seemed to deny that such commitments could be *gratifying*. For these reasons, Winstanley declared the ranters to be yet another "false savior," while ranters seemed to challenge precisely the piety and rage they brought out in Winstanley. To understand their differences, one needs to consider Winstanley's initial and basic attitude toward sex, which reveals so much else about him and became the most charged issue between them.

SEX AND MORALITY

When Winstanley wrote *The New Law of Righteousness,* he imagined that the elder brothers would accuse him of favoring theft, tumult, idleness, and "excessive community with women." As a moderate and loving Isaac, however, Winstanley dismissed such accusations as the projection of a covetous imagination. But he also insisted that the community of earth and spirit would abolish such behavior by "killing" covetousness:

> This universal power of a righteous law shall be so plainly writ in every ones heart that none shall desire to have more than another, or to be Lord over another, or to lay claim to anything as his; this phrase of *Mine and Thine* shall be swallowed up in the law of righteous actions one to another, for they shall all live as brethren, every one doing as he would be done by. (183)

When the righteous law rules within, he imagined, there will be an abundance of what is essential to life, and "pride and envy likewise [will be] killed," so that no one will scramble for precedence or for more than is necessary for survival:

> All shall cheerfully put to their hands to make these things that are needful, one helping another; there shall be none Lord over others, but everyone shall be a lord of him self, subject to the law of righteousness, reason and equity, which shall dwell and rule in him, which is the Lord. (184)

Winstanley's presumption was that the power of love and reason would create a harmony between desire and imagination so that people would not want more than what is righteous or appropriate to their nature and necessity as creatures.

Accordingly, to those who feared that abolishing "mine and thine" means endorsing or allowing "the community of women," that is, means the destruction of the family, Winstanley replied:

> For when man was made, he was made male and female, one man and one woman conjoined together by the law of love. . . . Reason did not make one man and many women, or one woman and many men to join together, to make the Creation perfect, but male and female in the singular number; this is enough to increase seed. And he or she that requires more wives or more husbands than one, walks contrary to the Law of Righteousness, and shall bear their shame. (185)

As with theft, so with promiscuity and adultery: the desire for superfluous goods or numerous sexual partners expresses an inappropriate reliance on "objects without" and reflects an inner hunger that nothing human or perishable can satisfy. As with labor, so with sexuality: Winstanley's notion of righteousness was meant to define the legitimate way to exerise a necessary human capacity so that people meet their needs in a way that makes them free. The necessity of procreation, he seemed to be saying, requires only one mate, and sexuality is legitimate only in relation to that mate. Monogamous heterosexuality is therefore the fruit of maturity: "Though this immoderate lust after strange flesh rules in the bodies of men now, while the first Adam is King, yet it shall not be so when the second man rises to reign, for then chastity is one glory of the Kingdom" (185).

Sexuality was included in the profound sense of limits animating Winstanley's notion of legitimacy. Legitimate sex was limited to marriage, and perhaps even to procreation, although his reference to what is "enough to increase seed" does not have to mean that sex may occur only for that reason. He confined sex to marriage partly because of his concern for "mutual preservation." To Winstanley, adultery and promiscuity qualified as exploitive behavior because neither really assures the "preservation" of the "strange flesh," and adultery would seem to disregard the preservation of one's mate as well. At the same time, he criticized husbands and fathers who treat wives and children like servants because love requires an equality that precludes domination or exploitation (159).

As with violence, so with sex: Winstanley sought to distinguish between impulses and actions that are "beastly" and those that are "human." Although acting "like men" does not require the purification of sexuality, as he would have people purify anger, there was in practice a comparable effort to integrate powerful, natural, and one could say instinct-laden impulses into moral relations with others. Like other activities (labor) and impulses (anger), sex involves other people and therefore has a moral quality that must be honored if it is to be legitimate. Just as he tried to transform violence into "experienced speech" between mutually recognized equals, so he intended to transform "lust after strange flesh" into a mutually enhancing sexual bond between covenanted equals. He did not value sex in its own right: he measured humanness or righteousness by how thoroughly people knit together desire and morality, or their nature and their choices, by finding "the reason" in impulses and relationships.

Thus, Winstanley was not ascetic in any simple way; but neither was his a Dionysian Christianity, like Norman O. Brown's. Winstanley did not embrace sexuality and its joys, and one imagines that his repeated language of "love" sublimated and universalized what otherwise might be expressed directly in sex. One could infer, then, that though he defended monogamy, he might have feared too intense and sexual an attachment to even one person. Indeed, Winstanley's effort to articulate a moral understanding of the life of humans as creatures may involve an unavoidable and underlying sense that sexual desire is a particularly troublesome aspect of human nature. To those who would be free within, the power of sexual desire and the power of those taken as sexual objects might be seen as threatening to the moderation and integrity of the self and to the righteous concern for the preservation of others. By defending monogamy, however, Winstanley meant to find the "reason at the bottom of love" so that it does not become "mere self-willedness of the flesh."

What he dismissed in *The New Law of Righteousness* as the covetous imagination of the elder brothers, however, appears in the flesh as the Beast overcoming the poor, thereby justifying the rulers' violent inclination to oppress the diggers. Ranters do represent a demonic version or parody of Winstanley's practices and principles, a return of his repressed, of the lust, rage, and selfishness he tries to purify through digging.

WINSTANLEY'S CRITIQUE OF THE RANTERS

It is tempting to consider Winstanley's response to the ranters as a new "stage" in the course of his learning. He began with what could be called an "oral" stage, as his language of sincere milk addressed issues of nourishment and what Erik Erikson calls "basic trust." Next, Winstanley attended to an "anal" stage, as his argument about manuring the earth addressed issues of self-control, work, and worldly accomplishment. Now, he attends to a "genital" stage, as he addresses issues of sexuality and commitment, facing the relationship between the self and the other in its most mature and difficult form.

One should not take such "stages" literally, but they do suggest the kinds of issues and arguments that Winstanley brings to bear on sexuality and the ranters. Having learned that freedom and happiness depend on trusting the Father within and reciprocating the love of the Common Mother, he now argues that freedom is realized through sexual and moral reciprocity with another person. In addition, his criticism of ranter sexuality recapitulates the imagery and arguments of his earlier texts. Oral and excremental metaphors disclose what he believes is wrong with ranters' relationships to their bodies and to others, but as before, they also suggest his own ambivalences.

When Winstanley characterizes the ranter practices that violate digger principles, he returns to his theory of the Fall:

> The ranter practice . . . is a kingdom that lies in objects, as in outward enjoyment of meat, drink, pleasures, and women; so that the man within can have no quiet rest unless he enjoy these outward objects in excess, all of which are vanishable. Therefore it is the devil's kingdom of darkness. (399)

Because the "immoderate ranting practice of the senses" rejects the guiding and moderating power of reason, says Winstanley, the ranters indulge in "abundant eating and drinking, and actual community with variety of women . . . which is the life of the beast." The ranters' voracious hunger for objects in the kingdom without "is destructive to the body, house, or temple wherein reason or the spiritual power dwells; it brings disease, infirmities, weakness, and rottenness upon the body and so ruins the house about a mans ears, that he cannot live in peace." Moreover, "diseases of the body cause sorrows of mind . . . for when you want your delight in excessive copulation with women, and in superabundant eating and drinking, which is a wasteful spending of the treasures of the earth, then anger, rage, and variety of vexations possess the mind or man within" (399–400).

Ranters are fallen Adams, driven by inner emptiness and rage to "spend" themselves in the pursuit of a satisfaction no object can provide. In the process, they turn the world and others into objects they "waste" immoderately and selfishly. As always, Winstanley sees powerfully attractive objects seducing men, who at the same time are compelled from within by their hunger and imagination. But ranters are different from the elder brothers, who seek to control sources of nourishment they anxiously need. In response to their methodical and ascetic accumulation of objects and their dutiful regulation of women and sexuality, ranters overthrow ascetic ideals, property, and marriage.

In turn, Winstanley argues that "letting go" of the Puritan conscience has freed ranters not only from guilt but also from self-control so that the self is overwhelmed by its desire. Rejection of orthodox forms leaves ranters wild, not regenerate. As they cast out the Puritan superego, ranters are devoured by the desire and the objects it is supposed to control. Because ranters represent the return of what the elder brothers would repress, Winstanley says that "this ranting power is the resurrection of the doggish, beastly nature . . . of the filthy unrighteous power in all his branches" (402).

Ranters still are covetous toward objects and people and therefore reveal the emotional core of Puritan practice: they have abolished property and marriage but do not heal inner hunger and possessiveness. Winstanley's language suggests that ranter rejection of Puritan forms exposes the childish impulses and fantasies that truly constitute the flesh. Indeed, Winstanley's proliferating images of consuming and devouring depict the ranter beast as if it were a child, a strange suggestion since children do not manifest genital sexuality. But Winstanley's oral image suggests what troubles him about the ranters' sexuality.

Imagine that the oral hunger of the ranter man, if expressed in sexual relationships, is greedy desire for a woman, as if she were an all-giving mother, a bountiful object, and not really a person with needs of her own. As a result, in his sexual conduct he will embrace sensuality but treat the woman as a maternal source of nourishment to be devoured, not nurtured. Imagine that the self-control associated with anality appears sexually in the anxious control of a woman, as if she were a dangerous temptress eliciting passions threatening to male autonomy. Sexuality under the dominion of "the back part" is a step forward in the sense that the woman is treated as a potentially moral agent, but at the price of sensuality. Her dangerous sexuality requires that both partners rigorously impose chastity and restrict sexuality to procreation. Accordingly, Puritans theorize a moral relationship between men and women, but sexuality is guilt-ridden and duty-bound, and women bear a special stigma and burden.

By overthrowing typically Puritan self-control and guilt, ranter men recover the sensuality associated with the idea of woman as nurturant. But since their desire is unrelated to her needs, she remains exclusively an object. Neither the orthodox nor the ranters conceive of an instinctual desire genuinely gratified by sex with another person whose own desire is recognized and gratified. In contrast, Winstanley appears to be defending a sexual relationship that is both sensual and moral, dominated neither by greed and oral hunger nor by guilt and control.[7]

For this reason, Winstanley anticipates Marx's argument that the developmental character of human desire is especially revealed in sexual relationships. In "the relation between man and woman," says Marx, one can find the "unambiguous, decisive, plain and undisguised" truth by which one can judge the whole level of human development:

> The direct, natural, and necessary relation of person to person is the relation of man and woman. . . . In this relationship . . . is sensuously manifested, reduced to an observable fact, the extent to which the human essence has become the human essence *for* man. . . . In this relationship is revealed too, the extent to which man's need has become a human need; the extent to which, therefore, the other person as a person has become for him a need— the extent to which he is in his individual existence at the same time a social being.[8]

Both theorists argue that because it is a natural impulse that involves others, sex typifies one's relationship to one's body and to others, and thus embodies the character of culture. Accordingly, Winstanley and Marx evaluate how natural drives are tied to moral relations, and they find in sexuality a measure of how civilized, or "human," people are. Their criterion is "humanness," that is, the extent to which the act of meeting needs involves the self-conscious recognition of others as subjects in their own right. Each theorist allows that sex can be a genuinely and mutually gratifying act, in which physical pleasure is heightened by a self-conscious need for the other as a person.

Both Winstanley and Marx therefore object to the "property relation" in which wife and children lose autonomy and become the servants of the husband, as sexual desire is attenuated by fear, guilt, and possessiveness. In addition, each theorist objects to a merely "negative transcendence" of private property and marriage because desire remains exploitive or "one-sided."[9]

7. Winstanley's response to the ranters and the orthodox suggests a view not unlike Nathaniel Hawthorne's in "The Maypole of Marrymount."
8. Karl Marx, *Marx-Engels Reader*, p. 83.
9. About "primitive communism," Marx says:

> The positive transcendence of private property—i.e. the sensuous appropriation for and by man of the human essence and of human life—is not to be considered merely in

But whereas Marx's idea of mutuality appears as the result of a historical progression and arises only by passing through primitive communism, Winstanley explicitly depicts genuinely reciprocal sexuality as an ever-present possibility from which men and women "fall" into beastly covetousness:

> The ranting practice is a peacebreaker; it breaks the peace in families and rents in pieces mankind. For when true love hath united a man and a woman to be husband and wife, and they live in peace, when the ranting power or king lust of flesh comes in, he separates those very friends, causing both to run into the sea of confusion, madness, and destruction, to leave each other and children, or to live in discontent with each other. (400)

The imagery of the sea suggests Winstanley's own fear of the Dionysian character of a certain kind of sexuality, and perhaps of sexuality as such. His fear, however, is related to his concern for moral reciprocity, and his warning about destruction refers not only to the self but also to women and children.

In this regard, Winstanley's language is striking:

> Therefore, know all ye lascivious feeders . . . that ye are breeders of foul, filthy, beastly, abominable children, which come into the world to preach to the nation in which they appear what . . . filthy sin or lascivious feeding heat hath begot, for lascivious feeding causeth lascivious acting. (403)

Evoking the Biblical tale of Ishmael, Winstanley calls the ranters' children "filthy and abominable." He uses excremental language to reject the poisoned fruit he finds shameful. Yet the children merely "preach to the nation" about the character of the parents. He warns that "the children begotten through this forced immoderate heat of lust prove furious and full of rage" (400). His apportioning of blame among the parents, however, suggests his overt and covert concerns.

Winstanley appears to blame male partners especially, for he views women as the chief victims of a "King Lust" that arises most powerfully in men:

> Mother and child are like to have the worst of it, for the men will be gone and leave them, and regard them no more than other women, like a bull that begets a calf, that never takes care neither for cow nor calf, after he hath had his pleasure. Therefore you women, beware. (401)

---

the sense of direct one-sided gratification, merely in the sense of possessing, having. . . . Private property has made us so stupid and one-sided that an object is ours only when we have it . . . when it is directly possessed, eaten, drunk, worn, inhabited, etc.—in short, when it is used by us. (87)

As before, the imagery of the cow denotes innocence victimized by beastliness, this time by lust, which for Winstanley is specifically a "false generating fire" because it is fueled by the unacknowledged desire to punish, use, and abandon. Like the children he fathers, the male is dominated by rage and hunger, which he directs at women, whom he treats as cows. Winstanley therefore warns, in verse:

> Beware you women of the ranting crew
> And call not freedom those things that are vain
> For if a child you get by ranting deeds
> The man is gone and leaves the child your gain.
> Then you and yours are left by such free men
> For other women are as free for them. (ESU/14)

These passages suggest that Winstanley deals with Hagars and Ishmaels, and the heirs of Ishmael, in a strikingly different way from that of the Puritans, who tend to punish them and exonerate Abraham. Whereas ministers reassert paternal power by demonizing women's sexuality, Winstanley declares men the chief culprits, whose lack of self-control prevents "true union" and victimizes children.

Yet the imagery of the cow also suggests Winstanley's ambivalence about women. Many ranters were women, who presumably chose the lusty life rather than a "union," true or otherwise. Winstanley rightly points to the ways they can be victimized by sexual liberty, but he does so by casting women as cows, symbols of nurturance, victims and objects of male desire, not agents of their own desire. By symbolizing women in this way, he suggests that they are not the lustful ones, an assertion that reveals, perhaps, his own wish that they be as he depicts them, willing and respected sources of nurturance, without lust. Thus, he overtly challenges the exploitation of women but also denies their own lusty agency because his idea of reverent reciprocity depends on idealization. He still needs to see women in a certain confining—and confined—way: like god and nature, women must be *safe* sources of nourishment.

Nonetheless, his symbolism of women enables him to transpose his argument about ranter sexuality into one about the ranter relationship to the wealth and labor of the community at large. What "distempers" a family also disrupts "whole nations":

> They that are the sons and daughters of that unrational power neither can nor will work, but live idle, . . . cheating others that are simple and of civil, flexible nature, so that by seeking their own freedom they inbondage others,

which is selfish but not universal love, for true love seeks the preservation of others as of oneself. (401)

A "true love" between conjugal partners corresponds to the community itself as a household in which members strive for their mutual preservation. Just as ranters seek liberty from Puritan sexual injunctions in a way that exploits women, so they seek liberty from the work ethic in a way that exploits others, or the community in general. For it is the ranter "nature" to "get what he can from others labor, to eat up others and make them poor, and then to laugh and rejoice in others poverty" (401). To "live idle on another mans labors" recapitulates the sin of the gentry and reveals again the exploitive and resentful motive at the heart of ranter liberty. Like the woman's body and being, the labor of others (the wealth of a community) is parasitically wasted and consumed. And just as the ranter Beast disrupts the spirit of mutual preservation within the family, so too it "inflames" people to "destructive" acts like "quarreling, killing, burning houses or corn" (400).[10]

To Winstanley, ranters combine aggrandizement rationalized as love, and weakness indulged as liberation; they resurrect and universalize the wantonness of childhood—they behave like bad children. They are unwilling or unable to form mature bonds, work for worldly accomplishment, or even feed themselves through their own labor; they refuse to act responsibly toward those they in fact need. Accordingly, they live, consume, and play in the context of utter dependency on the work and bodies of others. This dependency, which they call freedom, exposes the truth about them.

There is surely a temperamental element in Winstanley's critique. Winstanley does not shock, invert a stigma, or outrage the uptight; ranters are exuberantly excessive, theatrical, and immoderate. They are Groucho Marxists, whereas he is essentially a mild-mannered man, uncomfortable with excess, fanaticism, or display. Rather than "letting

10. In a parallel way, Marx describes

the bestial form of counterposing to marriage (certainly a form of exclusive private property) the community of women, in which a woman becomes a piece of communal and common property. It may be said that this idea of the community of women gives away the secret of this as yet crude and thoughtless communism. Just as the woman passes from marriage to a general prostitution, so the entire world of wealth . . . passes from the relationship of exclusive marriage with the owner of private property to a state of universal prostitution with the community. General envy, constituting itself as a power, is the disguise in which avarice re-establishes itself and satisfies itself, only in another way, in the form of envy and the urge to reduce to a common level. (82–83) go," he puts his energy into cooperative work and loving politics. Thus, he plays Apollo to their Dionysus, trying to hold together what they tear to pieces: his defense of the marriage bond bespeaks his commitment to the deeper marriage of head and heart, mind and senses, reason and emotion, discipline and liberty. His temperament and his commitment to empowering the poor require an alternative to both the Puritans' empire of repression and accumulation and the ranters' "primitive communism" of remission and envious resentment.

WINSTANLEY'S RESPONSE

To use a Biblical metaphor, Winstanley is in the wilderness and sees the ranters dancing around the golden calf of their desire. He understands and shares their desire not to go to a Canaan ruled by stern fathers and punitive law, but he believes they replicate the fathers' exploitation, leave intact the fathers' law, and undermine the commitments that could overthrow it. From Winstanley's point of view, ranters not only reject the fathers' exodus, so to speak, but also preclude the possibility of an exodus within and against that exodus.

Winstanley is especially concerned that many of the poor will be tempted to join in the dance. Those "most likely to be tempted and set upon and torn to pieces by this devouring beast," he warns, are "you that are merely civil and of a loving and flexible disposition, wanting in the strength of reason and the life of universal love" (403). The merely civil are not the orthodox, who are not of a loving and flexible disposition, but the young people who participated in the movement beyond and against Puritan orthodoxy. They will be tempted by the ranters not so much because of a repressed desire for sensual enjoyment as because of their inability and unwillingness to *judge:*

> Rather than proud civility be counted ignorant, it . . . first stands looking and saying, I can say nothing against this ranting practice, and then afterwards yields, and then is ensnared and taken by the subtle devouring ranting Beast. But he that obeys reasons law within shall escape that snare.

Civility appears as tolerance but is fearful of being left naked by changing fashions of the inner light. The refusal to judge expresses not only fear of the opinion of others but also the desire for remission from judgment altogether, and therefore from sin and guilt, which is precisely what the ranters offer: "The ranting power would make this covenant with all men, to put out their eyes . . . and to see by his eyes . . . and then he calls them high-lighted creatures; otherwise, he tells them they live below him" (401). Those who "yield" to the ranters are thereafter "ensnared" because they lack the autonomy that comes from commitment to the inward authority of reason.

Ranters will emerge and be found appealing because of the real difficulty of making judgments in a time when social and political upheaval unsettles and discredits moral standards, and because of the desire in such times to be released from all standards, which necessarily appear arbitrary and are likely to feel oppressive. Ranters feed on the impulse to rebel against traditional authority, which not only entails social criticism, individualism, and tolerance but also, in the context of political defeat, appears as the refusal to make judgments and commitments. The question Winstanley must address, then, is how to respond both to ranters and to those they seduce.[11]

Winstanley rejects the approach of the elder brothers, who wield the sword to force the stiff-necked and weak-willed to obey, for a "purge" only reenacts the paternal tyranny that is the real problem:

> Let none go about to suppress the ranting power by their punishing hand, for it is the work of the Righteous and Rational spirit within, not thy hand without, that must suppress it. But if thou wilt needs be punishing, then see thou be without sin thyself and then cast the first stone at the Ranter. (402)

Moreover, repression will only backfire, by intensifying the resentment of the poor: "to suppress sinners by force," he warns, "wilt thereby but increase their rage and thy own trouble." Therefore, "let everyone alone, to stand and fall to their own master."

11. When moral standards are seen to be conventional, and felt to be oppressive, but changing the world seems impossible, those who once agitated for social change are likely to express in cultural terms their political defiance and their despair. Powerlessness and rebellion can appear as loving life in the present, but it is a life narrowed to an absorption in the sensations of the body. As the 1960s demonstrated, cultural experimenters can emerge as part of a political movement of rebellion and can humanize it; but they only become "ranters" when political change fails or is repressed, or when people begin to despair of its efficacy. Whereas cultural revolt disavows politics, political rebels form rigidly ideological sects, like the Weather Underground. In the 1640s, too, a synthesis of cultural and political revolt broke apart, for along with ranters there were the Fifth Monarchists, who embraced violence in the name of "forcing the end." The separation of political action from cultural experiment tends to drive each toward violence and narcissism because activists lose a sense of ongoing participation in a public movement with shared values.

In these terms, Winstanley's response to this situation presents an especially interesting parallel with the ideas of Christopher Lasch, who has sought to rejoin culture and politics through an implicitly Puritan affirmation of moral authority and conscientious labor. Whereas Lasch associates renewal with paternal authority, however, Winstanley tries to build an ego strong enough to be liberated from paternal authority and therefore able to form a community that moves beyond Puritanism. For an account of the 1960s that resonates with the conflict between Winstanley and the ranters, see Michael Rogin, "In the Defense of the New Left," *democracy* (November 1983): 106–16.

Winstanley's response to the culture of despair accepts the aspiration for liberation in those whose "loving and flexible disposition" has made them susceptible to ranting. In contrast to Puritan fathers, he tries to formulate a discipline that truly liberates. Winstanley may be close to the ranters' Christian liberty, however much he thinks they have perverted it, but he has absorbed, not rejected, the original Puritan emphasis on moral self-discipline and regenerate community. Therefore, while he criticizes the Puritan form of conscience and community, he rejects neither moral judgment nor communal bonds. He responds to the ranters by affirming but transforming the disciplines they deny, but without acting like a Puritan father imposing his own fleshly inventions.

Winstanley's first antidote to the ranters is the cooperative work by which people feed themselves and "enrich" the commonwealth. This labor should not be a compulsive and enslaving form of penance; rather, "it is for the health of their bodies, it is pleasure to the mind, to be free in labor one with another" (593). Such "righteous, moderate working," he imagines, will promote personal efficacy and worldly ties, which "prevent the evil of idleness and the danger of the Ranter Power" (402). Winstanley says that "the earth ought to be a common treasury to all"; but concerning women he declares, "Let every man have his own wife and every woman her own husband" (366–67). Thus, his second antidote to the ranters is monogamous marriage based on choice and desire: "Every man and woman shall have the free liberty to marry whom they love, if they can obtain the love and liking of that party . . . and neither birth nor portion shall hinder the match" (599). The alternative to legalistic or arranged conjugal ties should be committed relationships, which would strengthen each member and protect them from the ranter power.

Winstanley insists that the genuinely gratifying *practice* of work and love, by making people "free within" and effective in the world, can counteract the conditions that give rise to the ranter beast. But he knows that some diggers, while engaging in practices that accord with "the reason" in creation, are still tempted. The key, then, is knowing self-consciously the reason in oneself and in one's practices. How can people come to learn and "own" that reason?

In part, he believes that reason is a capacity akin to prudence, and therefore can be learned best by experience. Accordingly, he takes a hands-off approach: "If any should be ensnared by the subtle devouring ranting beast, . . . I profess to have nothing to do with them, but leave them to their own master, who will pay them with torment of mind and diseases in their bodies" (367). He feels sure that once the "ranter power . . . shows himself a complete man of darkness," he will "come to judgement and so be cast out of heaven, that is, out of mankind" (402). To those who have not been ensnared yet, and perhaps to aid those who have, Winstanley also explicitly teaches the principle of mutual preservation, which animates digger practices. To exemplify mutual preservation while respecting the moral autonomy of those who deny it, he counsels: "Let not sinners punish others for sin, but let the power of thy reason and righteous action shame them, and so beat down their unrational actions." If diggers "keep close to the law of righteous reason," he anticipates that they "shall presently see a return of the Ranters; for that spirit within them must shame them, and turn them, and pull them out of darkness." But how can he expect to shame people who, declaring they have been released from all judgment, appear so utterly shameless? Such questions force Winstanley to deal with cynicism and the problem of justifying moral standards.

RESPONDING TO CYNICISM

In the name of conscience or the inner light, antinomians (including Winstanley) challenged the Puritans' effort to cement a new community judging itself by new criteria. Ranters and Winstanley saw the Puritan effort to create a new order as the imposition of a mistaken view of reality that would serve the interests of the few. An order that might appear natural, incontrovertible, and just to later generations appears to Winstanley and ranters as subjective, man-made, particular, and repressive.

But Winstanley and the ranters go in different directions from this point. Ranters attack the authority of all conventions and the validity of all standards. Sin and justice are "merely" arbitrary and subjective mental categories, they say, and therefore do not require particular kinds of action. To the pure, all is pure; what feels good is good. This belief partly reflects a liberation from ruling interpretations of justice and sin. But it also expresses a cynical way of dealing with the conventionality of standards and concepts. Ranters do not say that the meaning of justice, or right and wrong, entails certain actions different from those advocated by the elder brothers. Rather, they say there is no such thing as justice and sin, or that each person defines these concepts for himself or herself. As a result, these and other evaluative words are divorced from action and deprived of their meaning. In effect, ranters refuse to be responsible for meaning what they say (and for the meaning of what they say) and will not be held accountable for their actions. They will do whatever they want and call it whatever they want.

The valid insight of the ranters into the conventionality of standards like sin and justice and their defense of the inner light become a way for the individual to sanction any and all behavior. By dismissing standards as entirely personal or arbitrary, they renounce the effort to reason about, or justify, their own values while denying that any could be commonly valid. Thus, Winstanley condemns them for being "unrational" as well as "immoderate."

Clearly, ranters try to subvert the moral authority they rightly take as illegitimate. They may intend to say that "reason" is wholly ideological, convention unavoidably arbitrary, and "immoderate" behavior wholly natural. In part, though, they cynically use the conventionality of standards to overthrow all restraint and deny all accountability. Regardless of intention, their kind of rebellion creates a "devouring" process that negates all standards. Salutary resistance to authority becomes self-destructive: since all values are merely subjective and arbitrary, ranters deprive of authority even those values in whose name they rebel. Meanwhile, those "of a loving and flexible disposition" are "ensnared" because they cannot affirm the authority and validity of their own values. The personal consequence of ranting is that people lose the sense that there is or could be a legitimate and binding personal authority within them; the political consequence is that shared standards become impossible to define, let alone uphold.

This problem with the authority of standards and values taken as conventional, as evidenced by the ranters, may have inspired Hobbes's famous "state of nature." He too developed ranter insights and relativism, but he was horrified by the logic and consequences of rebellion. Hobbes can be seen as using the ranters (and the elder brothers) to construct a larger argument about conventions and language and the relationship between standards and actions. He makes the ranter case that meanings and definitions are arbitrary and subjective, that they disclose the truth not about the world but about human passions. To Hobbes, then, ranters reveal how everyone is really in a state of nature. As a political theorist, however, he also sees that the problem of conventions is social and systemic: conflicting interpretations of god, justice, and sin will proliferate among a socially divided and individualized people.

Hobbes responds to this situation by relying on logic and definition. Believing (at least intellectually) that conventions are arbitrary, his priority is to establish definitions that are sovereign and to which all agree. An atomized people can be reunited by their consent to use words according to the fixed and indisputable definitions provided by the sovereign. Though this approach implies that any definitions will do as long as people consent to them, Hobbes also professes to offer a science whose definitions are in fact "apt" to the world. He grants that fixing and enforcing definitions is a technical solution to order and meaning, but he considers it the best response to a social disintegration that seems to defy substantive resolution or agreement on the basis of extant understandings. He also hopes, however, that people will be changed by speaking his new language so that they will be transformed into "a real unity of them all."

Thus, Hobbes goes in a direction opposite to that of the ranters. Rather than sacrifice the idea of standards to the claims of sovereign selves, he conflates conscience and desire, subordinating both to rules or standards defined as true and just by the sovereign. Because of the ranters, Winstanley agrees with Hobbes that conscience does not suffice to validate the truth of ideas, the legitimacy of standards, the justness of what is called justice. In contrast to Hobbes, however, Winstanley hopes to address the problem typified by the ranters without depriving people of the right to make judgments about public norms and rules.

By defining god as the reason within the self and in creation, Winstanley tries to provide a substantive criterion by which individuals and the community can distinguish between liberty and license, pure and corrupt speech, just and fleshly conventions, or true motions of the spirit and those motions mistakenly (or cynically) claimed to be such. But if reason is the criterion by which to judge what is godly, how does one discover what accords with it? Fundamentally, Winstanley believes we honor reason when we preserve creatures according "to the nature and necessity" of each. Of course, proposing a standard of "mutual preservation" does not settle the question of what accords with the nature and necessity of humans. Consequently, Winstanley's idea of reason involves uncertainty and conflict, which raises or leaves unresolved the Hobbesian problem of anarchy.

But Winstanley's point is not to hold people together according to whatever definitions are commonly agreed on, nor to impose the kind of community he calls "merely civil," in which there is no inward allegiance to norms. Rather, he seeks a dialogue about the criteria implicit in a community's extant values and practices. As a standard present in people and already embodied in some of their activities, "mutual preservation" is a criterion that bridges the exercise of individual judgment and the ongoing endeavor to "knit together" with others.

Thus, mutual preservation appears in the traditional meaning of *commons*, and in the history and use of concepts such as *magistrate*, *tyrant*, and *public*. To some degree Winstanley transforms the common sense of a word's meaning, but to a large extent he recalls a meaning with which people are losing touch or for which they no longer take responsibility. This is to say he also affirms and protects the practices that made, or still could make, concepts meaningful. When Winstanley defines sin as the violation of mutual preservation and then says it is sinful to enclose land and hoard superfluous goods when others are starving, his definition makes sense of the experience of the poor, in whose lives it is rooted. He would reconcile common standards and a community of individual consciences, not through technical definitions divorced from daily life, but rather by taking seriously the substantive meanings regulating that life.

Perhaps Winstanley sees a substantive solution to the problem of values and anarchy because he knows by experience that community is not merely created, nor standards merely invented, that individuals are not separated entirely, and that language is not arbitrary because it is not disembodied from the life of those who speak it. Thus, he does not start from, or presume, an abstracted (and anarchic) state of nature in which conventions must be "invented." He tries to resolve conflict about conventions and definitions by beginning with actual people embedded in a particular history and culture.

In this way, one can address the question that began this discussion about standards and cynicism: how can Winstanley expect to shame and instruct ranters? For the same reason that Socrates was able to make Thrasymachus blush: ranters implicitly invoke and feel the standards they deny. They angrily attack the elder brothers precisely for the sinful violation of justice; only because of such standards do they feel *righteously* angry. That they will not honor or acknowledge those standards in their own action is the hypocrisy and fear in their cynicism.

Accordingly, Winstanley's response to the ranters also suggests an answer to the question of his relationship to Puritanism. In each chapter, I have argued that he works from Puritan premises, whether about pride and rebirth, work and autonomy, or political liberty through covenanting. But in each case he uses Puritan idioms to transform, or deepen and broaden, his Puritan antecedents. In contrast, ranters use many of the same idioms, but they seek to explode the Puritan project by destroying the commitments and practices at its base. Unlike the ranters, therefore, Winstanley addresses, and potentially encompasses, the experience of those around him. Thus, he exemplifies the radical possibilities that can inhere in a reverence for the very idioms and traditions one transforms.

In practice, Winstanley illustrates the fact that conventions and language are neither arbitrary (and therefore invented and imposed) nor god-given (and therefore revealed and owned), but inherited, meant, and revised by humans within the bonds of a historical culture. But in part, he escapes the snare of cynicism because he believes that the values and practices appropriate to human nature and necessity are also given by a god who writes his law in each of our hearts. As an activist and writer, Winstanley tries to shame the ranters by bearing witness to the concepts and values they invoke in their attack on the Puritans. But he has faith in the "return" of these prodigal children specifically because he believes they will be shamed by the reason of the Father within. It speaks to all in the same voice and calls them back to a household in which reality is manifest, conjecture unnecessary, and speech pure.[12]

THE SHAMEFUL RESIDUE AND THE DEMON OF POLITICS

If one were to jettison Winstanley's religious language, however, in an attempt to get at the secular core of his political practice, one would lose his understanding of precisely what reanimates a demoralized people. By calling the ranters back to the judgment of the Father within, Winstanley hopes to strengthen the Christ within them: in psychoanalytic terms, Winstanley's shaming is meant to strengthen the ego by strengthening a power of inward but conscious judgment that is akin to the superego. He does not impose the punitive, paternal superego of the Puritans, but neither is he wrong to believe that "owning" inward judgments is essential to moral autonomy and relationships of mutual preservation.

But his desire to invoke the Father within and shame the ranters also reveals the underside of Winstanley's political therapy. Ranters represent Winstanley's own lust and anger in immoderate (or unsublimated)

---

12. To be sure, the ranters (and Hobbes) are more radical than Winstanley because of their cynical insight into conventionality. Perhaps Machiavelli represents a third way: one could argue that without denying conventionality, he tries to overcome the cynicism that splits bodily need from moral values. See Hanna Fenichel Pitkin, *Fortune Is a Woman* (Berkeley and Los Angeles: University of California Press, 1982).

form. They act out the beastliness Winstanley says is transformed by the Father who feeds and empowers him. It is as if they say to him: you have not transformed and cannot transform what you consider beastly in yourself and, thus, in us; as a result, although you speak of returning us to the Father within, we proclaim the return of what you can only repress; we preach to the nations what you in your shame try to hide. As if in response, they elicit from Winstanley not only the language of love and restoration but also the language of angry expulsion, which expresses his own shame about aspects of himself.

Thus, in speaking of the ranters, Winstanley mixes oral, sexual, and excremental imagery. The "lascivious feeder" is also a "lascivious breeder," in both regards an "unclean, doggish, filthy" beast, fertile with "filthy" and "abominable" children. He describes the ranters through excremental language in order to assert that their oral and sexual impulses are contaminated by rage, but his language also suggests his own rage. He directs that rage against impulses he deems shameful, which he believes obstruct true union with the god within (and with others). The ranters represent the lascivious feeder and breeder in himself, whom he believes he must cast out if he is to be righteous and legitimate, chaste and at peace. Just as he wants to purge his body of anger and anality so it can be the temple of god, so he would purge it of lust and orality.

Whereas Winstanley is making a principled case about the legitimate way to express sexuality, ranters proclaim that their god blesses their angry, lusty beastliness. He tries to instruct them about sublimation, but they unnervingly attest to the sanctity of what is being sublimated, about which he is ashamed or ambivalent. Thus, he tries to shame them, speaking to their denial of values and standards they feel but will not own, while they try to shame him, revealing his denial of the impulses for which he also seeks legitimate form. In this light, they both have something to teach, but neither is able to listen.

Accordingly, one need not endorse ranterism as a way of life to learn from the ranters several important lessons about Winstanley. Most obviously, Winstanley's desire for "true union" expresses and promotes a troubling ambivalence about sexuality. He is uncomfortable with the disruptive power of sexual desire and the dangerous temptation of sexual pleasure. Though he would integrate these into a moral relationship, he imagines a union somehow unperturbed by sex, as if sexual desire could and should be wholly domesticated. He does not want to split love in its moral and physical senses, but he devalues passionate physical desire in his effort to make it legitimate and unthreatening. Because of his moral commitments and fears, he feels inclined to expel or purify what he must doubt he can integrate.

To return to Marx's argument in "On the Jewish Question," Winstanley does not fully embrace terrestrial desire, even as he acknowledges earthly need, and so he does not "confess his sins to be what they are." As a result, his effort to synthesize the spirit of love and the power of desire suggests the wish to *redeem* the sexual passion he otherwise must abhor. Like those Marx identifies as "Christian," Winstanley also imagines that he has the power to triumph over what he shamefully defines as dirty. One need not follow the ranters and abandon the Christian idea of mutual responsibility to affirm the validity of sexual desire, but neither must one follow Winstanley and moralize sexuality to affirm one's responsibility and power. There is a tension here, denied by Winstanley and the ranters but represented in their angry relationship. It instructs not only about the shame at work in Winstanley's moralizing impulse but also about his failure to explore the full sense in which humans are sexual creatures.

More deeply, perhaps, his early question, "And what more [than food, shelter, and clothing] can be desired on earth?" shows how his piety proscribes not only sexual passion but also desire, which he limits by nature to what one needs, arguing that desire beyond such a limit is illegitimate, inflamed by a covetous culture. After all, conjugal union, and food and clothing "gained freely by our labors," do not exhaust the human project, although they may provide what is basic to it, and do not represent complete human fulfillment, although they may suggest its essential constituents. Winstanley limits desire in this way, not just because he lives in a culture of scarcity, but also because of his inner religiosity. He fears that desire, when inflamed by imagination, leads people to violate the moral limits of what he deems is appropriate to them as creatures.

To be free within is a *summum bonum* of sorts. Based on a harmony between what we need and what we desire, this ideal requires a "chaste" imagination and limitations on our power. Since the ranters deny there is such an inner stasis, they feel entitled to break through moral boundaries and impiously claim god's sanction for their pursuit of the forbidden. They themselves consider it impossible to destroy inner harmony because it cannot exist; instead, they redefine needs, explore desires, and play with the imagination. In this way, they subvert Winstanley's assertion of a "natural" and god-given limit, showing it to be in fact the voice of culture.

As a result, the ranters open up possibilities beyond the horizon of cultural convention and what Winstanley himself calls "slavish fear." One can agree with Winstanley about the motives and consequences of their "restless pursuit of desire after desire," as Hobbes calls it. Nonetheless, they witness the "stiff-necked" powers of desire and imagination, which Winstanley piously tries to circumscribe or even stifle. As his demonic parody, perhaps they testify in fact to the subversive power of *his* desire and imagination, which led him past conventional horizons—a blasphemy for which he claims god's sanction.

Thus, the ranters' irreverence teaches another lesson by clarifying the tension between the life of impulse and the forms of culture. Since there is no such thing as a "pure" impulse, and ranters' desires are inflamed by resentment and thus still shaped by culture, one cannot romanticize them as either noble or ignoble savages, emblems of "nature." In this sense, and against Hobbes, Winstanley is right to call them creatures of covetous culture and not its natural alternative. However, by revealing that he is not an agent of nature either, the ranters expose the truth about his cultural project. They instruct Winstanley about what is dangerous and illusory in his dream of a seamless weave of culture and nature, or form and impulse. Although he does not surrender to his anger at them for ripping that fabric, they elicit the pride in his piety and the elements of control in his perfect union. They embody what must be excluded or exorcized from his household and thus reveal the anxieties on which it is based and the costs it must exact from its members.

The refusal of the ranters to be integrated into his marriage of nature and culture, their theatrical glorification of the body's functions, and their comic defiance of his moralizing discourse provide a refreshing—if necessarily perverse and self-destructive—perspective on Winstanley's earnest piety. In spite of their irresponsibility, one can learn from, and even admire, their refusal to be "reformed" by him. As self-proclaimed Ishmaels, they do expose the shameful secrets of even a regenerate culture and "preach" of the presumption at work in even the best-intentioned and most democratic of reformers. As orphans and outsiders, they remind us that we are, and to some extent should be, prodigal children of our parent culture. Perhaps ranters deserve the last word because these "devils" would teach Winstanley the pride and limitations of Apollo's vocation.

PART FOUR

The Meaning of Defeat

When I speak to you
Coldly and impersonally
Using the driest words
(I seemingly fail to recognize you
In your particular nature and difficulty)
I speak to you merely
Like reality itself
(Sober, not to be bribed by your particular nature
Tired of your difficulty)
Which in my view you seem not to recognize.

—*Brecht*

When these clay bodies are in the grave,
And children stand in place.
This shows we stood for truth and peace and freedom in
our days
And true-born sons we shall appear of England that's our
Mother.

—*epigraph to* Winstanley's New Year's Gift

DEFEAT

In January 1650 Winstanley's *New Year's Gift to Parliament and Army* recounted the December harassment of diggers, which army troops permitted and watched. Affirming the diggers' continuing resolve, he declared, "Those diggers that remain have made little hutches to lie in, like calf-cribs, and are cheerful; taking the spoiling of their goods patiently, and rejoicing that they are counted worthy to suffer persecution for the sake of righteousness" (393). They were not merely passive, however. He told his readers they "have planted diverse acres of wheat and rye . . . and resolve to preserve it by all the diligence they can." The only obstacle is external: "poverty is their greatest burden, and if anything do break them from the work, it will be that" (393).

In March Winstanley collected into one book his earliest pamphlets, including *The New Law of Righteousness,* to which he added a new preface. He also published *Fire in the Bush,* perhaps his most poetic and intensely spiritual work, directed specifically at the churches and ministers. Against those who think that Winstanley had become "secular" in some simple sense, both books testify to the fact that he still sought a synthesis between the kingdom within and the kingdom without. But *Fire in the Bush* did not mention digging and lacked an explicitly political argument about rights and title, conquest and contract: the book's passionate interior gaze lit up a worldly endeavor whose failure seemed likely.

As if the diggers were blessed by God, however, eleven acres were ready to harvest by early April. In a letter to raise food and money, dated April 4, Winstanley pleaded, "If the hearts of any be stirred up to cast anything into this treasury, to buy victuals to keep men alive, and to buy corn to cast into the ground, it will keep alive the beginning of public freedom to the whole land, which is otherwise ready to die again for want of help" (439). While trying to solicit material support, Winstanley also made a last effort to engage Platt in debate. "Friday of Easter week," he lamented in his last pamphlet, "he came and brought his answer," in the form of a cataclysmic, and to all appearances final, raid (433).

Winstanley's response, however, was unrepentant. At Easter time he reminded his enemies that just as "the Scribes and Pharisees of old" had rejoiced when "they put Jesus Christ to death," so too "these English Pharisees, because they have acted the power of the Beast, and seem to stand uppermost for a time, they say they have routed the diggers" (436). But diggers have been routed neither "by scriptures" nor "by law," and surely "not by dispute, for your impatient, covetous, and proud-swelling heart would not suffer you to plead rationally" (436). He grants that "the power of self-loving pride hath for the present trod down our weak flesh," but "the strength of our inward man hath overcome them" (437).

Like Christ, diggers "hath tried Priests and professors of religion, and hath ripped up the bottom of their religion, and proved it mere witchcraft and cosonage, for self-love and covetousness is their god or ruling power" (437). Even as he acknowledged temporal defeat, Winstanley found solace in the reaffirmation of his commitments:

> Though this work of digging upon the Commons have many enemies, yet I am assured of the righteousness of the work. And it shall take root in one

place or other before many years pass over Englands head. I can set no time, but I wait for the consolation of Israel to rise up and break forth in others, as I have a taste of him in myself. (432)

In looking back, one tends to fix history and imagine that events could not have occurred otherwise than they did. Winstanley, living at the time, was enraged and crushed by what he rightly saw as the choices of the elder brothers:

> If you do not run in the right channel of freedom, you must, nay you will, as you do, face about and turn back again to Egyptian Monarchy; and so your names in the days of posterity shall stink and be blasted with abhorred infamy for your unfaithfulness to common freedom; and the evil effects will be sharp upon the backs of posterity. (535)

His understanding of the Lamb's defeat as an act of crucifixion, his dreams of vengeance, and his insistence that the elder brothers will be shamed did not express merely personal feelings but carried a political import. For the crucifixion of Christ was the defeat of an alternative to "the powers of the Dragon," which will bring even the elder brothers into torment and bondage. This is not a curse Winstanley or god will impose on them, but the poisoned fruit of their own choices: their own works will turn against them.[1]

THE MEANING OF DEFEAT

The issue in Part IV, however, is not the meaning of the Dragon's victory or what actually happens to the elder brothers on the road they chose to take; rather, it is what defeat means to Winstanley and how he responds to it.

Borrowing terms Max Weber articulated in "Politics as a Vocation,"

---

1. Winstanley knew that his enemies could not permit him to dig because of their inner covetousness and worldly interests, but he also knew that the elder brothers could have permitted digging if they had understood more fully the freedom and sainthood they professed to honor. Therefore, he believed the elder brothers made choices for which they were responsible. Indeed, it was Winstanley's sense that they had betrayed promises they themselves took seriously and thereby had betrayed themselves. And the consequences of that betrayal, he argued, would be the loss of their own political freedom, sacrificed to a restored "Egyptian Monarchy."

As Marx was to argue in *The Eighteenth Brumaire*, Winstanley argued that the propertied had turned against the poor and the commitments entailed by their own political poetry of liberty in order to protect their social power and property. They consented to Parliament's subordination to the executive power. It is this development to which Hobbes gives logical form in his argument for a Leviathan. (For Marx's comparison of Cromwell and Bonaparte, see Marx, *Surveys from Exile: Political Writings*, vol. 2, p. 232.)

one can say that Winstanley began to dig as the good son of "the god of love," who is in irreconcilable tension with "the demon of politics." Weber, I take it, had in mind that politics involves the demonic manifestations of tragedy: the discrepancy between intentions and consequences; the violence arising from insurmountable differences; the responsibility for maintaining (often by force) conventions made fragile by human depravity; and the terror of creating a world amidst the uncertainties and contingencies of historical time. Winstanley regarded these realities as consequences of pride and therefore as fugitive shadows of a life that is passing away. And he insisted that good sons and daughters will not be implicated in the nightmare they seek to exorcize. He need not "grow old with the devil," as Weber put it, because Christ rising will "swallow up in love" these demons within and without.

As Winstanley faced irreconcilable differences, however, he developed a new understanding of plurality; as he confronted violence, he addressed the problem of transgression and of how to expiate it; as he debated the ranters, he attended to the recalcitrance of desire and the fragility of convention. He developed a citizen politics that expanded what we have called his horizon of reverence. To be sure, he continued to insist that he was wholly unlike Cain, untainted by particularity, imagination, and prideful invention. But pressing circumstances and Winstanley's own innovative responses tended not only to highlight but also to subvert the radical distinction on which he premised his legitimacy. Indeed, the theoretical fruitfulness of his year as an activist arose from this ever-deepening tension between the good son's commitment to the god of love and the citizen's encounter with the demon of politics, which also constituted the cross he bore.

Winstanley's defeat, however, destroyed the narrative of Christ rising and reversed the identifications on which he had based his legitimacy. It is Winstanley who is cast out like Ishmael, as if he were the tainted fruit of an illegitimate marriage. It is he who is punished and exiled like Cain, as if he had transgressed the family relations and worldly authority blessed by god. It is he who loses the blessing like Esau, as if he had "despised" the birthright of his father. Thus, Winstanley's defeat drives him into what should be considered a fourth wilderness condition.

Winstanley is no longer the instrument of a god whose purposes he knows and embodies in action. The spirit that was the basis of his identity and rebellion is now absent from the world; the earth that was to nourish and free all her children has become passive and even helpless, the victim of enclosure; the poor, that human earth he hoped would put forth blessed seed, are now barren of possibility. Winstanley no longer can believe in or enact the reconciliation of the self with history, flesh with spirit, and sons and daughters with God, the earth, and each other.

His defeat signifies that Christ has been crucified (in and as the poor), again "trod under foot," so that the power of darkness, or covetousness, is the undisputed ruler of actual existence and thus of the consciousness of most people. As the spirit is divorced from society and history and withdraws into interior spaces, the external world is drained of meaning (as Luther had found it), and Winstanley himself, cut off from history, ceases to join in his own action the inner and outer worlds. Unable to enact his testimony in the world, he is thrown back on himself. In such circumstances, what does it mean, and what is required, to go on living?

A year and a half after his defeat, in November 1651, the publication date of Hobbes's *Leviathan,* Winstanley completes *The Law of Freedom in a Platform; or, True Magistracy Restored,* a proposal for reform he hopes Cromwell will implement. Declaring in the preface that he had been "stirred up" to give his talent and words what he calls a "resurrection," Winstanley tells Cromwell, "I must speak plain to you, lest [my spirit] tell me another day, if thou had spoken plain, things might have been amended" (502–3). He gives Cromwell a "method" by which to resurrect "commonwealth's government, though [it] had been buried under clods of kingly covetousness and oppression a long time" (515).

Accordingly, *The Law of Freedom* does not testify that Christ is rising in the body and society to lift inner and outer bondage. Rather, it calls on Cromwell to become an "outer savior" who will construct a state and social institutions that will make the earth a common treasury and England a righteous commonwealth. Thus, Winstanley now theorizes as a political creator in a world without the historical promise of redemption: he never blames god for his defeat, but in his imagination he calls on humans to do the dirty work he once left to god. Having confronted his own "Machiavellian Moment," Winstanley puts his earlier insights into a different, perhaps more realistic or secular, form and takes full responsibility for creating and enforcing standards and practices he treats as conventional.

At the same time, however, Winstanley's sojourn in the wilderness has exacted an enormous price. He is overwhelmed by the powerlessness that leads him to write to Cromwell. No longer "holding a torch" to "the present state of the world that is burning up like parchment in the fire" (252), he has become a "watchman in the nighttime of the

world" (255), only able to offer Cromwell a book he calls "a candle."
As if his despair about the prospect of making a worldly difference overcomes his effort at resurrection, he ends the book with a poem in which
he longs for death:

> Truth appears in light, Falsehood rules in power;
> To see these things to be is cause of grief each hour.
> Knowledge why didst thou come, to wound and not to cure?
> I sent not for thee, thou didst me inlure.
> Where knowledge does increase, there sorrows multiply
> To see the great deceit in which the world doth lie.
> Man saying one thing now, unsaying it anon
> Breaking all's engagements, when deeds for him are done.
> Oh power where art thou, that must mend things amiss?
> Come change the heart of man and make him truth to kiss.
> O death where art thou? Wilt thou not tidings send?
> I fear thee not, thou art my loving friend.
> Come take this body and scatter it to the Four
> That I may dwell in One and rest in peace once more.

Lacking the power to "mend" the split of inner and outer worlds,
Winstanley's knowledge is impotent and therefore sorrowful. Despite
the voice that says "thou shalt not bury thy talent in the earth" (510)
Winstanley also must feel that his attempted resurrection of digger principles cannot bring to life a world that is deadened by the withdrawal of
spirit. Thus, his defeat as an actor enables him to become a creator, at
least in imagination, but his despair makes him into a certain sort of
creator. Absent from his text as actor, he therefore authors a proposal
for *others* to implement, but those proposals are poisoned by the defeat
that signifies the absence of god's spirit and his own agency. As a result,
he jeopardizes the freedom he means to promote.

Therefore, the relationship between the death of spirit and Winstanley's birth as a creator is central to the analysis of what is innovative and troubling in *The Law of Freedom*. Until recently, this discussion would have ended a narrative about Winstanley because virtually
nothing was known about the remaining twenty-five years of his life.
There was a certain poetic aptness in this disappearance, as if his political
defeat and wish for death led to a meaningful silence and his absence from
public life. How he lived those years, however, has been documented.

Little is known about Winstanley from 1651 until 1657, when his
father-in-law gave him and his wife Susan property near Cobham. But
she must have died, for in early 1665 local records show that a Gerrard
Winstanley recently married to Elizabeth Stanley, had established resi-

dence in a London suburb. By way of the estate he gained through his first wife's father, Winstanley apparently reestablished himself in Cobham as a landowner, and his second marriage was to the daughter of prominent Cobham gentry. Moreover, the Cobham parish register notes the baptism of two children, a daughter in 1667 and a son in 1670. More significantly, the documents reveal that Winstanley served as waywarden of Cobham parish in 1659 and 1666, overseer of the poor in 1660, churchwarden in 1667 and 1668, and chief constable in 1671. He died in 1676 as a Quaker.

Although *The Law of Freedom* may have failed as resurrection, it seems to have succeeded as an act of closure, and thus as a new beginning. As the documents suggest, the disinherited younger brother becomes a respected man of property, a father in his own right, and an officeholder in the very institutions he had criticized so powerfully. As a consequence, the following discussion about his imagined transformation of the Puritan household must become a halfway house to a final chapter about an unexpected rebirth, in which he literally returns as a father to the house of the fathers. The task of that chapter is to make sense of the astonishment J. D. Alsop expressed at his remarkable discoveries about Winstanley:

> It is difficult enough to credit that the millenarian who denounced trade in the 1640s as unjust and often dishonest eventually reentered London commerce as a Quaker. It would appear incredible that the outspoken heretical critic of established religion became a churchwarden, and the Digger agitator who disrupted society held office as a chief constable—particularly when these activities took place at Cobham, the scene of his radicalism. Yet the evidence is straightforward.[2]

The interpretation, of course, is not.

2. J. D. Alsop, "Gerrard Winstanley: Religion and Respectability," *The Historical Journal* 28, no. 3 (1985): 705–9.

CHAPTER VIII

Remaking the Fathers' House

It is a fearsome thing to kill.
But it is not granted to us not to kill.

—Brecht

Is it any wonder if, filled with the "political drive" as he
himself says he was, [Plato] attempted three times to . . . do
for all Greeks what Mohamed later did for his Arabs: to
determine customs in things great and small and especially to
regulate everyone's day-to-day mode of life. His ideas were as
surely *practical* as those of Mohamed were practical: after
all, far more incredible ideas, those of Christianity, have
proved practical! A couple of accidents here and a couple of
other accidents fewer—and the world would have seen the
Platonization of the European South. . . . But success eluded
him: and he was thus left with the reputation of being a
fanaticist and utopian—the more opprobrious epithets
perished with Athens.

—Nietzsche

The Law of Freedom is the fruit, mature and bitter, realistic and fan-
tastical, of Winstanley's defeat. In what senses has he, as Weber urged,
"grown old with the devil?" Has he, as Marx argued, admitted "his sins
to be what they are" and thus "struggled" against "his internal priest,
his own priestly nature"? *The Law of Freedom* surely is intended to
"resurrect" his talent and common freedom, but any resurrection presumes a death, and the question is how that death shapes his learning
and his last book.

Consider, first, how Hobbes and the Puritans interpreted the defeat
of the theodicy that had justified political rebellion. Hobbes premised
his science of conventionality on the assertion that theodicy, the idea

that history has a redemptive purpose, was a vainglorious and danger-ous error. In part, he called his great book *Leviathan* to invoke the Book of Job, for he "humbled the children of pride" by discrediting the idea that god had authored a purpose in history and human action to fulfill it. In this way, Hobbes revealed the conventionality of authority and thereby both the problem of disorder and the human invention that could provide salvation from it. He believed that once the idea of re-demptive history was exposed as a dangerous fantasy, rebels would fear their pride and therefore submit reverently to a state of their own crea-tion. In this way, he envisioned Promethean invention arising from the grave of redemptive history and radical politics.

Not coincidentally, Puritan sermons during the interregnum shifted in focus from the Book of Revelation, which foretells the resurrection of Christ and the creation of god's kingdom on earth, to the Book of Job, which defeats such dreams. Identifying themselves with Job, Puritans apparently felt unsure of god's purposes and justice; indeed, they had become fearful of the chaos caused by what they now deemed the prideful claim to god's sanction. As Puritans even used Hobbes's argu-ments, they abandoned a politics justified by the unfolding of god's spirit in history and expressed through the language of grace and lib-erty. Their crisis of faith and fear of disorder led them toward the de facto authority that assured order and property.

Winstanley's last book speaks to this political crisis experienced partly in spiritual terms. Never having believed in a transcendent god, Winstanley could find no solace when god withdrew from the world. Unlike Luther or the Puritans, Winstanley could not find life in a spirit that was merely internal, and thus, he could not find spirit in a life that was merely private. For this reason, his own crisis must have been far more profound than that faced by his elder brothers. As a result, how-ever, he resists their political response and Hobbes's teaching. Win-stanley's contention that England is returning to "Egyptian Monarchy" suggests not only his fear of political regression but also its relation to spiritual deadening, just as the image of pyramids suggests slave labor and the construction of a death-in-life, the absence of political self-determination and the burial of spirit. Thus, whereas the Puritans and Hobbes sever piety from collective action, Winstanley believes both are in jeopardy.

As Hobbes's arguments suggest, however, Winstanley's ability con-sciously to create conventions arises precisely from the defeat of re-demptive history. But he still relates inward autonomy to "freedom in the earth" and collective action, and therefore he still tries to "resur-

rect" the radical politics that Hobbes hopes to bury along with redemptive faith. Thus, Winstanley moves beyond the horizon of his earlier reverence, but in order to "resurrect" a "commonwealth's government"
that empowers the poor. In *The Law of Freedom* Winstanley no longer
bears witness to the history god authors and he enacts, but rather he
becomes the author of the narrative by which the poor can reach the
Promised Land. This change not only suggests his despair about redemptive history and his powerlessness politically, but also shows their
innovative fruits. Crucified as an activist, he is reborn as a theorist who
tries to reform a world deprived of god's empowering spirit, as well as
an artist who creates an imagined world in which falsehood does not
"rule in power."

Yet Winstanley becomes a certain kind of creator because the spirit in
people has been crucified: he tries to reconstruct, rather than supplant,
the house of the Puritan fathers. He returns to his Puritan antecedents,
imagining an extensive disciplinary apparatus, endorsing the pervasive
exercise of paternal power, and excluding women from any role in public life. What appear from one point of view as secular expedients, however, appear from another as integral to a commonwealth intended to
guarantee the reverence, nourishment, and unity he once deemed the
fruit of "God's work." Thus, a platform of human invention shaped by
realistic expedients and by a continuing dream of reverence is also a
dream of solace.

Winstanley still rejects propertied Puritanism, and he does not build
Leviathan. But the impact of his defeat, reflected by his view of paternal
authority, fraternal citizenship, and the role of women, will demonstrate
how and why his final book fails as politics and art.[1]

THE PREFACE: A POLITICAL THEORIST
SPEAKS TRUTH TO POWER

The body of the text of *The Law of Freedom* is sandwiched between
a preface written to Cromwell, in which Winstanley speaks of his powerlessness and tries to prepare Cromwell for what is to follow, and a final
poem longing for death. Winstanley's awareness that his only hope

---

1. This chapter provides an alternative to the views of two commentators on Winstanley. On the one hand, Christopher Hill basically reads *The Law of Freedom* as a welcome secularization of Winstanley's thought, an advance theoretically and politically. In
contrast, in *Utopia and the Ideal Society* (Cambridge: Cambridge University Press, 1981),
J. C. Davis mistakenly and intemperately argues that Winstanley's utopia is totalitarian.
The truth is not located in between these views but is of a totally different cast.

(however dim) lies in his enemy poignantly sets the tone for the book. His handling of this painful relationship reveals him speaking in the classic voice of a political theorist and suggests an instructive parallel with Thomas More in Book I of *Utopia*.

Like More, Winstanley now addresses the problems of power and counsel. Declaring his powerlessness to remedy directly "the confusion and thick darkness that hath overspread our brethren," he offers a "candle" to Cromwell but feels helpless to assure whether Cromwell will live by its light (510). Indeed, Winstanley knows that he and his ideas are likely to be dismissed. As he said before, "freedom comes clothed in clownish garments," but now he specifically plays the jester to a king: like More, he ironically casts himself as the fool. He warns Cromwell not to be put off by appearances: "Take off the clownish language, for under that you may see great beauty" (510). The problem of his marginality and the prejudice of others, evoked by the clothing metaphor, requires that *The Law of Freedom* be a teaching device that instructs Cromwell in a new way of seeing the world.

As Winstanley once warned that god's truths appear strange to those who are strangers to god, now he describes a "house" that appears strange: "Though thou understand it not at first sight, yet open the door and look into the house, for thou mayest see that which will satisfy thy heart" (515). As a house, *The Law of Freedom* is like the island in *Utopia*: both are transformative places because they estrange the reader from the familiar. To enter the house Winstanley has imagined is to see the world in a new way so that one can act differently. A fictional construction of a house, therefore, could teach Cromwell how to learn the right "method" of building an actual commonwealth. Thus, *The Law of Freedom* is not only a teaching device, a work of heuristic fiction, and an imaginary house but also the foundation for a real house, a platform for a practical program that is based on existing conditions and designed according to digger principles.

In both regards, Winstanley speaks to Cromwell as a potential Moses:

> God hath honored you with the highest honor of any man since Moses' time, to be Head of a People who have cast out an oppressing Pharaoh. . . . And God hath made you a successful instrument to cast out that Conqueror and to recover our land and liberties. (501)

Originally, Winstanley spoke Moses' words and insisted that they were authored by god; he had written from *within* the exodus narrative, which he insisted was being "materially fulfilled" by god and his own action. Now the exodus narrative has become a metaphor by which

Winstanley flatters Cromwell and teaches him what it means to be a Moses in his time.[2]

That teaching recapitulates Winstanley's earlier arguments, derived from "natural experience" and the "grievances and burdens of the poor" and illustrated by Scripture. Not surprisingly, Winstanley reminds Cromwell that the Hebrews treated Canaan "as a common treasury of livelihood to the whole commonwealth of Israel. They made provision for every tribe and for every family in every tribe, nay, for every particular man in a family." Only in this way was "Israel, in all his families and tribes made a free commonwealth in power as well as in name" (524–25).[3]

Winstanley's specific instructions to Cromwell suggest other parallels with More. To be a Moses, Cromwell must abolish clergy, tithes, and churches, lawyers and kingly law, and landlords and property. He also must institute a commonwealth in which communal production is distributed through "storehouses" according to need, and in which political power is based on yearly elections in parishes, counties, and the nation. Winstanley summarizes the platform to follow:

> Every family shall live apart as now they do; every man shall enjoy his own wife and every woman her own husband, as now they do; every trade shall be improved to more excellency than it now is; all children shall be educated and be trained up in subjection to parents and elder people more than now they are. The earth shall be planted and the fruits reaped and carried into storehouses by common assistance of every family; the riches of the storehouses shall be the common stock to every family: there shall be no idle person nor beggar in the land. And because offenses may arise from the spirit of unreasonable ignorance, therefore the law was added. (515)

Like More's character Hythlodaeus, Winstanley anticipates Cromwell's fears:

> Some hearing of this Common Freedom, think there must be a community of all the fruits of the earth whether they work or no, [and] therefore strive to live idle on other mens labors. Others, through the same unreasonable

2. Winstanley is in the position of other radicals facing a hostile regime once opposition has failed. For example, Proudhon made a similar appeal to Bonaparte after the coup of 1851. Moreover, it is tactically the case that the dependence of the propertied on Cromwell could have given Cromwell room for independent action.

3. Offering what will be his final definition of freedom, Winstanley says, "Freedom lies where a man receives nourishment and preservation, and that is in the use of the Earth: for as man is compounded of the four materials of the creation, fire, water, earth, and air, so is he preserved by the compounded bodies of these four, which are the fruits of the earth [without which] he cannot live" (519). Since "a man had better to have no body than to have no food for it," he continues, "this restraining of the earth from brethren by brethren is oppression and bondage, but the free enjoyment thereof is true freedom" (520).

beastly ignorance, think there must be a community of all men and women for copulation, and so strive to live a bestial life. Others think there will be no law, but that everything will run into confusion for want of government. . . . Therefore, because transgression doth and may arise from ignorant and rude fancy in man, is the law added. (526)

The fears of the propertied, no longer groundless, suggest the necessity of law and punishment:

If any say this will nurse idleness, I answer: . . . idle persons and beggars will be made to work. If any say this will make some men to take goods from others by violence and call it theirs, because the earth and fruits are a common stock, I answer: though storehouses and public shops be commonly furnished by every family's assistance and for every family's use . . . if any man endeavor to take away [another's] house, furniture, food, wife, children . . . such a one is a transgressor, and shall suffer punishment. If any man do force or abuse women in folly, pleading community, the following laws do punish such ignorant and unrational practice, for the laws of the commonwealth are laws of moderate diligence and purity of manners. (527)

Located between the Puritans who fear idleness, anarchy, and promiscuity and the ranters who endorse such behavior, Winstanley promises to respond to both, but through a commonwealth that shares the earth and political power.[4]

Like Book I of More's *Utopia*, Winstanley's preface introduces the practical goals of reform while beginning to reorder deeper perceptions about what is necessary and possible. Unlike More, however, Winstanley has resigned himself to the role of counsel only after the failure of the redemptive history that he believed would abolish kings and thereby counselors.

Consider, then, the changes that have led Winstanley to turn toward Cromwell and sound like More. As he says toward the end of *The Law*

4. Like the character Morus in More's *Utopia*, the fictional Cromwell offers principled objections: he argues that tithes and property are the fruit of a "righteous" law of mine and thine, so that Winstanley's proposals rob men of their just due. Like Hytholodaeus, Winstanley inverts these claims. On the one hand, he argues that tithes and wealth are "stolen goods" and that a property system enshrines "theft, violence, and continual cheating." Moreover, since clergy, lawyers, and landlords "live at ease, feeding and clothing themselves by the labors of other men, not their own," their rank "is their shame not their nobility." On the other hand, he argues that a true commonwealth would make it possible to fulfill the Christian morality that Cromwell professes to honor (512–16). Winstanley also means to answer Cromwell's practical objections, which parallel those of Morus: sharing the earth will create poverty, idleness, anarchy, and—here he differs from Morus—promiscuity and "community of women." In response, Winstanley promises to enforce a common obligation to work, and to create a private sphere that other individuals cannot invade: "The commonwealths laws are to preserve a mans peace in his person and his private dwelling, against the rudeness and ignorance . . . in mankind" (527).

of Freedom, "seeing the child is come to birth, now let it appear . . . whether you will receive Christ, who is the spreading spirit of freedom . . . or whether you will return to monarchy, to embrace Egyptian Bondage" (585). Winstanley still is committed to a moral community that honors the Golden Rule, but the "child" that is born is variously described as the "name" of commonwealth or a "law" of righteousness or freedom. Whereas Christ was once a power in the heart that would enable men and women to refashion their government (from below), now Christ is simply a standard, powerless in itself, that becomes powerful only if enacted into law *by* government (from above). Whether the helpless child actually will grow up and knit people together depends now on Cromwell and government, not god.

These changes entail other crucial changes in Winstanley's premises. First, he no longer presumes the inner regeneration of sons and daughters. The failure of Christ to rise automatically and universally means that fallen men must be taken as they are. For the first time in Winstanley's writings, order is a necessity as essential as sincere milk and food. Secondly, since history and nature no longer automatically produce righteousness in each person, people must use their own hands and minds to fashion the righteous laws that address the problem of covetousness and the necessity of order. Christ's spirit does not disappear, but it can reappear only by way of the Mosaic government that was its antithesis.

Thirdly, punishment thus has become essential to the common preservation Winstanley still seeks. His willingness to punish reflects his awareness that god's withdrawal requires precisely the acts his piety once forbade: freed from the need to be god's loving servant, he no longer denies his anger or disavows punishment. As always, however, his concern is to meet necessities in a way that makes people free: the necessity of order requires law; law requires punishment; and only if people make law and take on punishment in the right sort of way can they protect their freedom without jeopardizing it.

These changes create dilemmas that the preface does not address but that are suggested by Marx's response to the defeat of 1851 and made explicit by Lenin. Marx and Winstanley initially premised political action on a faith that people's direct experience would disclose the truth about their world. Believing that "Christ rising" and class consciousness emerged as it were automatically from experience, each theorist imagined that philosophy, political education, and political leadership would be rendered superfluous. For each, the defeat of this dream led to valuable innovations, but ones fraught with danger.

After *The Eighteenth Brumaire* Marx saw that direct experience deceived people, so that theory and political education became necessary. He withdrew from politics to seek truth through theory: he wrote *Capital*. Since history no longer could be relied on to provide truth and thus to supply workers with a consciousness appropriate to making a revolution, Marx made theory the locus of a truth not manifest to the senses. Correspondingly, he built a party that, by becoming the source of workers' consciousness and action, could replace existence and history as the motor of class struggle. As thought and action no longer were united in the workers, there developed a split between a conscious party and workers submerged in a mystified social life.[5]

After 1905 Lenin exemplified these tensions implicit in Marx's work. Most important, he manifested an ambiguity about the workers, for his advocacy of theory and the party was premised on a profound mistrust of their "spontaneity." Indeed, in the effort to wean workers from bourgeois ideology, Lenin's vanguard appeared like the god who refuses to pity or indulge the creature's weakness and suffering because redemption is at stake. The dangers here are obvious: the vanguard (and theorist) may disown the consciousness of its subject, so that theory and political education become a means of domination, if the elect creates an orthodoxy they protect from the popular thought and action they consider contaminating.

Just as Marx and his heirs resurrected philosophy and invented a party after history failed to generate class consciousness, so Winstanley had to provide theory and create leadership once Christ no longer was rising in sons and daughters. To be sure, defeat led Winstanley to accept the human invention that Marx and Lenin were to embrace from the beginning. Marx and Lenin, however, reveal the crucial issues and problematic responses engendered by the failure of Winstanley's initial historical vision.[6]

After all, in *The Law of Freedom* Winstanley implicitly plays god to

---

5. For the arguments about Marx that have shaped my reading of Winstanley's final changes, see Jerrold Seigel, *Marx's Fate* (Princeton: Princeton University Press, 1978) and Harold Rosenberg, "The Pathos of the Proletariat," in *Act and Actor* (New York: World Publishing, 1970).

6. By revealing the spirit in matter, Winstanley's conversion brought him into politics to "own" it in action. That an inner conversion should animate the world and create a political connection to it—should join inner and outer kingdoms—might seem paradoxical to Marx, who understood "spirit" only as evidence of an interior split off and alienated from the world. For Marx, the world is not alive, but politics and human action can animate it, bring it to life. This is the position toward which Winstanley is propelled by his defeat; but since he moves there under the pressure of believing that the world has been deadened by god's withdrawal, he does not really believe he can bring it to life.

Cromwell's Moses and explicitly calls on Cromwell to be a "man-savior" to the people. In addition, Winstanley's turn to a human creator is premised on a doubt about the piety or spirit he intends to promote, and it is not clear in the preface whether the "head of power" simply rules a social body without spirit or brings that spirit to life. Has Winstanley written a script in which Cromwell imposes orthodoxy, or founds freedom?

Winstanley initially worked out the relationship between creature and creator internally and psychologically so that his inner religiosity was shaped by the tensions between reverence and freedom, submission and empowerment, purification and transformation. Now these tensions are suggested by the relationship between Cromwell and the poor. In what ways are the poor empowered as creators to define, feed, and discipline themselves as creatures? In what ways do they remain merely creatures, passively taking the form given them by their human creator?

SETTING THE REFORMATION IN MOTION

Now that social change does not originate with the direct action of the poor authorized by god, it must originate in Moses, who is the "head" of the "body of the people." After the preface, however, Cromwell is never mentioned. As the exodus story shows Moses authorizing each tribe to appoint elders, who later become the rulers of Israel, so Winstanley imagines Cromwell initiating a process of self-governance and rendering himself superfluous. At the moment, Cromwell is the "head" of the people, but his role requires that he create another and different head, one more closely linked to the body: "Therefore, seeing England declared a free commonwealth, and the name thereof established in law, surely then the greatest work is now to be done . . . that the power and the name may agree together" (535).

Cromwell is to initiate the transition Winstanley still believes is the heart of reformation: turning a kingdom into a commonwealth. The text makes clear that Parliament (and not Cromwell) is to become the real "father of the land": "For as a father's tender care is to remove all grievances from the oppressed children, not respecting one before another, so a Parliament is to remove all burdens from the people of a land." And like a father, its "eye and care must be principally to relieve the oppressed ones" (536). Parliament can be "tender hearted," however, only if Cromwell restores "successive Parliaments" and reforms the franchise. Once Parliament is a legitimate head of power, the social body, or "root of power," can be reformed.

Winstanley argues that "all those interested in monarchical power and government ought neither to choose nor be chosen officers to manage the commonwealth's affairs, for those cannot be friends to common freedom" (542). The criteria for exclusion are lending money to the king's army, fighting in that army, or buying and selling crown and church lands. Since these men are "members of the covetous generation of self-seekers" who "take away other mens rights," and "lest that ignorant spirit of revenge break out in them to interrupt the common peace," they are "for the present . . . unfit to be chosen officers or to choose" (542–43). Winstanley addresses the Machiavellian problem of what to do with the enemies of innovation by undermining the political power of "monarchy men" and preventing them from extending their enclosure of the earth. Exclusion is not permanent, however, and Winstanley's motives are not vindictive:

> I do not say that they should be made servants, as the conquered usually are . . . for they are our Brothers and what they did, no doubt, they did in conscienable zeal, though in ignorance. And seeing but few of the Parliaments friends understand their common freedom, though they own the name commonwealth, thereby they . . . ought to bear with the ignorance of the Kings party . . . though for the present they be excluded. (542)

Though he characterizes the people as "charmed, fooled, and besotted" by ignorance and indoctrination, he does not call them covetous, and he believes they have an interest in freedom and therefore considers them eligible to vote. Accordingly, he recommends the criteria they should use for choosing leaders from among themselves. In general, "unfit to be chosen" are

> all uncivil livers, as drunkards, quarrelers, fearful ignorant men who dare not speak the truth lest they anger other men; likewise all who are wholly given to pleasure and sports, or men who are full of talk. All these are empty of substance, and cannot be experienced men. (542)

Though not "fit," such people are not legally precluded from being chosen, and they still "have a voice in choosing." They become the foil by which he defines those who are "fit to be chosen." First, he advises, "Choose such as have a long time given testimony by their actions to be promoters of common freedom" regardless of their religious views or church membership. Second, "Choose such as have suffered under kingly oppression," even if they weren't active supporters of Parliament, because "they will be fellow feelers of others bondages." Third, "Choose officers out of . . . those men who are forty years of age, for these are most likely to be experienced men." In general, he concludes, all these are likely to be "men of courage, truly dealing, and hating covetousness" (542).

Winstanley's presumption appears to be that a righteous vanguard will be created because the poor at least can recognize their own necessities and those who would meet them faithfully:

> For indeed, the necessity of the people choose a Parliament to help them in their weakness, and where it sees a danger like to impoverish or enslave one part of the people to another, [it is] to give warning and so prevent that danger, for [it is] the eyes of the land. And surely those are blind eyes that lead the people into bogs, to be entangled in the mud again, after they are pulled out.

Winstanley now believes that people must admit their "weakness and necessity" and rely on the eyes of men who are courageous, experienced, and less subject to "the slavish fear of men." Nonetheless, the people do more than choose their officers but are totally involved in the process of lifting bondage. They constantly deliberate in the parishes about their grievances, and after discussion, they ratify or block Parliament's proposed responses. "Because people must all be subject to the law, under pain of punishment," Winstanley insists, "therefore it is reason they should know it before it be enacted, that if there be anything of . . . oppression in it, it may be discovered and amended" (558).

As this advice suggests, Winstanley does not put blind faith in rulers: representatives all too easily become corrupt. He insists on frequent elections because "the heart of man is so subject to be overspread with the clouds of covetousness, pride, and vainglory" that "public officers" long in office "will degenerate from the bounds of humility, honesty and tender care of brethren" (540). He also argues "that whereas many have their portions to obey, so many have their turns to rule" in order to encourage all men "to advance righteousness and good manners in the hopes of honor," to develop "able and experienced men, fit to govern," and to enhance "the health of our nation and the education of our children" (540–41).

But the political framework of republican government, local participation, and rotation in office does not comprise a sufficient response to covetousness and ignorance. Like More, Winstanley links the political and social project of eliminating outer bondage to the social and psychological project of counteracting pride. The issue, then, is not what a founder imposes on the people but the horizon of reverence citizens themselves create and obey: in the absence of god's spirit, how do they try to nurture and free themselves?

FAMILY AND SOCIETY: CREATING A NEW HOUSEHOLD

Winstanley exemplifies a moment in history when the individuating aspects of modernity had not yet fully dissolved the corporate sensibility of feudalism. Therefore, his social platform democratizes the corporate body of the feudal order and rejects the feudal idea of treating the individual only in terms of an ascribed place in a fixed hierarchy. Winstanley gives each individual one vote and equality in production, yet he rejects individualism and retains the feudal idea of membership in a social body.

The true commonwealth is functionally differentiated into various types of agriculture and manufacturing, which operate without the mediation of the market. In contrast to the Puritans and Hobbes, Winstanley proposes that farms, storehouses, and guilds be organized communally and directed by locally elected officials. As he democratizes the economy, so too he proposes that people elect political officials at the parish, county, and national levels. By covenanting to establish "foundation freedoms," he says, the English can establish a society in which

> Every freeman shall have a freedom in the earth, to plant or build, to fetch from the storehouses anything he wants, and shall enjoy the fruits of his labors without restraints from any. He shall not pay rent to any landlord and he shall be capable of being chosen any officer if he be above forty years of age, and he shall have a voice to choose officers though he be under forty. (597)

Winstanley no longer believes, however, that these freedoms suffice to address the problem of order. Repeating his earlier rhetorical question, he asks, "Having food and rayment, lodging and the comfortable society of his own kind, what more can a man desire in the days of his travel?" But now he responds, "Indeed, covetous, proud, beastly minded men desire more." He returns to his Puritan antecedents: he no longer rejects paternal authority, social discipline, law, or punishment. One should keep in mind, though, that in crucial ways Winstanley *always* was Puritan in his temperament and premises. Indeed, because of his seriousness about the Puritan commitment to self-determination, he tries to fashion a worldly authority that is genuinely democratic and whose discipline will empower. He therefore becomes a creator very different from Hobbes, but the despair about the spirit that makes his innovations necessary and possible also renders them problematic.

Like most feudal, early modern, and Puritan theorists, Winstanley begins in the family household, which he takes as the basic unit of life and the model for society: "The original root of magistracy is common preservation, and it rose up first in the family" (536). In contrast to Hobbes, who insists on parental willfulness or "paternal despotism," Winstanley subjects paternal authority to democratic and moral limitations. "A father in a family is a commonwealths officer," but like all other officers, he "is to be a chosen one, by them who are in necessity, and who judge him fit for that work" (538). Thus, the legitimacy of authority depends both on consent and on its faithfulness in "meeting the childrens necessities." These include love, education, and discipline, as well as the physical protection that Hobbes emphasizes. Winstanley writes:

> A father is to cherish his children til they grow wise and strong, and then as a master he is to instruct them in reading, in learning languages, arts, and sciences, and to bring them up to labor . . . in some trade, or cause them to be instructed therein. . . . He is to command them in their work . . . and not suffer them to live idle. He is either to reprove by words or whip those who offend, for the rod is prepared to bring the unreasonable ones to experience and moderation. That so children may not quarrel like beasts but live in peace like rational men. (545)

Though the father is granted a right to discipline children, he does not rule unilaterally in the home. Upon complaints from children, other citizens, apprentices, or elected "overseers" of production, he can be reproved or, if necessary, relieved of responsibility. The father is bound by the rules of an observant community, and his children have a right to oppose him by invoking those rules.

Winstanley's account of the family proceeds, however, as if women had no part in parental authority. When he says that the family's privacy is assured if the father fulfills his duty, and that children should be taken from a delinquent father, it is as if the mother did not exist. Indeed, Winstanley only addresses women explicitly when he declares their legal right to a husband of their choice and their legal obligation to nurse their own children.

The absence of women, the pronounced emphasis on paternal discipline, and the concern about the legitimacy of authority extend to the "bigger family, called a parish." Because "the body of the people are confused and disordered," says Winstanley, "offenses do arise." Therefore, every year the parish chooses officers to be "overseers." In part, they monitor social life and use persuasion to settle conflicts, without resort to legal adjudication; in part, overseers monitor economic life and supervise the work in households, shops, and storehouses. Through rotation in office, people in the parish are to share in production of life's necessities and self-government, thereby learning virtue. Winstanley's account of this parish life emphasizes discipline:

> Mankind in the days of his youth is like a young colt, wanton and foolish, til he be broke by education and correction, and the neglect of his care or the want of wisdom in the performance of it, hath been and is the cause of much division and trouble in the world. (576)

But his goal is that children be "brought up like men, and not like beasts, that so the commonwealth may be planted with laborious and wise men, and not with idle fools" (576). Discipline is meant to provide the basis of education and ultimately freedom.

Once weaned, says Winstanley, a child should go to school "to learn to read the laws of the commonwealth, to ripen his wits . . . and so to proceed in his learning, til he be acquainted with all arts and languages." Then "they may be better able to govern themselves like rational men" (576). School is only one aspect of education, however, and is limited in duration:

> One sort of children shall not be trained up only to book learning and not other employment, called scholars as they are in the government of monarchy. For then . . . they spend their time finding out policies to advance themselves to be lords and masters over their laboring brethren. (577)

To prevent the social division of mental and manual labor and its political consequences, Winstanley requires that schooling be followed by work in "such trades, arts, and sciences as their bodies and wits are capable of" (577), which continues until the age of forty.[7]

Winstanley endorses a division of labor and power between the sexes. He proposes a different kind of education for each sex: "And as boys are to be trained up in learning and trades, so all maids shall be trained up in reading, sewing, knitting, spinning of wool or linen, music and all other neat easy works, either to furnish the storehouses with linen and woolen cloth, or for the ornament of particular houses" (579). Correspondingly, Winstanley is anxious that young men become good heads of household: "No man shall be suffered to keep house and have

---

7. Winstanley's animus against "scholars" is not anti-intellectual. Indeed, he believes that removing property and eliminating poverty will generate an explosion in learning. "If men are sure of food and rayment," he imagines, "their reason will be ripe and ready to dive into the secrets of creation, that they may learn to see and know God in all his works" (580). As in More's *Utopia*, those over forty are entitled to devote themselves to learning as well as ruling, and the entire populace enjoys a "seventh day" set aside for parish discussions of "the arts and sciences."

servants under him til he hath served seven years under the command of a master himself. The reason is this, that a man may be of age, and of rational carriage, before he be a governor of a family" (600). By extension, only male heads of household will become citizens entitled to vote, and only elders (males over forty years of age) are entitled to be chosen as lawmakers.

Women are not rendered entirely powerless. Though envisioned as domestic, deferential, and passive, they are not without rights: girls get the same broad education as boys; young women work and are entitled to marry whom they choose; wives and mothers are not servants or slaves, for they explicitly retain their freedom if the husband is punished for any "offenses" (597). Nonetheless, women are excluded from public life and from Winstanley's language. His specific references to women, however, suggest the reason for their exclusion and the meaning of their absence: their position is not merely unfortunate, but it reveals what is troubling in his way of conceiving the political relationship between fathers and sons.

Winstanley's demand that mothers nurse their own children would protect poor women from the common and exploitive practice of nursing the children of the wealthy, but it also suggests his renewed anxiety about assuring nourishment. Likewise, he proposes the death penalty for rape, which would protect women's "bodily freedom"; but by stipulating also that the partner of a woman who begets a child must marry her, Winstanley shows his anxiety about her autonomy. Perhaps it seems to him that women's public role outside the family makes them available and tempting to men and frees them to consent to the desire they elicit.

But their role as dutiful sources of milk and love suggests a good deal more. Most obviously, just as the earth now appears as the passive and powerless source of nurturance requiring the protection provided by fathers and law, so, too, women become the protected and therefore captive providers of nourishment within a family ruled by a father. In both regards the authority of the actual fathers is meant to guarantee nourishment for all the children. But in the name of protection, women are *made* powerless and private by men anxious to control their bodies, love, and milk. As Winstanley once taught, anxiety about real food and literal milk discloses far deeper problems.

The sincere milk of god, I have argued, was an internal source of nourishment that made possible Winstanley's visceral connection to nature and the body, his sense of the beneficence of life itself, and, not least, his acknowledgment of the autonomy of women. No longer able to trust that god will nourish and protect him, Winstanley perhaps has turned back toward real women as if to control them, who are the source of life. The absence of spirit in the world, which he experiences as his separation from the Father's breasts within, appears as the separation of women from the world. What he once embodied personally is now embodied by women, whose confinement makes trust possible once again. Thus, Winstanley's absence as an actor empowered by god is signified by the absence of women from public life, and hence their powerlessness signifies his own.

But in the absence of god's spirit, and therefore in the shadow of absent women, Winstanley becomes a builder: his platform proposes that fathers and sons become the birthing partners in the creation of culture. By way of a humanly invented reverence, he now fashions a world in which sons can be assured of what he once experienced internally and considered the *natural* inheritance of every human being. Indeed, he says he will not "meddle" with the interior drama of redemption, by which men and women who were the captives of culture had allied with nature and been empowered by the spirit animating it.[8]

Now rebirth becomes an exclusively male art, as fraternal citizens and paternal authorities create a culture that uses education and punishment to stand against unregenerate nature as well as covetous culture. Once authentic piety and loving nature no longer provide an alternative to culture, Winstanley tries through his art to supplant nature and implant piety, which could be called the dream of culture. This dream appears as the externalization of Winstanley's religiosity. Instead of the androgynous god whose breasts provided the love and reasoned discipline that fed the soul and engendered Christ rising, one sees disciplinarian fathers and loving mothers who enable men under forty to become "sons of freedom." Through his own imaginary invention Winstanley seeks to secure for other sons the autonomy, earth, and power that he failed to gain from a real father or as the good son of god and the earth. Thus, Winstanley is the son who creates a paternal authority that substitutes for the god within, but he also is the powerful and devoted fa-

---

8. Winstanley says in the preface:

I speak now in relation between oppressors and oppressed: the inward bondage I meddle not with in this place, though I am sure that if it be searched into, the inward bondage of the mind, as covetousness, pride, envy, hypocrisy, sorrows, fears, desperation, and madness are all occasioned by the outward bondage that one sort of people lay on another. (520)

ther, legitimated by the necessities and consent of the sons. In both regards, as we will see, Winstanley imagines how men can create the
grounds and limits of their worldly freedom. But since god cannot be
trusted to nurture the soul of each, and the soul cannot be trusted to
submit reverently to god, it then appears that fathers and sons replicate
the domestication of women.

THE STATE AND THE SWORD

Winstanley now establishes freedom through a politics in which citizens voluntarily enact and enforce law. They must build a government
that is "a wise and free ordering of the earth, and of the manners
of mankind, by observation of particular laws or rules that all the inhabitants may live peaceably in plenty and freedom" (528). Indeed,
Winstanley's reliance on law is intensified by his fear of disorder: "There
must be suitable laws for every occasion, for almost every action that
men do, for one law cannot serve all seasons, but every season and action have their particular laws attending thereunto for the preservation
of right order" (528).

That law is a necessity, and necessarily extensive, however, makes
Winstanley even more anxious about its legitimacy. Laws are legitimate
only when fashioned by an annually elected Parliament, consented to by
people in the parish, and appropriate to the nature, necessity, and grievances of every person. Winstanley says that when fathers make laws in
this way, they act as servants of "the great lawgiver in the commonwealth, [which is] the spirit of universal righteousness." Then the people
"are engaged by love and faithfulness to cleave close to" the fathers and
the law (554). Fathers and sons should bind themselves to the law they
choose, manifesting the reverence Winstanley once accorded to the god
within.

Whereas Puritans and republicans build covenanted government on
customary freehold and limited suffrage, Winstanley establishes political participation on a different basis. His "foundation-freedom" in the
earth performs the same function as freehold and household, but for a
different class. It frees the poor from personal subjection and thereby
liberates them for public action and civic virtue. Therefore, he does not,
like Puritans and republicans, feel compelled to exclude the poor from
politics.

Like Puritanism and republicanism, however, Winstanley rearms the political vocation he once tried to disarm. In the face of usurpation or conquest, he declares:

> The necessity of common preservation, by reason of foreign invasion or in-bred oppression, [does] move the people to arise in the army, to cut and tear to pieces either degenerated officers or rude people, who seek their own inter-est and not common freedom, . . . to enslave both the land and the people to their particular wills and lusts. (572)

With specific relevance to his present, citizens are obliged to fight only for a government that "rules well," and they legitimately may rebel against one that is corrupt. Like Machiavelli, Winstanley now believes that virtue requires people willing to fight and die for their liberties and earth, to act literally as soldiers.

The "necessity of common peace" also requires citizens to form a "ruling army," to "cause the unruly ones, for whom only the law was added, to be subject to it" (539):

> And here all officers, from the father in a family to the Parliament in a land are but the heads and leaders of an army, and all the people arising to protect and assist their officers in defense of a right-ordered government are but the body of an army. (572)

Even though Winstanley maintains that only some will be "unruly ones for whom only the law was added," a few selections from the list of laws, offenses, and punishments reveal his underlying anxiety about dis-order and his new willingness to punish, even with death. Sounding like Hobbes, Winstanley says: "If there were no power in the hands of offi-cers, the spirit of rudeness would not be obedient to any law or govern-ment but its own will" (552). Although Winstanley insists that "no man shall be troubled for his judgment or practice in the things of his god, so long as he lives quiet in the land" (591), he no longer advocates the evangel message of not returning evil for evil: "He who strikes a neigh-bor shall be struck himself by the executioner blow for blow, and shall lose eye for eye, tooth for tooth, limb for limb, and life for life; and the reason is that many may be tender of one anothers bodies, doing as they would be done by" (591). He goes so far as to punish those who speak "reviling or provoking words" or "stir up contention," but his criteria reflect his longstanding concerns.

Whereas those who call "the earth his and not his brothers" shall be shamed publicly and "made a servant," those who actually "do buy and sell the earth or the fruits thereof" or "administer justice for money" shall be executed "as traitors to the peace of the commonwealth" (595). Whoever preaches for money, rather than engaging in free discourse among peers, "shall be put to death for a witch and a cheater" (597). And not surprisingly, Winstanley anticipates transgressions that concern sexual relations: "If any man lie with a maid and beget a child, he shall marry her. If a man forcibly lie with a woman and she cry out and give no consent . . . he shall be put to death and the woman let go free; for it is robbery of a woman's bodily freedom" (599). Certain kinds of crimes jeopardize the foundation-freedoms of everyone. Buying and selling, preaching, and rape (acts committed by Winstanley's most threatening enemies) challenge the deepest values of the commonwealth. They also violate what is most sacred to people as creatures: their earth, their minds, and their bodies. To these acts he will not turn the other cheek.

Despite his willingness to punish, however, there are no grounds to argue that government imposes its inventions on an unwilling populace: no autonomous state power or standing army coerces people into a community of one heart and one mind. Like Hobbes, Winstanley is now acutely aware of the fragility of order, and yet unlike Hobbes, he unmistakably insists that people exercise power in unmediated and public ways. Thus, Hobbes arms the state, whereas Winstanley arms the people directly as a citizen militia. As a result, Winstanley declares hopefully, "If Parliament were not the representative of the people, who indeed is the body of all power, the army would not obey its orders" (562). Winstanley's realism consists in the insight that choice and consent are the only basis of a durable order: it is this insight he invariably emphasizes when he contrasts kingdoms and commonwealths.[9]

Thus, the goal of the fathers' discipline is the freedom to make and keep covenants, which is achieved when the law citizens give themselves becomes what is most sacred to them. At the same time, citizens learn that the principle of "mutual preservation" must animate those laws and covenants if all are to be fed and empowered. With the right to consent to law, however, comes not only the duty to subject oneself to it but

9. Because kingly power is not founded and reaffirmed continually by popular consent and action, "if it had not a club law to support it," says Winstanley, "there would be no order at all" (529). Thus, he insists to Cromwell:

> I do not say, nor desire, that everyone shall be compelled to practice this commonwealths government; for the spirits of some will be enemies at first, though afterwards will prove most cordial and true friends thereunto. Yet I desire that . . . the ancient commons and waste lands and the lands newly got in by the armies victories . . . may be set free to all that have lent assistance . . . and to all that are willing to come into the practice of this Government. . . . And for others who are not willing, let them stay in the way of buying and selling . . . til they be willing. (513)

also the duty to punish transgressions in others. Just as Winstanley once argued that suffering the consequences of transgression taught Adam the reverence for limits that engendered freedom, so *The Law of Freedom* requires citizens to use punishment to instruct each other in the meaning of responsibility and mutuality. This is the sobering but fullest expression of membership in a "free commonwealth."

Since citizens consensually create and enforce a horizon of reverence, the problem in the text is not political tyranny. The issue is not the absence of consent, but what it is to which people consent, why they consent, and with what consequences; not the presence of worldly authority, but its character; not punishment, but its motives. That is, the problem lies in Winstanley's conceptions of authority, reverence, and righteousness, for even as he tries to constitute them democratically, he drains his platform of the spirit of rebellion to which he once testified.

REVERENCE AND FREEDOM

Unlike women, sons literally constitute the authority to which they consent. In an ongoing way, they are entitled to criticize and replace officers, participate in deliberation, change laws by withholding consent, and object when a law is administered improperly. In extreme circumstances, Winstanley reserves to them the right to rebel. And of course, they can expect to become fathers themselves, who are eligible for office. Nonetheless, his metaphors and the example of women indicate what is troubling in the voluntary subjection of sons and fathers.

Winstanley's metaphors suggest that men are to replicate the "knitting together" that god once fostered and that women do literally, but only in private. "King's law," says Winstanley, "is the soldier who cuts Christ's garment into pieces, which was to have remained uncut and without seam," so that covetousness "moves people to fight against one another for those pieces, viz, for the several enclosures of the earth, who shall possess the earth and who shall rule over others." In contrast, a righteous government "unites Gentile and Jew into one brotherhood and rejects none; this makes Christs garment whole again and makes the kingdoms of the world to become commonwealths" (589).

Like women, too, sons are enjoined "upon pain of punishment" to "cleave" to the legitimate authority of the fathers:

> All these officers are links in a chain; they arise from one and same root, which is the necessity of common peace, and all their works tend to preserve common peace. Therefore they are to assist each other, and all others are to

assist them, as need requires, upon pain of punishment. . . . And the rule of right government, being thus observed, may make a whole land, nay, the whole fabric of the earth, to become one family of mankind and one well-governed commonwealth, as Israel was one house . . . though it consisted of many tribes, nations, and families. (544)

Like women, sons willingly serve and sacrifice in obedience to the fathers; but whereas women are enjoined to nurture, sons are enjoined to discipline and punish. Plurality is knit together by mutual preservation, but this political art now requires punishing the transgressions that rip the fabric of reverence and threaten the commonwealth family.

Thus, Winstanley's inner struggle to submit to god by purifying himself now takes on a more punitive outer form: the law god once wrote and burned into the heart to cast out covetousness is created now by citizens and inscribed by them on each others' bodies. As a result, Winstanley's acceptance of violence is not brazen like Machiavelli's, or compulsively logical like Hobbes's, but stern and moralistic. Like the Puritan fathers whose inner need to punish he once diagnosed, Winstanley calls on good citizens to punish the particularity he still associates with Cain and Ishmael.

Part of what is troubling in *The Law of Freedom* appears here, for he has become a creator in the absence of god's inner authority and therefore in the presence of a deep fear about nature and self-control. As a result, Winstanley's newfound capacity to invent is put in male terms and turned against the life, desire, uncertainty, bodily knowledge, and power signified by the women these inventors protect and control. Partly, then, the book squelches the spirit that animated his own rebellion because he does not rely on, and indeed tries to control, what he believes is no longer being nurtured—and ordered—by god. Fathers and sons mutually tyrannize the kingdom within, whose motions no longer can be trusted to provide "inward understanding," and themselves as a social body, for they no longer can trust that inner piety will enable them to nourish themselves righteously. Thus, the willingness to punish and be punished suggests that fathers and sons anxiously and self-righteously build a "family" in order to wall in their own dangerous desires, just as they confine women. In this sense, *The Law of Freedom* does not so much betray Winstanley's radicalism as disclose that his sense of betrayal has cut the heart, and thus the women, out of it.

But fear of disorder does not suffice to explain what is troubling about the way Winstanley externalizes god's authority. Winstanley manifests the inner need to justify violence unequivocally and moralistically: the necessity of violence intensifies his anxious insistence that it is surely righteousness his sword defends. Indeed, he dreams of constructing a morally perfect, ethically rational universe in which men know what is evil and only the evil suffer.

This dream requires at its foundation a certainty about righteousness, which becomes the basis on which fathers and sons cast out covetousness so as to knit together. As the necessity of order raises the problem of punishment, so the need to punish raises the problem of legitimacy; as the need to be legitimate raises the problem of establishing a common ground or justification, so the need for a common ground raises the problem of agreement. In the face of ongoing covetousness Winstanley tries to establish agreement about righteousness so that transgressions can be known and punished with moral certainty. Given covetousness and plurality, however, how can Winstanley imagine agreement about righteousness? Like Hobbes, he is aware of the problem, but he asserts:

> You will say . . . men will differ so in their judgments that we shall never agree. I answer: there is but bondage and freedom, particular interest and common interest; and he who pleads particular interest into a free commonwealth will presently be seen and cast out. (559)

The point is not so much that this is an unrealistic and unwarranted assertion, but rather that precisely this assumption liberates Winstanley to create, while it shapes that creation in troubling ways.[10]

Winstanley can take on the judgment and vengeance of god and become a builder only by presuming the certain moral grounds god once provided him. With this faith he mobilizes impulses he once hoped to purify altogether: anger, invention, contention, accusation, and even the desire for honor are welcome and legitimate if directed against "particular interest" and channeled to serve "common preservation." Thus, fathers and sons engage in a purification process, on the presumption that what they punish in themselves and others is really "covetous" and that what they serve is truly righteous. As Winstanley continues to

---

10. Taken as such, the effort to find a ground for his legitimacy as a builder is perfectly reasonable. And in part, his definition of *common* is also reasonable. Winstanley wants to say, All should agree that what is common is to be sought; that what is common includes "every particular body," at least for what is important. Moreover, he appears to believe that certain basic conflicts can be eliminated if men acknowledge that certain needs are common, or conversely, apply to needs the principle of the Golden Rule. That all require access to the earth and that guaranteed access depends, in turn, on sharing it, is still linked to his idea of god: "I cannot believe that our righteous creator should be so partial in his dispensation of the earth, seeing our bodies cannot live upon the earth without the use of [it]" (569).

split off, and now punish, the pride he associates with Cain, so he embodies his own will to purity in his vision of a transformed household. In this sense, he does not so much betray his radicalism as disclose the pastoral dream that always was troubling about it.

Holding to this dream after his defeat, however, represents for Winstanley a massive denial of his experience. When he lost the providential support of his historical narrative, he might have faced the pride in his claim to righteousness; unable to believe that he was the wholly reverent son of god, he might have granted that righteousness is not a matter of certain knowledge and that he lacked a guaranteed moral sanction. With this humility, he might have devised a politics in which what people revere, or the limits by which they define legitimacy, would *emerge* only through the moral risk and conflict that he precludes.

If reverence were not innately and introspectively recognized, but the uncertain and changing gift of conflict, then those who act could not presume certain moral warrant when they profess to defend justice or attack corrupt power in its name. Indeed, all actors would be at great risk themselves of transgressing because it may turn out that they are neither defending what is righteous nor punishing the guilty. Righteousness and reverence could not be separated so simply from the risk of transgression; reverence and rebellion could not be divorced from each other. Citizens then could not demonize those they punish for transgressions. Indeed, awareness that those they punish could embody an unappreciated good, a valid point of view, an essential value or interest, would give proper political form to the injunction "Love thine enemy."

But when Winstanley lost god's sanction, he continued to believe that he was a good son who had not transgressed god's truths. One can share his sense that he had not done wrong, yet one sees his continuing need to deny his own pride. After all, he had transgressed human law in the name of a divine law he could not prove; he proudly had insisted that the universe conformed to his conceptions of righteousness; by way of his god, he resentfully had raised himself above brothers he judged; he had endorsed bloodshed he could not redeem and had been responsible for suffering he could not expiate. An actual blood crime had enabled Cain to know the nature of his transgression, so that his exile deepened him, but Winstanley's certainty about the righteousness of sharing the earth prevents him from seeing the ways he is nonetheless bound to Cain as well as Ishmael and Esau.

For this reason, Winstanley's last book does not reflect the tragic self-recognition of Cain, who acknowledged his complicity in his plight and perhaps built a city accordingly. Nor does it represent the tragic viewpoint of the Book of Job, in which there is unavoidable, valid, and valuable conflict between the perspectives of god and man, or authority and its subjects. Instead, Winstanley manifests the combination of anxiety, piety, and vengeance that he analyzed in the Puritans. Because of his fear of disorder and his dream of a righteousness immaculately conceived and piously defended, one therefore expects a city awash in blood. But Winstanley repeatedly asserts that punishment is only a last resort, and only for the obviously covetous few. In fact, his disciplinary system is extraordinarily restrained in severity, even if extensive.[11]

Precisely in these regards, however, one finds what may be most troubling about *The Law of Freedom*. Winstanley believes that punishment is only for the few because he hopes to shape people who not only agree to a common standard but also conform to such an extent that transgression is radically reduced and punishment rendered virtually unnecessary. The romance behind the realism of Winstanley's household extends, then, from faith in a morally certain standard to the idea of constructing a morally perfect world, the project of fashioning people who internalize its standards in a way that preempts the need for coercion.

It is in this regard, too, that parallels with Thomas More are so striking. Like More, Winstanley links the elimination of private property to social institutions that will undermine the internal basis of covetousness in pride and, thus, in particularity. By narrowing the scope of the ego and the avenues of its possible aggrandizement, and by depriving the family and parish of functions that would promote exclusive kinds of identification, both theorists reduce radically the ways a person could constitute himself or herself as a being distinct from, and opposed to, others. Rather than privatize men, proscribe politics, and confront a liberated egoism with an awesome state, as does Hobbes, More and

---

11. The system is based on a graduated series of responses to "offenders," who are "admonished" in private discussions and then, if there is a repetition of the offense, in public remonstrance. A third offense indicates that persuasion and shame have failed, and official judicial proceedings are initiated. In the meantime, the offender is not imprisoned: Winstanley says he wants to prevent the "cruelty" of prisons, and hopes that while awaiting trial, an offender "may remember himself and amend his ways." Even if found guilty, the offender is not imprisoned but set to work at hard labor. Even repeated offenses of most crimes result in hard labor, despite Winstanley's reference to "an eye for an eye." The death penalty is applied only for those crimes that threaten "foundation-freedoms." Surely this violates Winstanley's own ethical canon, for he could have imposed the punishment of servitude. Nonetheless, Winstanley's discipline is unbelievably mild compared to the brutality of the penal system at that time.

Winstanley proscribe egoism and politicize daily life so that social power can be exercised communally.

Thus, More and Winstanley rely on shame as the inner basis of "knitting together." In *The Law of Freedom* social life proceeds wholly in the eyes of others, and exposure to public gaze is central to the text: the family is like a fishbowl; the key to discipline is public remonstrances; the key to the usual punishment of hard labor is not pain but the shame of wearing different clothing and doing the most degrading work. In a passage startlingly reminiscent of More, Winstanley declares:

> All those who have lost their freedom shall be clothed in woolen cloth, that they may be distinguished from the others. They shall be under the government of a taskmaster who shall apppoint them to be porters or laborers, to do any work that any freeman wants done. (597)

"To what end is this," he asks rhetorically, "but to kill their pride and unreasonableness, that they may become useful men in the commonwealth?" (597).

Winstanley does seek inner recognition of the reasons for law. He does intend to create "courageous men" undeterred by "slavish fear" and therefore able to defend new truths and challenge unjust authority. But there is a tension between his reliance on inwardness and his reliance on the censure of others. Perhaps guilt is now problematic to him: it can promote conflict, or at least a sense of one's separateness; it is manifested in the "conscienable zeal" of those who follow what they mistakenly believe is their inner light. As a result, he appears to rely on shame more than guilt, and it may be that he leaves the conscience unregulated precisely because it is not crucial to knitting people together.

Accordingly, one fears that the pressure of the social voice could overwhelm the otherness of the inner voice. Living in the scrutinizing glare of others' watchful eyes may restrict damaging forms of self-expression, but it does so by effacing particularity altogether. If one follows the argument of Marx's "On the Jewish Question," the materialism of "the Jew" might be the route to an emancipation that abolishes external forms of property; but that emancipation abolishes the "Jewish" sense of particularity, the self-possessed ego, which is rooted in the separateness of the body, as in the separateness of a people who stand apart.

That Winstanley proposes the mutual tyrannizing of shameful censure in the name of reason and love should be taken seriously. For behind his hostility to "reviling words," hypocrisy, selfishness, vanity, and irresponsibility is the underlying "reason" that these violate the ideal of neighbor love. Especially after his defeat by these and other, less petty vices, Winstanley wishes for no one to be wrongfully hurt, to suffer as he did. Just as the anger in the text is released in the name of preventing harm, so the mutual surveillance of citizens arises out of love, but as the obsessive, stifling, and ultimately killing desire to protect one another from harm.

Finally, however, their desire to be their brethren's keeper is not the strongest motive compelling allegiance and conformity to law. What really obviates punishment and motivates conformity is not fear of physical punishment, love for the fathers, or love of others but rather the desire to be loved by one's neighbors and a corresponding fear of exile. Thus, whereas Parliament is the "father to the land," there is also a mother—though actual mothers are confined to the household, and the earth is not a loving presence. The mother of the commonwealth is the sons themselves, the "body of power," the fraternity that, as Norman O. Brown rightly says, is always a mother. As the confinement of women also suggests, the author of *The Law of Freedom,* defeated and spurned, disinherited by men and abandoned by god, might feel the need to be loved in particularly acute way.

Thus, the platform jeopardizes autonomy not just because the soul in each man, like the women, must be domesticated, and not just because Winstanley tries to resurrect his certainty about righteousness. In addition, the need for love, no longer satisfied internally, encourages a worldly submission that does not engender freedom. But this suggests how the authority of the brethren operates on the same terms as the god within. As his god never affirmed rebellion but fed only the submissive, feminine, and childlike soul, promising nurturance only to creatures who were internally submissive, so Winstanley felt ashamed of the ways in which he was a "being for himself," which he associated with rebellion. In other words, the need to be loved precluded any contention or even distance between himself and god.

Whereas god's love and Winstanley's own submission in fact encouraged his rebellion, his platform does not. Since he continues to disown his rebelliousness when he constructs a world in the absence of god, he premises nurturance and legitimacy on submission but without affirming rebellion and particularity. Because he still disavows the pride that was central to his piety, he theorizes a reverence toward worldly authority that promotes only obedience. In this sense, one can say that Winstanley does betray his radicalism, since he becomes a creator who subverts the very inwardness and particularity, the risk and rebellion, that once made his own radicalism possible.

Winstanley's need for love and certainty suggest that his platform fails to sponsor freedom for the same reason that it fails to include women. Their absence and his final poem attest to the withdrawal of the spirit that animated the rebellion witnessed by his earlier texts. That spirit was not only reverent but also necessarily rebellious. Although he always denied his rebelliousness, it was the tension between his reverent declarations and subversive intent that brought his texts to life. Now that he is no longer a rebel, his reverence appears only in the guise of worldly authority; his spirit of righteousness appears without the rebellion that animated it. One sees the resurrection of reverence, but without the rebellion it authorized. Indeed, that resurrection presumes the death and burial of rebellion: as a result, Winstanley builds not a temple for the spirit but a tomb.

The text of *The Law of Freedom* fails artistically for the same reason the commonwealth fails politically: the lack of playfulness and rebellion in the commonwealth, as brethren anxiously watch over each other, bespeaks the lack of playfulness in the author himself, as if he were prescribing a strict regimen of truth and neighbor love to sickly souls. Here is the key difference between More, or Plato, and Winstanley. Like them, he intends to induce a perspective shift in his readers, by illustrating a "house" and "foundation." Like them, his desire to make this fiction real, to make corporeal a work of the imagination, leads to a specificity of detail that can create the impression of a deadening still life. (Indeed, readers tend to see these fictions as blueprints.) However, More and Plato create utopias that, like good still lifes, enhance or intensify our sense of life and choice. Their fictions stop time, but in order to take us deeper into our own time; their fictions seem inanimate, but heighten our awareness of the fictions that animate (and deaden) our lives. Winstanley's text does not accomplish this.

In part, the liveliness of Winstanley's text is undermined by its utopian form and detail. But the text also is deadened by his own confusion about its status as blueprint or fiction: his effort to create a house in the imagination is a desperate effort literally to resurrect the program that was defeated in the world. Whether as blueprint or work of the imagination, however, the text is also deadened by his despair, which leads him to fix life in a death-like dream. But one must say that More and Plato knew of the hopelessness of their political positions, and this awareness did not drain life from their texts. Indeed, one could say that their hopelessness and alienation allowed them, even liberated them, to invest their life in a truth they consciously depicted as fiction.

Winstanley cannot do this. He still locates meaning only in lived action and hence cannot invest meaning in a text. Always insistent on the radical difference between god's truth and human fiction, how could he embody his truth in something he knew, or feared, was "merely" imaginary? He lacked the temperament or understanding, finally, to embody truth in a fiction he could take as such. As a result, he is no more playful with a text than he is with the commonwealth, or than citizens are with their own conventions, which they cannot take as fictions.[12]

Thus, the text is of a piece politically and artistically: unable to see that reverence emerges by way of rebellion and that righteousness emerges only by risking transgression, Winstanley also cannot see that truths emerge by way of fictions. Just as the commonwealth fails politically because he disavows the rebellion to which it could have testified, so the text fails artistically because he disavows the imagination to which it actually does testify. Perhaps one could say, then, that the text fails not so much because of Winstanley's emptiness as because he never took his own full measure.

12. The parallels to More are striking, although there is no evidence that Winstanley ever read *Utopia*. By far the most brilliant analysis of More is by Stephen Greenblatt in his *Renaissance Self-Fashioning* (Chicago: University of Chicago Press, 1978). Greenblatt sees More pushing to an extreme the connection between eliminating private property and effacing the deeply inward, guilty, self-conscious ego. The paradox for More, however, is that this self-effacement is enacted as the ultimate self-conscious act, canceled in its turn by the book itself as a monument to his genius. It is unlikely that Winstanley intentionally effaced his own inwardness or the particularity that made him a rebel; it is more likely that *The Law of Freedom* reflects his despair about the spirit. But even if he had not been defeated, he would never have appreciated the imagination, and therefore he never could have achieved as self-consciously playful, artful, and subversive a book as *Utopia*.

CHAPTER IX

From the Lamb
to the Dragon

When does the butterfly in flight
read what is written on its wings?

—*Pablo Neruda*

We should be able also to stand *above* morality—and not
only to stand with the anxious stiffness of a man who is
afraid of slipping and falling any moment, but also to float
above it and *play*. How then could we possibly dispense with
art—and with the fool? . . . And as long as you are in any
way *ashamed* before yourselves, you do not yet belong
with us.

—*Nietzsche*

LATER LIFE

After his defeat as a digger, Winstanley was disinherited in a double
sense: exiled from the household of the fathers, he had lost as well the
household of the true parents and regenerated children. Still believing
that he was the good son who had honored and not transgressed god's
truths, he built a city in his imagination, to create in his text a household
from which he would not be exiled. His final poem, however, suggests
his despair about a life he only could dream of transforming. Overcome
by the impotence of his sorrowful knowledge, Winstanley longed for
death: he did not know what it meant to live once forsaken by his god.

But Winstanley was not a Christ; he did not die. Nor was he an Abel,
who died by Cain's hand. From one point of view he was more like
Cain, who survived his rebellion to lead another life. From a different
point of view, however, he ends up more like Isaac than he ever could
have imagined in 1651, for he was not sacrificed, and he gained the inheritance and blessing of the fathers. What, then, is the relationship between his radicalism and his later life?

To James Alsop, quoted in the introduction to Part IV, it seemed that

Winstanley chose the way he led his later life and therefore wilfully and irrevocably broke with his earlier radicalism. Indeed, Alsop believes that Winstanley's radicalism was a momentary aberration in a life otherwise characterized by conformity. What he means is suggested by his un-critical textual use of ranter Clarkson's denunciation of Winstanley:

> I made it appear to Gerrard Winstanley there was a self-love and vain-glory nursed in his heart, that if possible, by digging to have gained people to him, by which his name might be great among the Commonality of the Nation, as afterwards appeared in him a most shameful retreat from Georges-Hill, with a spirit of pretended universality, to become a real Tithe-gatherer of propriety.[1]

By way of Clarkson, who had his personal reasons to hate Winstanley, Alsop implies that Winstanley always wanted an inheritance and the es-teem of others. Thus, the motives that radicalized Winstanley also led him back to conformity: once he realized he could not gain the applause of the poor, but discovered that he had an inheritance and could earn the esteem of the propertied, this opportunist abandoned radical poli-tics. In a concluding sentence that sounds triumphant, if not spiteful, Alsop declares: "The foremost radical of the English Revolution had be-come respectable."[2] One suspects that Alsop takes satisfaction in this fact; but certainly he believes that Winstanley's later life sheds a sober-ing and disenchanting light on his radical period, if not on all radicals.

Whereas Clarkson's self-righteous scream of betrayal and hypocrisy suggests one stereotypical response to the later life, Alsop himself repre-sents a second: smug "reality teachers" have always reduced radicalism to personal resentment and expected the inevitable return of prodigal children. A third stereotypical response is represented by Christopher Hill and T. Wilson Hayes: to detach Winstanley's radicalism from his later life, they depict him as a defeated victim who chooses silence. Like Alsop, they seek consistency—he by devaluing radicalism, they by imag-ining Winstanley as inwardly unrepentant and alienated.[3]

1. Alsop, "Gerrard Winstanley," p. 708.
2. Alsop, "Gerrard Winstanley," p. 709.
3. Hayes argues that Winstanley could not accept the "tyrannical alternatives" repre-sented by the "champions of propertied society" or the "fanatical Fifth Monarchists." Therefore, he concludes, Winstanley soberly gave up public life: "He had spoken; he had acted. No more could be expected of him" (*Winstanley the Digger*, p. 219). Although Hayes is right that Winstanley's silence might have been an act of wisdom, he himself wisely stays silent about Winstanley's apparent conformity to "the champions of proper-tied society" and the fanatical state church. Christopher Hill simply says, "Where else could he go after it became clear that Christ was not going to rise in Charles II's En-gland?" But Hill makes an argument about Quakers that he chooses not to apply to Winstanley, even though Winstanley ends a Quaker. Hill argues that defeat changed people's *inner* orientation so that they *chose* withdrawal, quietism, and life in the market (*The World Turned Upside Down*, pp. 299–306). To Hayes, Alsop rightly responds:

G. E. Aylmer offers a less self-serving point of view, arguing quite simply that there is a contradiction between Winstanley's earlier radicalism and his later life and that one should evaluate the validity of Winstanley's ideas and actions on their own terms.[4] Surely this is the soundest approach, and I shall return to it shortly, but it leaves unasked the really interesting and important question: is there a connection between his earlier radicalism and his later life? Although inferences about Winstanley seem to disclose more about his interpreters than about him, there is evidence for a different inference about how his radicalism shaped his later choices. In retrospect, at least, *The Law of Freedom* seems like a halfway house: it suggests the inner connection between Winstanley's radicalism and his respectability.

In a truly uncanny way, the book foreshadows Winstanley's rebirth, the new life he begins to live. As it presumes the death of spirit and enjoins the absence of women, so it is followed by the death of his first wife. As it represents the death of his rebellion and turns against the piety that once animated him, so it is followed by a life characterized by outward conformity to the institutions he once criticized. As it signals the reassertion of family, private life and paternal power, so it is followed by remarriage, progeny, and an apparent focus on domesticity. As it describes the legitimate grounds for worldly authority, so it is followed by his accession to public offices in the very parish that had been the scene of his rebellion. As it is animated by his desire to belong and be esteemed by his peers, so it is followed by a life in which he gains respectability. As it reflects heightened anxiety about earthly nourishment and the misery of deprivation, so it is followed by a life in which he secures an independent source of nourishment and perhaps lifts the shame and inner sorrows he associates with poverty and wage labor.

In general, then, as *The Law of Freedom* represents Winstanley's dream of a reconstituted household in which he is a legitimate father and worldly authority, so it is followed by his literal return to the father's house, and as a father in his own right. He surely could not anticipate how his later life would parallel, and even fulfill, the deeper impulses that his last book manifests, but we can use the book to help us understand that life.

"The question is not what posterity expected of Winstanley, but what did he expect of himself?" And Alsop rightly concludes that Hill avoids the problems posed by the actual choices he made.

4. G. E. Aylmer, "The Religion of Gerrard Winstanley," in *Radical Religion in the English Revolution*, ed. J. F. McGregor and B. Reay (Oxford: Oxford University Press, 1984), p. 116.

Did Winstanley perhaps recognize the element of pride in his dream of salvation in historical time? And did perhaps the failure of the poor to transcend their own history lead him to see that he could not transcend his own? Forced to relinquish the idea of salvation, he might have reconceived his responsibilities and his reverence for god within a social order it is not god's will to change. Accordingly, he authentically might have changed his sense of what god required and permitted.

There is every reason to think that he might have continued to define himself as the dutiful son and therefore as a reverent father (and office-holder). Indeed, his need to serve and revere might have led him back to conformity with authorities he once attacked. At the same time, that conformity could reflect his acknowledgment of what he always had wanted for himself, since he could not gain it for others. Stripped of his prophetic mantle, he might have felt he had permission to affirm what he once felt pressured to disavow—paternity, domesticity, and power in his unreformed world. A reduction in the scope of his calling might be considered a betrayal from one point of view but could as easily be read as a sign that he has integrated what he once had denied.

To be sure, just as *The Law of Freedom* manifested a split between worldly reform and the spirit within, so his later life, like Quaker inwardness, *presumes* the disjunction between spirit and flesh, god's truths and historical circumstance, human dreams and social reality. This lack of reconciliation is precisely the truth taught by his defeat, which he must address if he is to go on living at all. Hence there is no reason to assume he was entirely at peace, however modestly he prospered. Of course, no one can know. But a simple view of the prodigal's return and inner peace, like the simple view that he remained silently alienated, makes too neat what only could have been messy. I offer a more complicated view if only to suggest that his later choices should be considered in a way more sensitive to the history of his concerns and the meaning of his defeat. But even a more complex view lacks the proof of his own words to testify to his own understanding. So where are we left?

MEMORY AND LAUGHTER

As Aylmer rightly insists, "Setting aside both his earlier and later career in business, Winstanley's ideas should surely stand and fall in their own right."[5] What is the value of those ideas?

5. Aylmer, "The Religion of Gerrard Winstanley," p. 94.

Most obviously, Winstanley is enormously instructive because of what he explicitly intended to teach. His is the best analysis I have found of propertied Puritan radicalism, of its psychological, social, and political nature. He understood the causes, flaws, and limitations of its character, but he also took seriously its language and developed his critique from inside its idiom. Moreover, he understood the ways in which its successes and failures would lead to a certain kind of future: personal anxiety and social division not only created an ascetic and punitive, mystified and limited radicalism but also, when that radicalism failed, warranted and promoted the market and strong state defended by Hobbes. Finally, he lived through and worked out an alternative radicalism, which truly reached the roots of the problems he identified so acutely.

His ideas and actions, however, are not merely of historical value, which is why merely textual or contextual approaches are insufficient. One loses too much by "trodding under foot" the losers in the battles of history or by "preserving" them as if one were a taxidermist. The road not taken still exists in a certain dimension. Therefore, one can return to Winstanley's landmark to recover possibilities, not nostalgically to mourn losses.

Thus, I have suggested parallels with modern theorists specifically to emphasize what is special and unusual about Winstanley. Precisely because he was present at the origins of modern politics and was not himself fully "modern," he exemplifies a different *voice*, from which modern readers can learn particular lessons. What made it possible for him to synthesize psychological and social arguments and to criticize "kingly," Puritan, and protoliberal politics was precisely the rare character of his language, which was related to the extraordinary sensibility I have called "reverence."

To begin with, Winstanley's metaphoric language enabled him to find and express the connections between the inner life and worldly action. His excremental, oral, and parental metaphors literally embodied the connections he sought to disclose and diagnose. He found those connections in the idioms of his time, in the speech of his contemporaries, so that his works demonstrate how language can be a medium of revelation and not only concealment. Because he was so sensitive to the meaning of words, Winstanley became a witness to the necessities and realities, as well as the capacity for choice, that are disclosed by language. Thus, even as he rooted thought and action in psychological and social reality, in the necessities of the body and in social interests, he also took seriously people's intentionality and freedom. In this effort, he fused his bodily metaphors with the scriptural language of his time, defining a human project located in the personal struggle for self-determination and in the social struggle to overcome estrangement, and embedding these in Biblical history. In turn, that history was about the ongoing struggle over the discourse and covenant that defined identity and membership, inheritance and title. Thus, Winstanley became a great *political* theorist specifically because he integrated an analysis of underlying causes and history with an analysis of, and commitment to, speech and choice. As he "testified" to the necessities, conflicts, and possibilities revealed by language and history, he also exemplified what it means to be a citizen. In the name of a covenant that recognized the needs and rights of all, he fashioned a politics based on dialogue and directed toward the problem of power and the pressure of necessity.

Winstanley's ingenious reinterpretations of common idioms yielded a remarkable political theory and practice, which achievement in turn demonstrates a larger point. The Revolution occurred in England not only because people were discontented or had interests they wished to pursue, but specifically because evocative and even poetic language articulated desire and grievance into dreams, principles, and causes. Winstanley's commitment to the power of the word verged on the alchemical, but his speech, like the language of his time, did transmute the "base" matter of necessity into the revolutionary act of turning the world upside down. The discovery that one can give voice to one's experience is itself the fundamentally empowering insight behind a popular politics. Thus, the power and poetry of his speech also reveals what is lost when men and women become "modern" in their disenchanted or cynical view of political speech and in their enchanted pursuit of a language uncontaminated by human subjectivity.

Winstanley's bodily metaphors and Biblical idiom enabled him to do what no political theorist, perhaps, has accomplished so well: to join a theory of personal autonomy and a radical, yet dialogic, form of collective action. But language does not suffice to explain how Winstanley made these connections in theory or exemplified them in practice. His "experienced speech" did embody how humans are creatures who live simultaneously in the kingdoms within and without; but this achievement also was possible because of his primordial perception of the ways in which humans are *embedded* creatures, not only in a body that must "subsist" with nature and others, but also in a history and a language.

As he located the self in the body and nature, history and culture, and found god's spirit in these, Winstanley could argue about the ways in which humans are grounded and yet animated, rooted but also parented, moved as well as called by their needs, capacities, and social forms. In relation to such "givens," which humans themselves have not invented, Winstanley developed the insights about freedom that characterize each "moment" in his development. For him, freedom only emerges as people learn to digest and claim, own and honor, and witness and exemplify what defines them as creatures. Hence humans learn freedom only through the transgressions that disclose the needs and bonds they come to recognize as authoritative limits and truths.

In turn, as people serve or uphold what defines and binds them, they learn to establish a healthy kind of autonomy and a form of collective action that is neither murderous nor self-destructive. Winstanley represents a "road not taken" especially because this idea of conditioned freedom is an alternative to the liberal and radical models of collective self-fashioning. As a voice and sensibility that opposed and still illuminates the Promethean shaping of self and society, he provides an important counterpoint in the tradition of political thought and deserves a more respected place among its members.[6]

Even as I have emphasized the value of Winstanley's reverence, however, I also have resisted as a weakness and flaw the idea of god that Winstanley surely considered its basis. But how can I urge the importance of his contribution to political theory when it is inseparable from an idea of god I have questioned so seriously? In part, the earthly and this-worldly character of Winstanley's "spiritual" premises invites their translation into secular terms. More to the point perhaps, the argument for a reverent radicalism in his final book makes that translation and no longer hinges on Christ rising for its justification and enactment.

And yet that book is seriously flawed and even poisoned by the absence of god, or at least by Winstanley's despair about spirit in the

6. Winstanley speaks to concerns that now animate current critics of the modernization process pursued since Winstanley's time. The insights expressed in his idea of reverence evoke the recent theoretical efforts of psychoanalysts to ground the ego in mutuality and love, of ecologists to ground culture in reverence for nature, and of feminists to restore to politics what has been called an ethic of care. Similarly, Winstanley's model of activism exemplifies the efforts of those trying to resurrect a "populist" politics of localism, based on lived tradition and experienced speech; a "Gandhian" commitment to nonviolence, based on the power of exemplary action; and a commitment to direct democracy, based on the political competence of those who are not experts and technicians. The current challenge to a top-down, elite model of political and social change recapitulates the arguments and concerns Winstanley developed against the Puritan radicalism that Walzer rightly considers the prototype of vanguard politics.

world. Does *The Law of Freedom* actually caution against relating his reverence to more modern and secular concerns? In this regard, finally, Winstanley's tale may be most instructive. The value of his ideas resides not only in what he meant to teach: we can learn from the tale as well as from the teller.

Central to Winstanley's idea of god was the belief that this spirit of reason and love feeds only the soul that is submissive. This idea is at the core of his insights and difficulties. Because he accepted what he called his feminine and created being, his passive and sentient self, and desired union with the maternal aspects of inner authority, he avoided the vicissitudes of modern attitudes about autonomy, creativity, will, and power. He found that what is passive and receptive as well as needy and hungry is not to be controlled, but is to be fed and loved. By discovering that a loving inner authority could empower him, he realized that (his own need for) love was not a snare but the essential ground of his development.

As a result, his theory did not split love and need from freedom but instead disclosed their relationship. Consequently, he accepted the equality of women and developed a politics that tried to "knit together" autonomy and connectedness with nature, others, and history. That is why Winstanley's synthesis of Old and New testaments is so important: just as he found the basis of autonomy in the soul's submission to god, so he found the seed of freedom in precisely what rooted people in the earth and tradition. In each case, he generated the unprecedented out of reverence for what he believed was defining and nurturing body, soul, and community.

Yet Winstanley's understanding of reverence also entailed a troubling kind of submission. He felt he could be legitimate only if he acted exclusively in terms of what he revered, wholly as an instrument of the tradition and spirit that parented his agency. By his reckoning, if he were the creator of the ideas, values, and practices for which he rebelled, then he would be merely another fallen Adam, another Cain, rather than a good son. Thus, his reverence imposed the extraordinary—and prideful—demand that he "cast out" ambition, imaginative invention, and anger.

Inwardly, these signs of particularity contaminated the passivity or union that he believed was the condition for being loved, fed, and empowered. Politically, conflict and the creation of conventions appeared only as a pride destructive to the reverence he associated with freedom. He explored the relationship between dependence and autonomy, reverence and freedom, but he himself radically dissociated freedom from the pride that is indeed essential to it. Thus, Winstanley's guilt and ambivalence, his self-deception, self-denial, and finally self-sacrifice, were also the fruits of his reverence.

Accordingly, Winstanley's idea of reverence is especially instructive about the dilemmas of being a creator. Those theorists who willfully embrace the artistry of human creation often deny that humans do and must act (to some extent) in terms of what is given to them, which they cannot create. When thinkers and activists seek a reverent politics, however, they can become like Winstanley, both driven and led to certain contrasting devaluations of the aspects of themselves and nature that appear to jeopardize their piety or challenge the authority, limits, and ideals they construe as the horizon of their action.

In the context of this split between creator and creature, which is represented in styles of radicalism, Winstanley's story, as opposed to his explicit teaching, is most compelling. In his political life he had to confront the tension between his commitment to humans as creatures and the impulses, demands, and capacities that are represented by humans as creators. As he came to extend his sense of human necessity, and thus of what constituted legitimate action, one can witness his developing effort to integrate creature and creator in himself, his theory, and his politics. By the end of the digging experiment, the tension between creator and creature had intensified and therefore become most fruitful; but the bent bow snapped in *The Law of Freedom*, partly because Winstanley felt abandoned by god and partly because he felt he could not rely on the submissive spirit in men and women to gain god's love. As he became a creator who no longer could trust god or the creature in man, he sought to supplant god and control the creature from without.

What is the lesson here? The problems in *The Law of Freedom* do arise because Winstanley tried as a human creator to replace god as a source of sincere milk and social order. Yet those problems result not from the inevitable failure of a secularizing translation of his religiosity but rather from the particular character of his ideas of god and reverence. Still not accepting the rebelliousness in himself (and in others) and still believing that only dutiful receptivity is the basis of righteousness, Winstanley created a worldly authority opposed to the same aspects of self and existence he once stigmatized in the name of god: *The Law of Freedom* fails to the extent it does because of the same religiosity that led to his earlier self-denials.

Rather than substantiate the assertion that a reverent politics requires something like Winstanley's idea of god, the ongoing self-denial in his radicalism and the flaws in his final book suggest the need to salvage his radicalism from his religiosity (even while understanding their connection). In hindsight one sees that the impulses, transgressions, and risks he always tried to deny were indeed inextricably part of the reverence he so powerfully defended. Thus, his transition from radical activism to *The Law of Freedom* does provide a cautionary tale, but one about the relationship between reverence and learning, and thus about reverence and laughter.

Winstanley's theory manifests the ongoing tension between his assertion that there are timeless truths given by god, toward which we must be reverent if we are to be free, and his contrasting assertion that our lives are constituted by our learning, which is to say by error and change— what Winstanley called "the experimental knowledge of Christ." The theodicy that was Winstanley's Puritan legacy enabled him to understand the human capacity for blindness and error, and thus for recognition and change. Because of his theodicy he could address, and even invite the elder brother to confront, the contradictions and self-righteousness he associated with covetousness. But like his god, Winstanley could forgive error, covetousness, and pride only by treating them as the means to a final and stable reverence for an unassailable and unchanging truth.

In Winstanley's life, however, each development in his thought and action was made possible by partial truth and error, not final truth. For he changed his understanding of reverence as he learned more about human necessities. But he never became self-conscious of his own learning process: it was fostered by a theodicy that bound him to an idea of a fixed truth that ultimately devalued error and interpretation. He could not make conscious the fact that error and interpretation actually were constitutive of what he took as truth.

Thus, Winstanley became a political creator who, like his god, could not be playful about, let alone affirm, the ongoing ways that life defies moral reasoning and righteousness. Externalizing his faith in an utterly rational god who could be known by reason and who promised to shape creatures wholly in accord with it, he dreamed of a community that did not wink at frailty, welcome contradiction, or praise contention. When he imagined building a world on the basis of god's truths, he therefore enshrined an orthodoxy. The truths in *The Law of Freedom* were in fact "experimental," but they would be taught as doctrine to sons and daughters who could not discover them through the risk and change he himself experienced.

Winstanley could not see or affirm what startles us in his story: reverence is learned only by way of error and transgression. If from the outside the story of his reverence appears as a history of errors, then one is forced toward the idea that reverence must presume a provisional and changing idea of truth and therefore must affirm the experiment and risk that engender and transform it. Accordingly, one should be cautious in condemning his later life, for then one would make Winstanley's own mistake about truth. What Nietzsche says "in favor of criticism" applies as well to Winstanley's life:

> Now something that you formerly loved as truth . . . strikes you as an error; you shed it and fancy that this represents a victory for your reason. But perhaps this error was as necessary for you then, when you were still a different person—you are always a different person—as are all your present "truths," being a skin as it were, that concealed and covered a great deal that you were not yet permitted to see. What killed that opinion for you was your new life and not your reason: *you no longer need it,* and now it collapses and unreason crawls out of it into the light like a worm. When we criticize something, this is no arbitrary and impersonal event; it is, at least very often, evidence of vital energies in us that are growing and shedding a skin. We negate and must negate because something in us wants to live and affirm—something that we perhaps do not know or see as yet.[7]

Since error is inextricable from learning, so is laughter. When Milan Kundera described the wisdom of the novel, he referred to a Jewish proverb, "Man thinks, God laughs":

> But why does God laugh at the sight of man thinking? Because man thinks and truth escapes him. Because the more men think the more one man's thought diverges from another's. And finally, because man is never what he thinks he is.[8]

Kundera refers to Rabelais, who invented the word *ageliste* to describe men who do not laugh: "Never having heard God's laughter, the agelistes are convinced that truth is obvious, that all men necessarily think the same thing, and that they themselves are exactly what they think they are." Winstanley depicted elder brothers who were *agelistes;* but Winstanley of course could not see himself in this way, and indeed he dreamed of a world in which error, disagreement, and deception— including self-deception—would be cast out. Accordingly, Winstanley and the elder brothers are twinned because, in the name of certainty and

---

7. Friedrich Nietzsche, *The Gay Science,* trans. Walter Kaufman (New York: Vintage, 1974), p. 246.
8. Milan Kundera, "Man Thinks; God Laughs," *New York Review of Books,* July 13, 1985.

in self-righteous tones, they turned against the irreverence of those who laugh.

Thus, the issue of laughter is not simply temperamental, for freedom itself is at stake. After all, it was Winstanley's irreverence toward the orthodoxy of the elder brothers that made him autonomous, and it was his refusal to play the ageliste that enabled him, until *The Law of Freedom,* to accept the irreverence of others. But his rebellion and his tolerance were based on a theodicy that promised to end the irreverence, alienation, and contradiction that had brought him into print and politics. Winstanley's reverence was subversive of authority but was itself an authority defended against subversion. To be sure, any revolt presumes an authority or horizon that requires defense, but any defense of an authority might recall—and value—its origins in revolt and transgression.

Perhaps it is unfair to expect so profoundly a religious man to cultivate irony or humor. Perhaps these are secular versions of grace, or forms of solace for the disenchanted, available only to those who know they live in a history without redemptive purpose. But the issue is not Winstanley's religiosity. Indeed, when the defeat of digging shattered his theodicy, Winstanley acquired neither the ironic sense that god had set him up in what was a cruel joke nor the tragic sense that human and divine purposes were irreconcilable. Rather, his anger was unleashed in the dream of a commonwealth that punished irreverence.

Thus, the absence of laughter may link Winstanley's earlier radicalism to what is substantively troubling in *The Law of Freedom* and also may disclose the inner connection between Winstanley's radicalism and his later life. It seems unlikely that Winstanley merely changed the god he self-righteously served while continuing to punish whatever contradicted his reverence. But it does seem likely that he became a conformist because his inner demand for pious service, certainty, and wholehearted reverence, when deprived of a ground in god's certainties, apparently found another ground—in the very authorities he once criticized.

Given that Winstanley's genius and radicalism are inseparable from his earnest effort to be righteous, and given the logic of Puritan sensibility, the reality of civil war and violence, and the fact that no one can step outside of one's time, my point is neither to fault him nor to argue that radicals must "lighten up." But it is important to identify the problematic underside of a politics based on reverence, whether articulated in explicitly religious or in secular terms. A politics neither animated nor tempered by laughter, neither chastened nor softened by irony, will be at war with the awareness that truth might not be unitary, that men might never agree, and that those who act might not be who they think they are.

To make this point is only to take seriously Winstanley's own warnings about the danger of becoming like one's enemy. In the context of his own effort in this regard, one needs to address the poignant fact of his final closeness to the Puritans, and to Hobbes. The issue, then, is to identify what bound Winstanley to his enemies, which has taken us from the lessons of learning to the meaning of laughter, and which now returns us to the problem of pride.

FORGETTING AND POWER:
WINSTANLEY AND HOBBES

I have argued that Winstanley's theory represents an alternative to Hobbes's and thus a road not taken in our history. But Winstanley's last book and later life appear to collapse this distinction. Indeed, they seem to exemplify the narrative in Hobbes's argument. In *The Law of Freedom* Winstanley did not build a mortal god, but he did create an imaginary orthodoxy to which he imagined citizens reverently conforming. In addition, one can begin down the road taken by following Winstanley's choices in his later life: his embracing of the patriarchal family, his absorption in the market, his outward conformity (and perhaps inner allegiance) to a state church and sovereign power are tokens of Winstanley's defeat and constituents of life in the belly of Hobbes's whale.

In Hobbes's argument, this narrative hinges on the loss of faith in the redemptive history that sanctioned revolt, which leads men to submit consciously to conventional authority. From this point of view, the search for an authority to revere was the constant that inspired Winstanley's rebellion and then conformity. But more deeply, the power of Hobbes's argument arises from his insights into pride and the consequences of denying or avoiding it.

It was the problem of pride that shaped Puritan politics and Winstanley's antinomian critique; it was the exposure of the pride the Puritans continued to deny that justified Hobbes's mortal god. Complicity in the sin of pride always will give Hobbes a theoretical opening; the denial of pride always makes rebels vulnerable to Hobbes's critique; and fear of pride always can transform rebellion into obedience. Winstanley was not defeated in history because he tried to avoid the sin of pride, but the reverence that denied it did shape his rebellion and, once defeated, led him in Hobbes's direction, toward a political creation that devalued rebellion and, ultimately, toward actual conformity.

Winstanley's last book and his later life, however, do not prove Hobbes "right" about life and politics. Rather, the criticisms I have made of Winstanley's reverent religiosity are even more apt to Hobbes's Promethean science and sovereign invention. After all, Hobbes attacked theodicy not out of a spirit that welcomed the ambiguity and freedom brought by the absence of a supreme arbitrator but because theodicy failed to secure "peace and truth." Enacting a faith in truth no less religious than Winstanley's, Hobbes revered a science that was no less at war with life, and no more open to ambiguity, than Winstanley's spirit. Thus, Hobbes's unsmiling rebelliousness and anxious acts of creation no more affirmed transgression than did Winstanley's dutiful radicalism and earnest love.

As a result, Hobbes's mortal god, like Winstanley's Father, was an authority at war with the irreverent rebelliousness that in fact animated him. Their fear of pride generated strangely symmetrical dreams of what can and must be accomplished by reverence for authority, however differently they constructed it. Therefore, the problems I have identified in Winstanley's reverence are not confined to a religious sensibility; indeed, they profoundly shape one of its greatest critics.

Accordingly, Hobbes's theory reveals not only a truth about the pride humans deny at their own risk but also the dangerous logic in any effort to simply "humble" or overcome it. Hobbes will always be a powerful theorist because he always will remind people of their pride. But his project is not a necessary conclusion to the confrontation with pride, and indeed it is a prideful fantasy that never can be carried out fully. Humans are not machines: although sociological creatures, they are also agents and creators; they continue to use language and political judgment—even if not often enough in public—in ways that he ruled out.

It is for this reason that Winstanley's difference from Hobbes matters so much. Winstanley sought an authority to revere, but always because he sought a reverence that would free; therefore, even in *The Law of Freedom*, he addressed and tried to strengthen the human capacity to judge, criticize, and rebel. Accordingly, he can help illuminate the desire for wholeness, the capacity for experienced speech, and the need for meaningful commitment that a Hobbesian world can neither squelch nor satisfy. What Hobbes tried to sacrifice and bury is still available: there is always a road not taken.

Of course, any political path, especially one informed by a theoretical spirit, will provide abundant ironies for the traveler. Winstanley's life compels us toward an ironic, but not cynical, view of the gap between moral claims and natural impulses, political dreams and historical reality, self-definitions and actual motives, abiding commitments and actual choices, our need for meaning and the ways of an inscrutable god. We have witnessed the inevitable defeat not of hope or rebellion but of the effort to justify a life by continually defining its calling. This warrants neither vain despair nor smug satisfaction, but rather the saving laughter of self-recognition.

Bibliography

BOOKS

Aeschylus. *Prometheus Bound*. Edited and translated by David Green and Richmond Lattimore. New York: Washington Square Press, 1967.

Arendt, Hanna. *The Jew as Pariah*. New York: Grove Press, 1973.

Augustine. *The City of God*. Garden City, N.Y.: Doubleday, 1958.

Aylmer, G. E., ed. *The Interregnum*. London: Macmillan, 1972.

Benjamin, Jessica. *The Bonds of Love*. New York: Pantheon, 1988.

Bernstein, Eduard. *Cromwell and Communism*. Translated by H. J. Sterling. London: George Allen and Unwin, 1930.

Brecht, Bertolt. *Poems, 1913–1956*. Translated and edited by John Willet and Ralph Manheim. New York: Methuen, 1976.

———. *Saint Joan of the Stockyards*. Translated by Frank Jones. Bloomington: Indiana University Press, 1969.

Brown, Norman O. *Life Against Death*. Middletown, Conn.: Wesleyan University Press, 1959.

———. *Love's Body*. New York: Random House, 1960.

Bynum, Carolyn Walker. *Jesus as Mother*. Berkeley and Los Angeles: University of California Press, 1982.

Camus, Albert. *The Rebel*. Translated by Anthony Bower. New York: Random House, 1956.

Cavell, Stanley. *Must We Mean What We Say?* Cambridge: Cambridge University Press, 1978.

Davis, J. C. *Utopia and the Ideal Society*. Cambridge: Cambridge University Press, 1981.

Dinnerstein, Dorothy. *The Mermaid and the Minotaur*. New York: Harper and Row, 1976.

Elton, G. R. *Reform and Reformation*. Cambridge: Harvard University Press, 1977.

Erikson, Erik. *Gandhi's Truth*. New York: Norton, 1969.

———. *Young Man Luther*. New York: Norton, 1958.

Greenblatt, Stephen. *Renaissance Self-Fashioning*. Chicago: University of Chicago Press, 1978.

Griffin, Susan. *Pornography and Silence*. New York: Harper and Row, 1981.

Haller, William. *Leveller Tracts*. New York: Columbia University Press, 1944.

———. *Liberty and Reformation in the Puritan Revolution*. New York: Columbia University Press, 1955.

———. *The Rise of Puritanism*. New York: Columbia University Press, 1938.

Hanson, Donald W. *From Kingdom to Commonwealth*. Cambridge: Harvard University Press, 1970.

Hayes, T. Wilson. *Winstanley the Digger*. Cambridge: Cambridge University Press, 1979.

Hill, Christopher. *The Antichrist in 17th Century England*. London: Oxford University Press, 1971.

———. *Continuity and Change in 17th Century England*. Cambridge: Harvard University Press, 1975.

———. *God's Englishman: Oliver Cromwell and the English Revolution*. New York: Dial Press, 1970.

———. *Milton and the English Revolution*. New York: Penguin, 1978.

———. *Puritanism and Revolution*. New York: Schocken, 1958.

———. *Society and Puritanism*. New York: Schocken, 1967.

———. *The World Turned Upside Down*. New York: Viking Press, 1972.

Hobbes, Thomas. *Behemoth*. Edited by Ferdinand Tonines. London: Frank Cass, 1969.

———. *Body, Man, and Citizen*. Edited by Richard Peters. New York: Collier, 1962.

———. *Leviathan*. Edited by Michael Oakeshott. New York: Collier, 1962.

———. *Man and Citizen*. New York: Anchor, 1972.

Jacobson, Norman. *Pride and Solace*. Berkeley and Los Angeles: University of California Press, 1978.

Kovel, Joel. *White Racism: A Psychohistory*. New York: Random House, 1970.

Lenin, V. I. *What Is to Be Done?* Translated by Joe Fineberg and George Hanna. New York: International Publishers, 1969.

Macpherson, C. B. *The Political Theory of Possessive Individualism*. London: Oxford University Press, 1962.

Marx, Karl. *Surveys from Exile: Political Writings*, vol. 2. Edited by Donald Fernbach. New York: Random House, 1974.

Marx, Karl, and Friedrich Engels. *Marx-Engels Reader*. Edited by Robert Tucker. New York: Norton, 1978.

Miller, Perry. *The New England Mind: The Seventeenth Century*. Boston: Beacon Press, 1961.

Nietzsche, Friedrich. *Beyond Good and Evil*. Translated by Walter Kaufman. New York: Random House, 1966.

———. *The Gay Science*. Translated by Walter Kaufman. New York: Random House, 1974.

———. *Thus Spoke Zarathustra*. Translated by R. J. Hollingdale. New York: Penguin, 1968.

Petergorsky, David. *Left-Wing Democracy in the English Civil War*. London: Victor Gollanz, 1940.

Pitkin, Hanna Fenichel. *Fortune Is a Woman*. Berkeley and Los Angeles: University of California Press, 1982.

———. *Wittgenstein and Justice*. Berkeley and Los Angeles: University of California Press, 1972.

Pocock, J. G. A. *The Machiavellian Moment*. Princeton: Princeton University Press, 1975.

Rogin, Michael. *Ronald Reagan, the Movie*. Berkeley and Los Angeles: University of California Press, 1986.

Rosenberg, Harold. *Act and Actor*. Chicago: University of Chicago Press, 1986.

Schneidau, Herbert. *Sacred Discontent*. Berkeley and Los Angeles: University of California Press, 1976.

Siegel, Gerrold. *Marx's Fate*. Princeton: Princeton University Press, 1978.

Underdown, David. *Pride's Purge*. London: George Allen and Unwin, 1984.

Walzer, Michael. *Exodus and Revolution*. New York: Basic Books, 1985.

———. *The Revolution of the Saints*. New York: Atheneum, 1968.

Weber, Max. *From Max Weber*. Edited by H. H. Gerth and C. Wright Mills. New York: Oxford, 1946.

Winstanley, Gerrard. *Collected Works*. Edited by George Sabine. Ithaca: Cornell University Press, 1941.

———. *England's Spirit Unfolded*. Reprinted in *Past and Present* 40 (July 1968).

———. *Law of Freedom in a Platform and Other Works*. Edited by Christopher Hill. Cambridge: Cambridge University Press, 1982.

Wolfe, Dan M. *Leveller Manifestos of the Puritan Revolution*. New York: Thomas Nelson, 1944.

Zagorin, Perez. *A History of Political Thought in the English Revolution*. London: Routlege and Kegan Paul, 1954.

ARTICLES

Alsop, J. D. "Gerrard Winstanley: Religion and Respectability." *The Historical Journal* 28, no. 3 (1985).

Ashcraft, Richard. "Leviathan Triumphant: Thomas Hobbes and the Politics of Wild Men." In *The Wild Man Within*, edited by Edward Dudley and Maximillian E. Novak. Pittsburgh: University of Pittsburgh Press, 1972.

Aylmer, G. E. "The Religion of Gerrard Winstanley." In *Radical Religion in the English Revolution*, edited by J. F. McGregor and B. Reay. Oxford: Oxford University Press, 1984.

Benjamin, Jessica. "A Desire of One's Own." In *Feminist Studies/Critical Studies*, edited by Teresa de Laurentis. Bloomington: Indiana University Press, 1986.

————. "The Oedipal Riddle." In *The Problem of Authority in America,* edited by Mark E. Kann. Philadelphia: Temple University Press, 1981.

Domhoff, William. "The Two Luthers: The Traditional and the Heretical in Freudian Psychology." *Psychoanalytic Review* (1970).

Fingarette, Herbert. "The Ego and Mystic Selflessness." In *Identity and Anxiety,* edited by Maurice Stein, Arthur Vidich, and David White. New York: The Free Press, 1960.

Griffin, Susan. "The Way of All Ideology." *Signs* 7, no. 3 (Spring 1982).

Hill, Christopher. "The Religion of Gerrard Winstanley." *Past and Present* (Supplement 5, 1978).

Hudson, W. S. "Economic and Social Thought of Gerrard Winstanley." *Journal of Modern History* 17 (1946).

Juretic, George. "Digger No Millenarian." *Journal of the History of Ideas* 36 (1975).

Mulligan, L., J. K. Graham, and J. Richards. "Winstanley: A Case for the Man as He Said He Was." *Journal of Ecclesiastical History* 27 (1970).

Pitkin, Hanna Fenichel. "Justice: On Relating Public and Private." *Political Theory* 9 (August 1981).

Schwartz, Peter. "The Maternal Christ as Redeemer: Speech and Gender in the Thought of Martin Luther." *The Journal of Psychohistory* 12, no. 4 (Spring 1985).

Skinner, Quentin. "History and Ideology in the English Revolution." *The Historical Journal* 8, no. 2 (1965).

Wolin, Sheldon. "Hobbes and the Epic Tradition of Political Theory." William Andrews Clark Memorial Library, University of California, Los Angeles, 1970.

Index

Compositor:	G & S Typesetters, Inc.
Text:	10/13 Sabon
Display:	Sabon
Printer:	Braun-Brumfield, Inc.
Binder:	Braun-Brumfield, Inc.